IMAGES
of America

SHREWSBURY

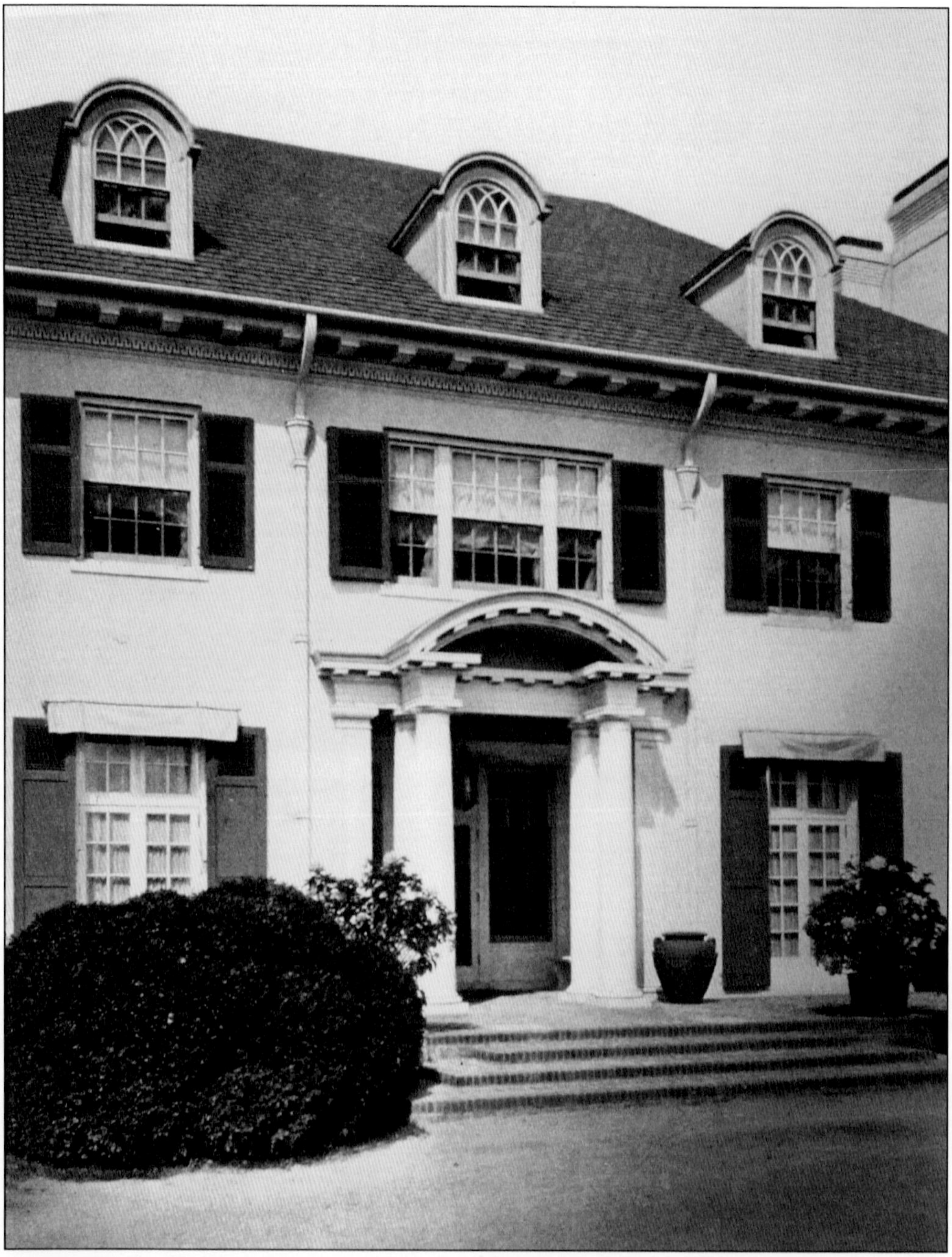

Shadow Brook, the finest house ever built in Shrewsbury, merits a separate chapter. It begins on p. 35.

Cover Photograph: See p. 72.

IMAGES
of America

SHREWSBURY

Randall Gabrielan

ARCADIA
PUBLISHING

ISBN 978-0-7385-6420-3

Published by Arcadia Publishing
Charleston SC, Chicago IL, Portsmouth NH, San Francisco CA

Printed in the United States of America

Library of Congress Catalog Card Number: 2008941198

For all general information contact Arcadia Publishing at:
Telephone 843-853-2070
Fax 843-853-0044
E-mail sales@arcadiapublishing.com
For customer service and orders:
Toll-Free 1-888-313-2665

Visit us on the Internet at www.arcadiapublishing.com

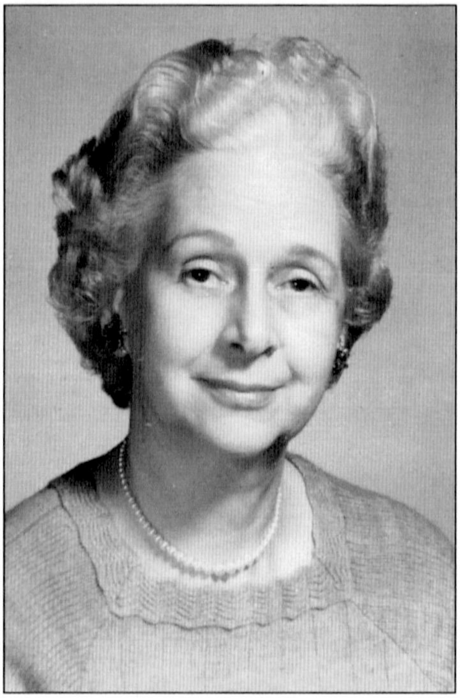

This book is dedicated to J. Louise Jost, teacher and historian.
Miss Jost began a second teaching career in Shrewsbury Borough School,
adopting Monmouth County as her own, and she instilled an appreciation for its history
in a generation of students. One product of her inspiration and their devotion
can be seen on pp. 118–19, but The Mosaic can be better-witnessed by visiting the school.
Miss Jost's single-minded efforts in cultivating Shrewsbury's history
culminated in the establishment of the Shrewsbury Historical Society Museum,
Education, and Research Center, a facility she continues to head
as the long-term president of the Shrewsbury Historical Society.

Contents

Acknowledgments

The cooperation and encouragement of the Shrewsbury Historical Society was the springboard for this project. It was completed through the participation and generous loans of a number of Shrewsbury families and collectors in several Monmouth towns. My deepest thanks and gratitude to the historical society and to its president, J. Louise Jost, for liberal access to their collections, including their pictures and research notes.

Local families are usually essential links to a representative book. The Bordens have a three-century tie to Shrewsbury. Francis and Margaret Borden provided material of extraordinary interest from the family archives. I am thankful and grateful for their assistance, as this is a finer book as a result of their generosity. Anna Louise Campbell Rudner also provided pictures of exceptional merit.

Photography Unlimited by Dorn's continues to tap its extensive holdings of long-unseen negatives. Their contributions of 1950s images provided a needed link of the recent past to the ancient town, and reflect pride of place, as Shrewsbury is the former Dorn home.

I extend my sincere thanks to Joseph W. Hammond, a fine Monmouth scholar and historian, who not only assisted with pictures, but also gave me access to his research that produced a successful nomination for listing Christ Church on the National and New Jersey Registers of Historic Places. His work awaiting publication, *Christ Church in Shrewsbury, New Jersey and the Church Designs of Robert Smith*, was also generously shared. This work has provided new and accurate insight into the past of one of Shrewsbury's most venerable institutions.

My thanks and gratitude to the many collectors and residents for their pictures, whether one or many, whose generosity and support earn them stature as co-producers of this volume: Catherine Attridge, Olga Boeckel, Christ Church, Donald Dewey, Joseph Eid, Esther Hymer, Robert and Mary Johnson, Harriet Kodama, Patricia Keiper Kurdyla, Robert Manson and the family of Dorothy Blair Manson, Monroe Marx, the Monmouth County Historical Association, John Rhody, Rutgers University Libraries–Special Collections and Archives, Robert A. Schoeffling, Karen L. Schnitzspahn, and Grace Tetley.

Introduction

Shrewsbury was settled around 1665 (the exact date will probably never be known) as one of the Two Towns of the Navesink. Arguably, it was the cradle of civilization in Monmouth County. Its Four Corners—the intersection of Broad Street (the former Kings Highway) and Sycamore Avenue (the former Indian Burlington Path)—is Monmouth's most historic place. No other small area contains as many significant early institutions and aged buildings.

Its naming, likely chosen by an unknown settler to honor his home in England, is another, perhaps unsolvable, mystery. A theory involving Shrewsbury's geographical similarities to its English namesake has been advanced to link the names. However, the English town is surrounded by a loop of the Severn River, while New Jersey's Shrewsbury is some distance from its local rivers.

Shrewsbury was organized in 1693 as one of the three original Monmouth County townships. It embraced a vast area that included present-day eastern Monmouth County (south of the Navesink River) and all of Ocean County. The major section that became Ocean County was separated in the colonial era. Large parts formed Howell Township in 1801 and Ocean Township in 1849, the latter in an era when most large, early townships in New Jersey were reduced to administratively manageable size.

The division of Shrewsbury Township in the late nineteenth and early twentieth centuries is a fascinating and unstudied aspect of Monmouth's political history, a process ending with the formation of Shrewsbury borough, an issue closely linked to Shrewsbury's social history.

The historic core of Shrewsbury village was long interested in the development patterns of its surroundings, including the spread of small lot sub-divisions, annexation threats, or any change threatening a settlement widely perceived as "aristocratic." Thus, the building of Fahnestock's Shadowbrook estate was seen as a buffer against the spread of small-lot housing, as was occurring in southern Red Bank.

The earliest citation of "aristocratic" applicable to Shrewsbury that the author has found occurred in 1886. The term, not unjustified, was used regularly in the 1920s as the village center withdrew from Shrewsbury Township. Be mindful that by 1870, when Rumson Road was a sandy path through farmland and Navesink River Road was being built among Middletown Township's riverfront farms, Sycamore Avenue was attracting wealthy urbanites. When agriculture was a means to prosperity, Shrewsbury could boast of some of the richest examples. Thus, one can assert the 1926 formation of the borough was zoning by municipal organization. The new borough adopted a zoning law in 1930. The early formation of social/

cultural organizations and the ascendancy of its churches justifiably enhanced the "aristocratic" reputation.

Shrewsbury prospered when agriculture was business. However, when Holmes Borden built up his retail store in the 1870s, the *Monmouth Democrat* could report his rise by asserting that Shrewsbury business had been "dead" for a generation. The town takes historic pride in Hazard's ketchup factory, which brought wide recognition to the town's name; it endured only a half-century, however, making one suspect an upscale shopping center could be the borough's business high point.

"Progress" is inevitable and one expects two views of it in a little-changed town. Newcomers may find all that they had been seeking in a still-sylvan setting, while some with long memories regret each newly turned spade of earth. The view of Shrewsbury from the other of the two towns is that of a little-changed place with great historic stature, a town with the hoped-for and expected stewardship to preserve what made it great.

The strong interest in Shrewsbury's history and the number of unaccessed sources will create an opportunity for a second Shrewsbury book. The author is seeking loans of additional photographs and would appreciate willing lenders contacting him at: 71 Fish Hawk Drive, Middletown, New Jersey, 07748, or 908 671-2645.

One

The Four Corners

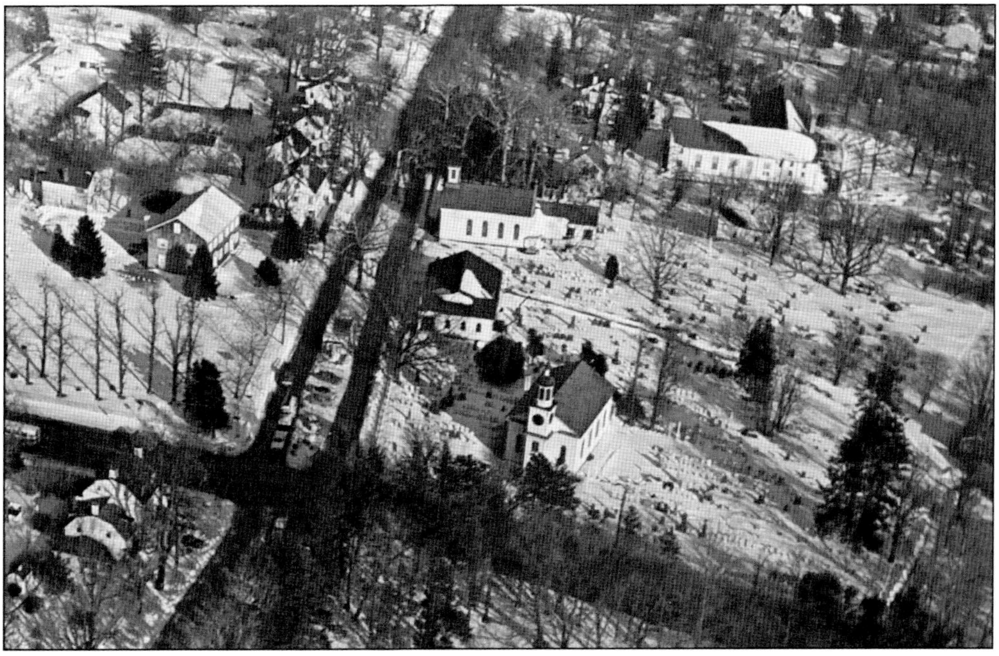

The intersection of Broad Street (running horizontally) and Sycamore Avenue (running vertically) has changed little, with its basic fabric in place for nearly 175 years. The post office (p. 25) stood when this postcard was made for New Jersey's 1964 tercentenary, with the island still wide enough to park cars perpendicular to the street. The structures close to the corner clockwise from lower left are: the Allen House (p. 26–31), the Quaker Meeting House (p. 20), the Benjamin White House (p. 102), the Presbyterian church (p. 18–19), the Christ Church Hall, and Christ Church (p. 10–17). The wheelwright and blacksmith shop is long-gone, with the lower right corner's Borough Hall omitted from the picture.

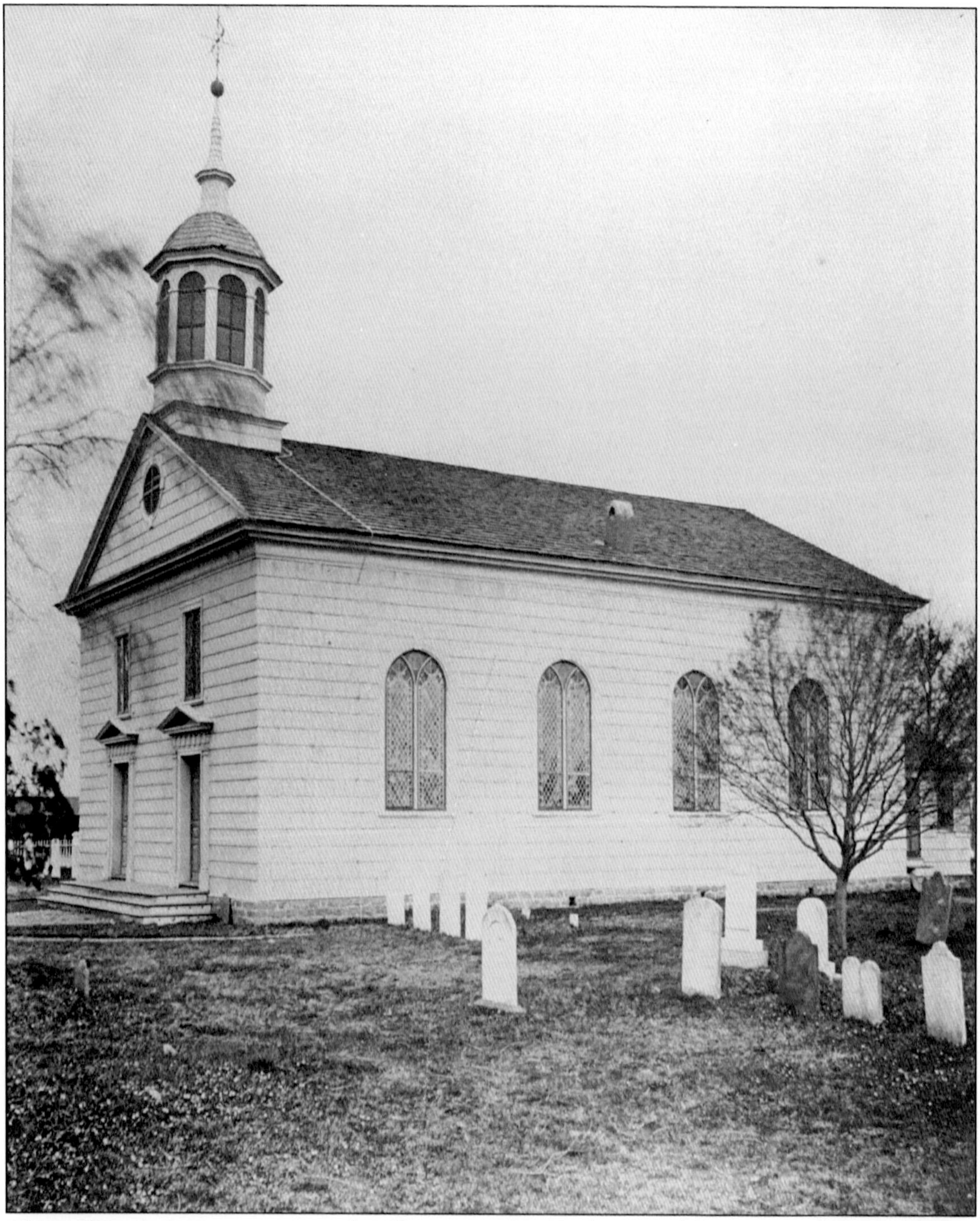

Christ Church dates its origin to the Christmas 1702 Eucharist celebration at the Lewis Morris Tinton Falls residence. In 1706, the church purchased 1.6 acres at the southeast corner of Broad Street and Sycamore Avenue. The lot remained vacant until 1732, when a brick church was erected there. This *c.* 1870 view is likely the earliest extant photograph of the existing church, built between the years 1769 and 1774, and designed by prominent Philadelphia builder-architect Robert Smith (1722–1777). The front (or western) facade featured two Doric order doorway surrounds.

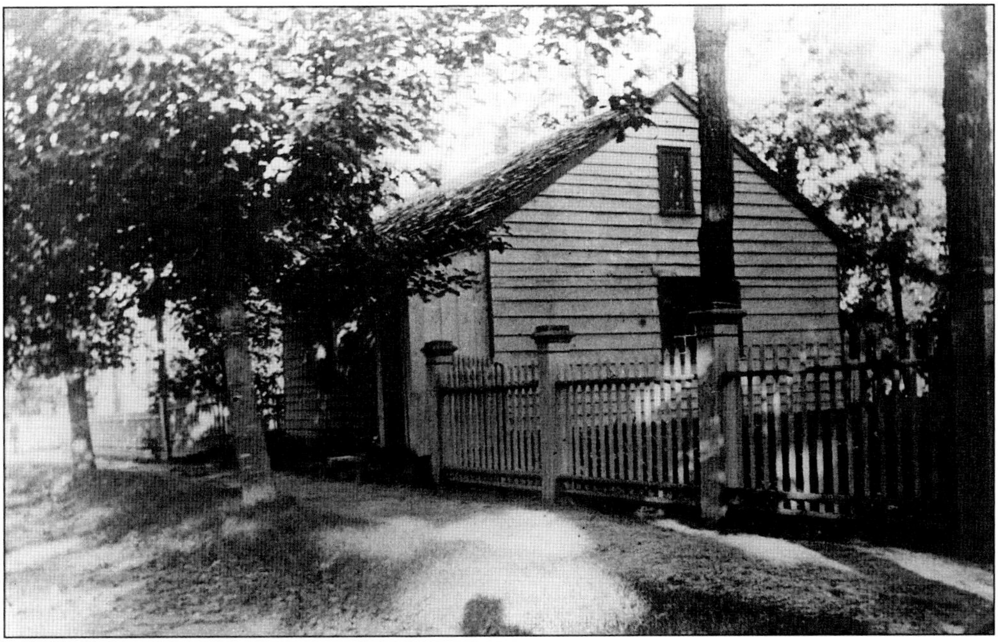

The 1770 joiners shop was used by Josiah Halstead for building the interior finishing of the present church. Occupied as a public school *c.* 1810–30, the building was later a parish house and Sunday school. President Grant was entertained here during the 1869 church centennial celebration. The building was removed in 1898 for the construction of the first part of the present parish house, adjacent to the church on the east. (Christ Church Archives.)

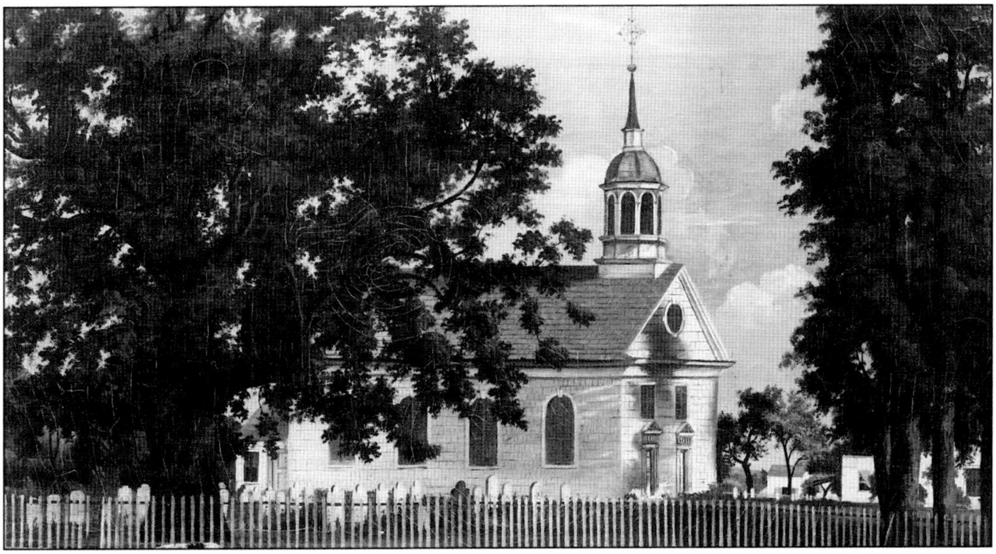

An 1855 oil on canvas in the collection of the Monmouth County Historical Association reflects the construction and finishing changes over the prior twenty years. The chancel was extended in 1844 and the paling fence was erected in 1852. The church was painted white in 1836 and the shutters green in 1839. The design of the Christ Church cupola was repeated by Robert Smith. One identical in every detail was built on Carpenters' Hall, Philadelphia, around the same time as Christ Church, with later examples at the first American Hospital for the Insane in Williamsburg, Virginia, and the Walnut Street Prison in Philadelphia.

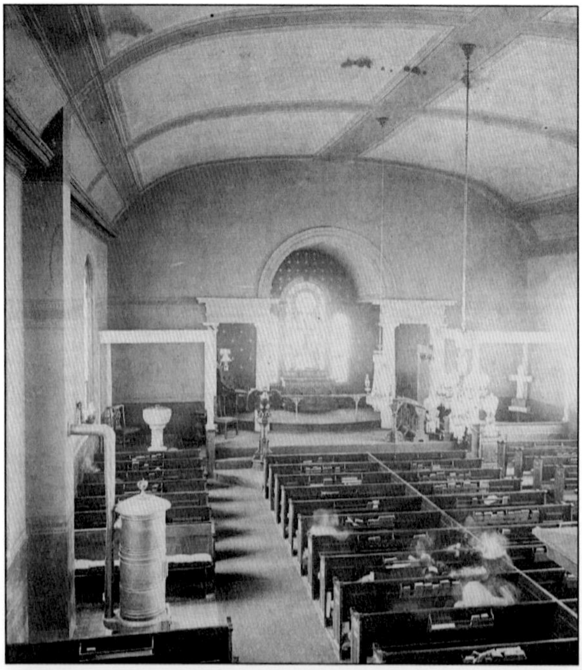

This 1880s photograph follows interior changes made early in the decade, directed by New York ecclesiastical decorator Edward J. Neville Stent. The interior was painted in 1881 with elaborate stenciling on the ceiling, the same year the cut-crystal, etched-glass chandelier donated by George De Haert Gillespie was installed. Other gifts in 1882 of the Gillespie family and supporters included a carved altar of butternut wood, bronze communion railings, an eagle lectern, and prayer stalls. Note the new baptismal font installed in one of two canopied pews (see p. 17). (Monmouth County Historical Association Collection.)

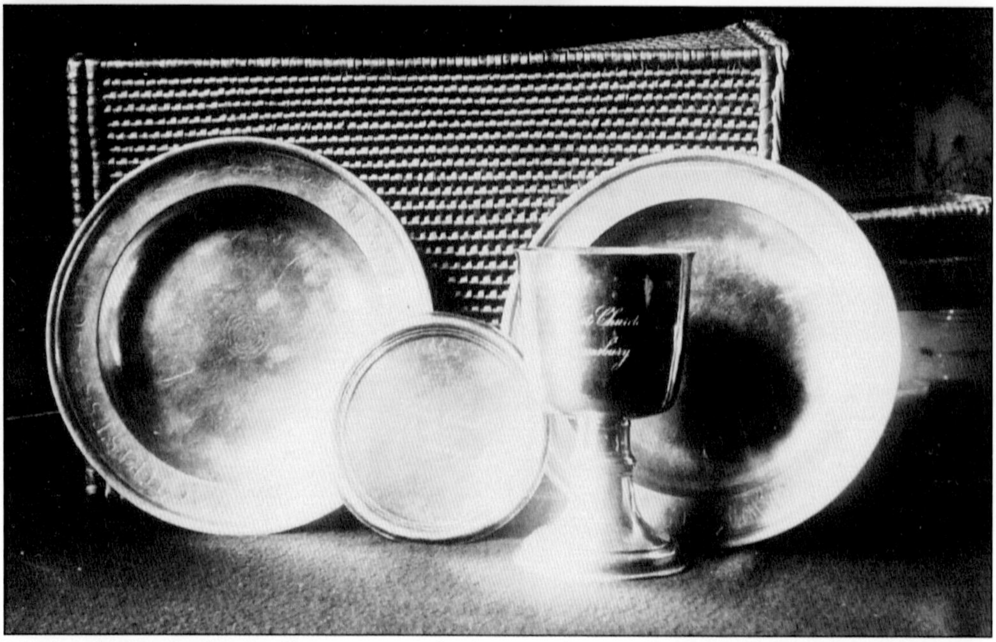

The Lord Chamberlain's office gave standard issue gifts to colonial governors for presentation to the parish of the governor's choice as demonstrated by this c. 1900 photograph. Joseph Hammond's research has revealed issuance of sixty-three sets dating from 1694 to 1779. The chalice and paten were given to Christ Church in 1738, the year Lewis Morris became governor and the parish charter was issued. The large plates are pewter, made in the 1790s by John Townsend in London. They hang on the church wall, while the silver chalice and paten are stored in a bank vault, and are returned to the church only for special ceremonial occasions. (Special Collections and Archives, Rutgers University Libraries.)

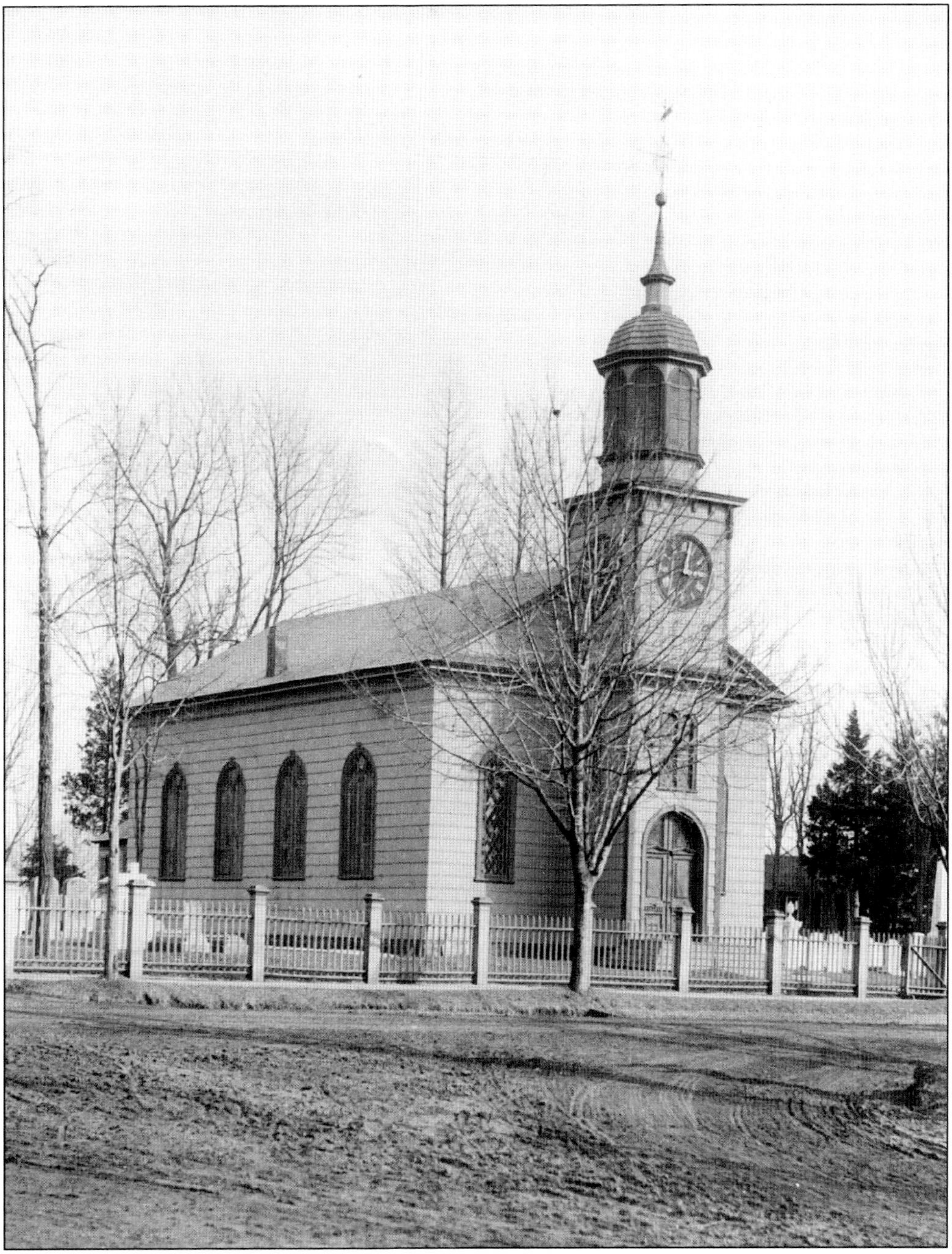

The most visible of changes to Christ Church was the 1874 addition of a 10-foot-square tower to the west facade, built by local master carpenter Lambert Borden and shown in this c. 1880s photograph. His framing is consistent with the original church, with Borden retaining the early character by moving the cupola forward to the new tower. A clock from the renowned E. Howard Clock Company of Boston, with faces on the north, west, and south sides, was provided by private subscription. The clock remains operative and is wound weekly by hand. New stained-glass windows on the west imitated existing openings on the sides. The two former front doors were removed, with the single entrance into the tower aiding winter heating.

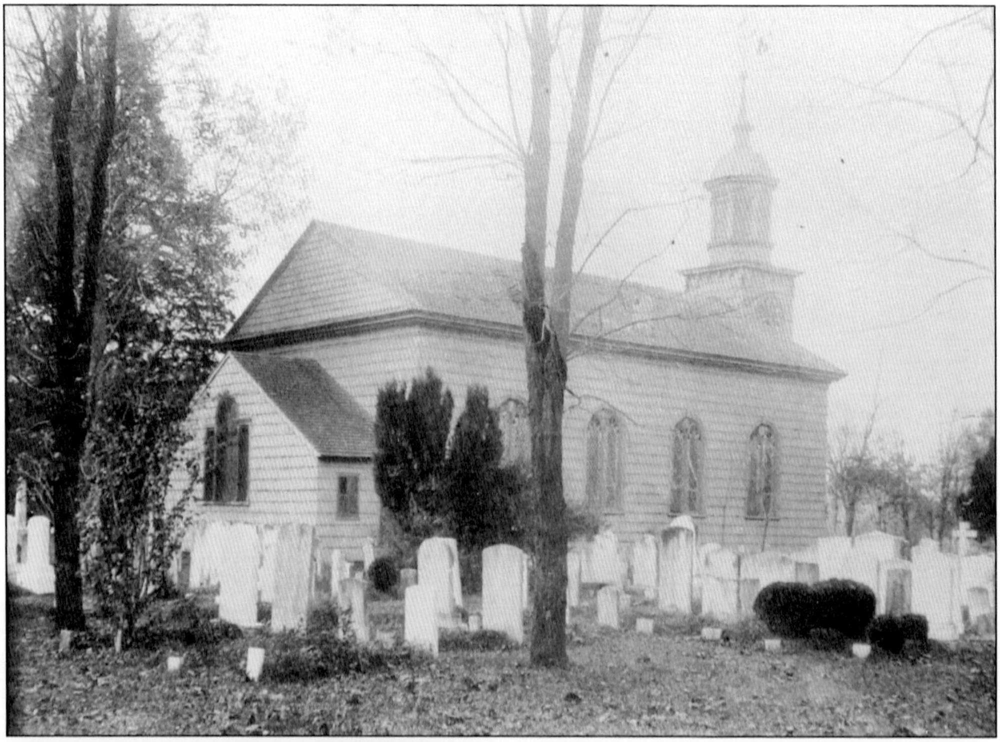

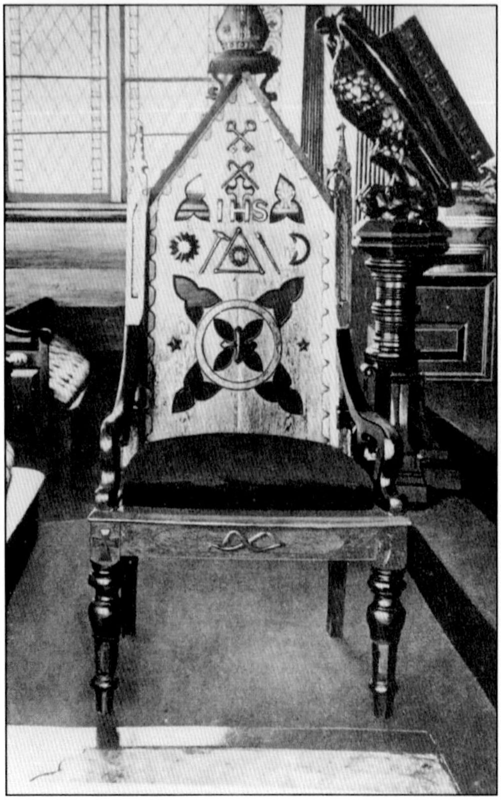

The first significant nineteenth-century alteration to Christ Church was the 1844 addition of a 10-by-20-foot chancel recess on the east, built by Peter K. Hadden, a Shrewsbury master carpenter. It was raised four steps from the main floor level and flanked by two small rooms for the clergy and vestry. The addition is visible in this c. 1895 photograph by W. H. Richardson of Philadelphia. (Special Collections and Archives, Rutgers University Libraries.)

The Christ Church Bishop's Chair was made by Robert Holmes White, likely in the 1860s, from a large oak once standing north of the church and visible on the bottom of p. 11. The chair, shown in this c. 1910 postcard, contains a bishop's miter on the crest and various Christian and Masonic symbols.To this day, use of the chair is reserved for bishops. White, a carpenter who was responsible with his brother for church maintenance, made a similar chair without the symbolism. (John Rhody Collection.)

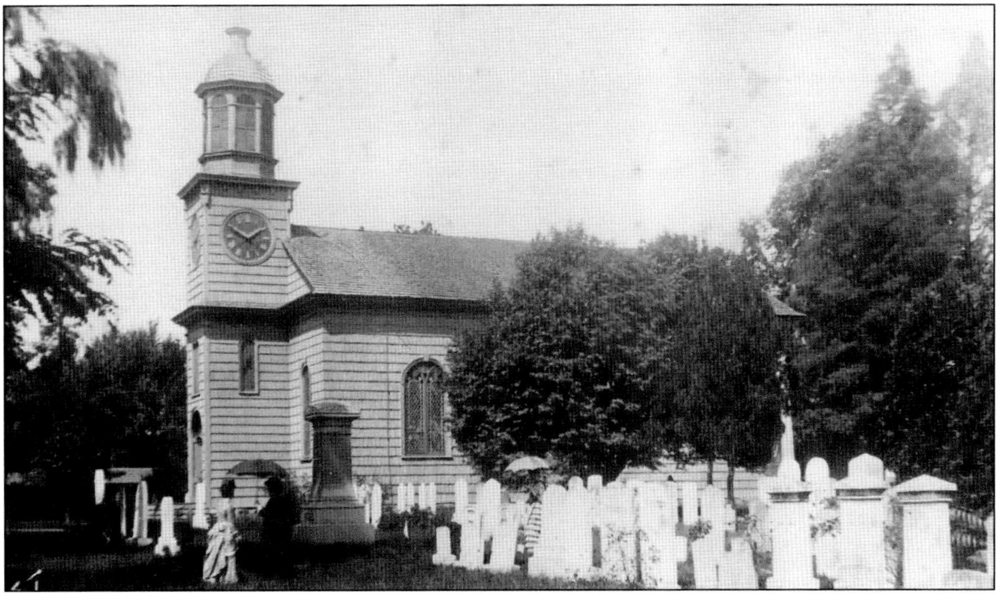

Edward Taylor, a noted amateur photographer of Middletown, took this view of the south elevation August 17, 1886. Internments in the cemetery began c. 1720, prior to the erection of the first church. Many prominent citizens are buried here. Tombstones in slate, sandstone, marble, and granite represent a full range of styles of the past three centuries. Three tombstones set in the floor of the church in 1769 memorialize Elizabeth Ashfield (1729–1762), Theodosius Bartow (1692–1746), and Henry Leonard (1756–1761). They died prior to the erection of the present church and are presumably buried somewhere in the graveyard.

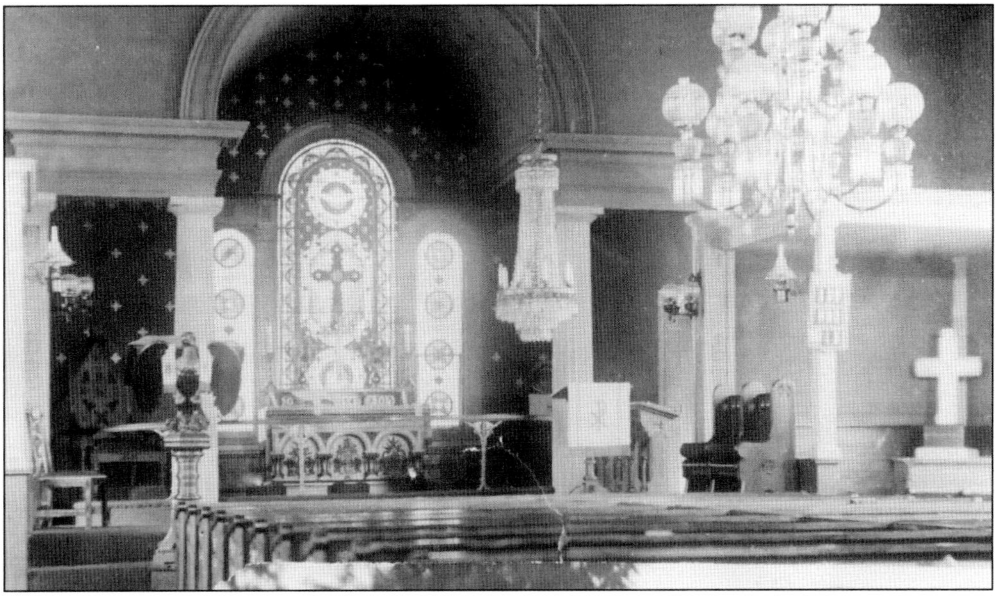

Edward Taylor's September 27, 1886 photograph depicts a closer view of the 1881 carved butternut wood altar, bronze communion rails, and eagle lectern, among the gifts in 1882 by Gillespie and supporters. Not visible here at the east end of the church is the two-manual replacement pipe organ purchased in 1879. The pews were given a layer of dark mahogany graining in this period.

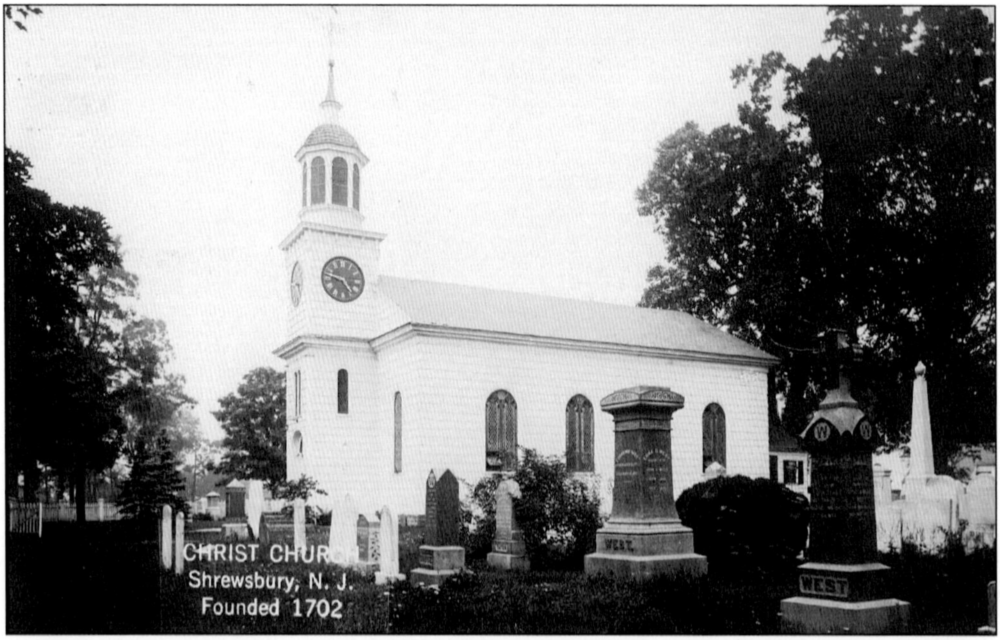

A 1920s postcard portrays a new white exterior painting. The medium beige trim was painted dark green in 1881, reflecting then current tastes. The earlier fence was removed in 1907, but was replaced in the 1924–25 renovations.

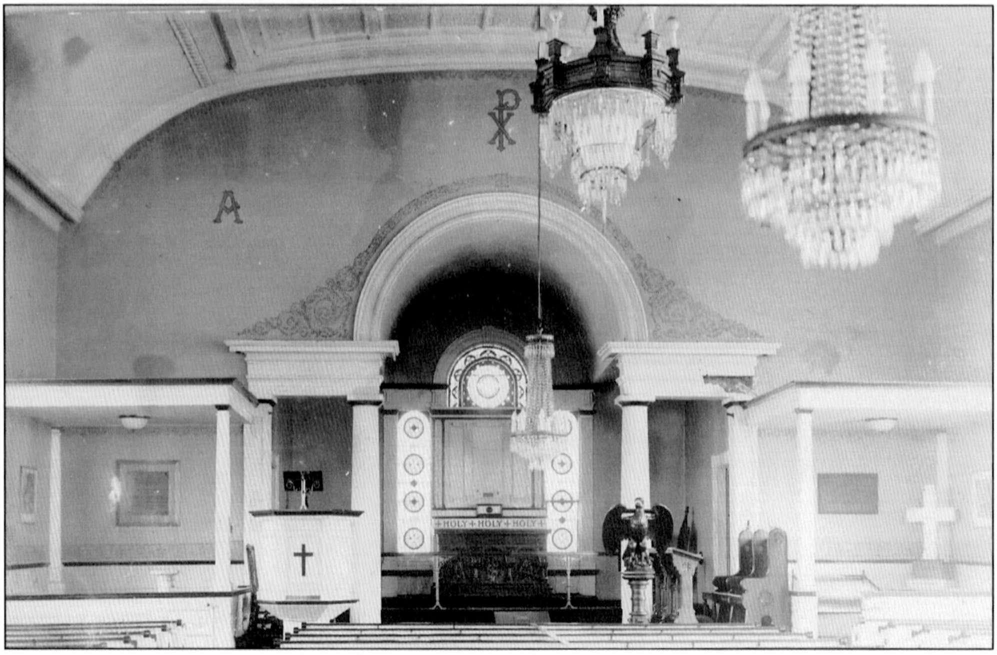

An interior companion card to the one above, this view by noted Red Bank photographer Charles Foxwell depicts a newly electrified church and the installation of a pulpit, present for the first time since 1844. The font was repositioned in the rear of the sanctuary. The plastered ceiling was replaced in 1906 by one of pressed metal, installed by Daniel H. Cook of Tinton Falls, a specialist with many such local installations.

Canopy-covered pews, 7-by-8 feet, were built on both sides of the east end of the sanctuary. They were likely used by any important visitors, tradition notwithstanding. The canopies are supported by fluted pilasters and a free-standing column. Church records indicate the rector owned pew #1. No governor was known to have visited Christ Church while in office. Christ Church's canopied pews may be the sole original survivors of a fairly common installation in colonial churches, as shown in this contemporary view. (Christ Church Collection.)

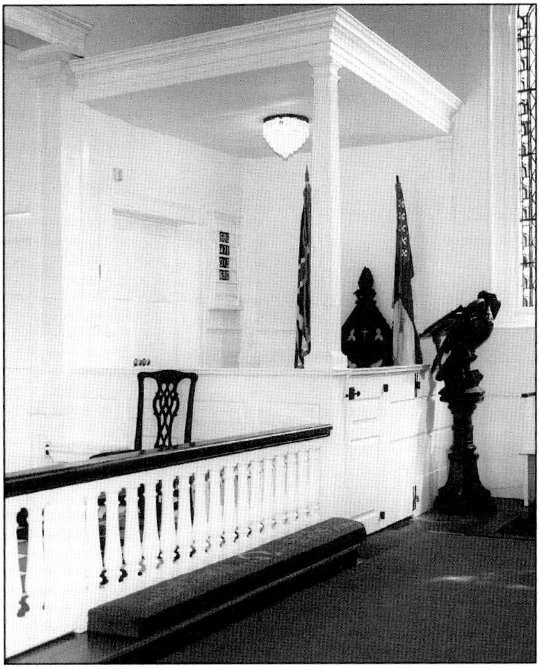

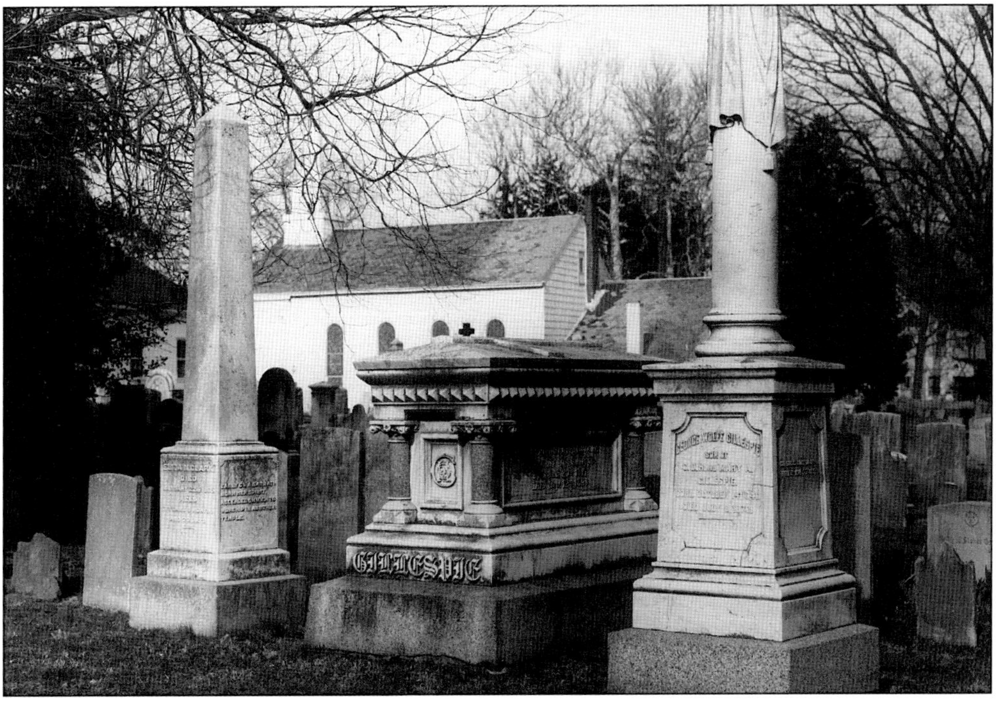

George De Haert Gillespie, New York businessman and owner of a vast Rumson estate, worshiped at Christ Church and was its major nineteenth-century benefactor. His sarcophagus is one of the most attractive monuments in the church's cemetery. To the right are the graves of his two sons, their early deaths reflected by shrouded half-columns. The visible one bears the poignant inscription on the side, "His Sun Is Gone Down/While It Was Yet Day." (Christ Church Collection.)

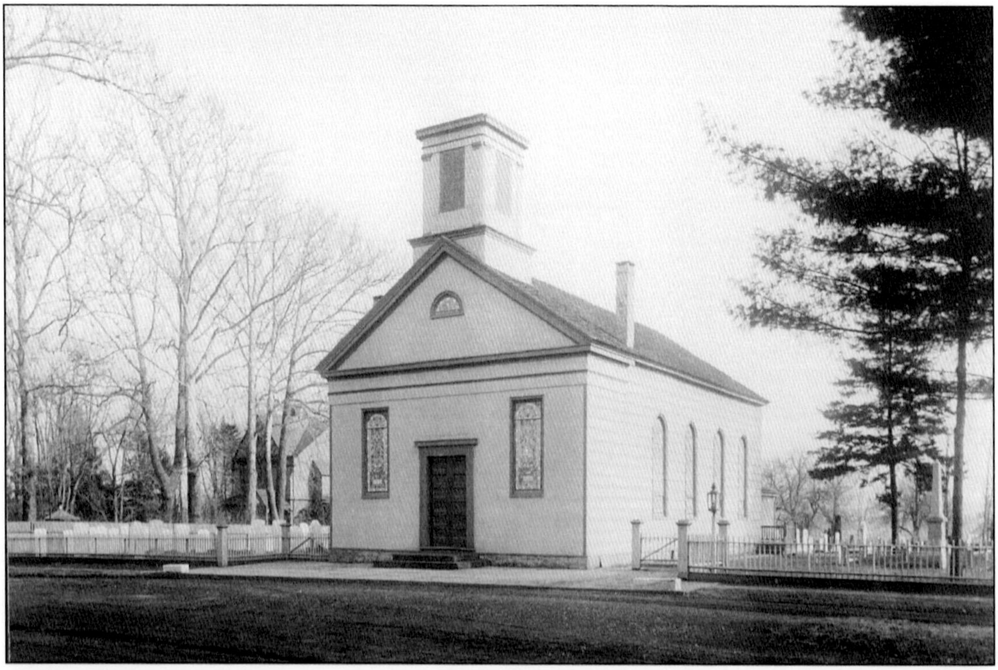

The Presbyterian church at Shrewsbury has established its founding as 1732, but notes that Presbyterian activity in the area can be traced at least to 1705 when John Boyd was licensed as the first minister to be ordained by the first Presbytery in this county. A charter was obtained in 1750; an early church was built, deteriorated, and was torn down. Services were held elsewhere, including Christ Church. Funds for a new church were raised in 1821, with the present Greek Revival edifice dedicated September 29, 1822. This image shows the Presbyterian church c. 1900.

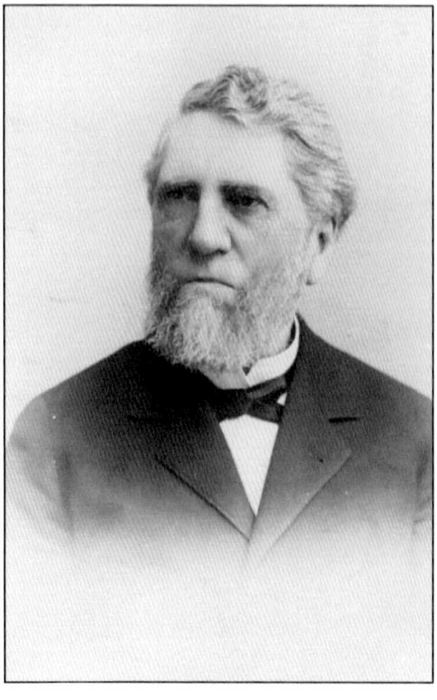

The Reverend Dr. Thaddeus Wilson, born 1824 near Walkill, New York, served the Shrewsbury Presbyterian Church forty-five years as pastor. Graduating from Amherst in 1843 and the Princeton Theological Seminary in 1846, Wilson began his ministry at Centerville, New York, coming to Shrewsbury in 1852. Shown here c. 1890, Reverend Wilson supported educational matters and was recognized for his interest in civic betterment. Wilson married Charlotte A. Miller. One of their children was the noted lawyer Edmund Wilson of Red Bank, who was father of the famed writer of the same name. Upon retiring in 1897, Reverend Wilson was named pastor emeritus, and moved to Spring Lake, where he died in 1904. (Shrewsbury Historical Society Collection.)

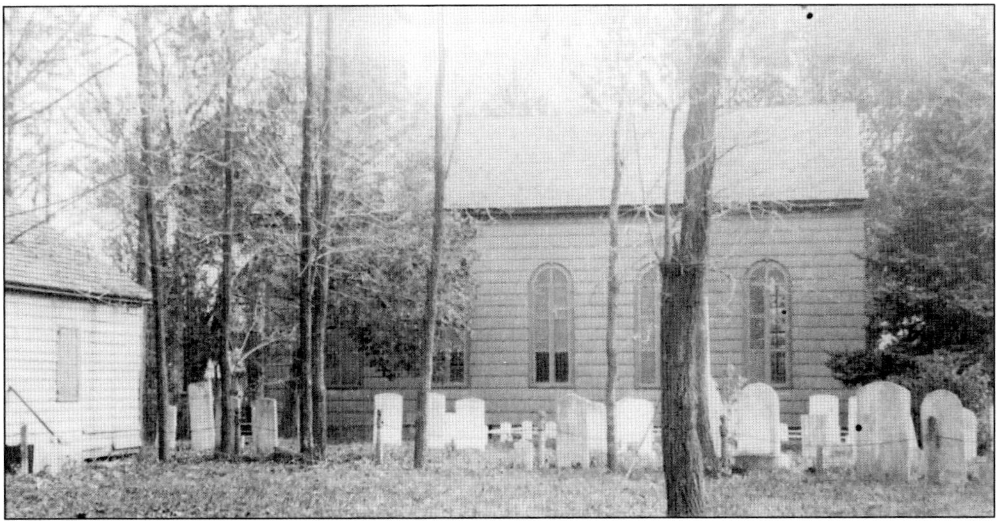

The Presbyterian church has been altered several times as demonstrated in this 1890s photograph. It appears that the northernmost window opening was removed, perhaps in an 1895 remodeling when the social room was added and the interior was remodeled in oak. That year, eleven stained-glass windows were installed, four on each side, two on the front and one in the belfry. The latter was given by Wolff & Williams of New York, the firm that made the windows. Services were held in the Sunday school room during the project. (Special Collections and Archives, Rutgers University Libraries.)

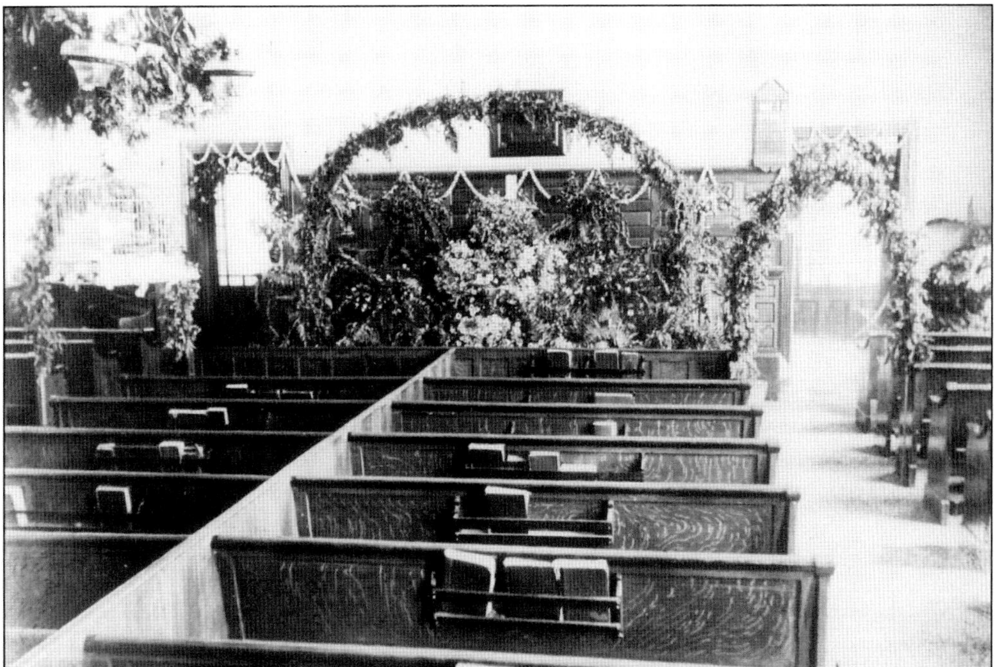

This picture predates the 1951 interior remodeling intended to restore the "colonial character" of the building. A new pipe organ and chimes were added, the lighting fixtures changed, and a new pulpit was installed. During this period the General Van Vliet house was purchased for use as a manse and a new church house was planned, with Blair Hall completed in 1959.

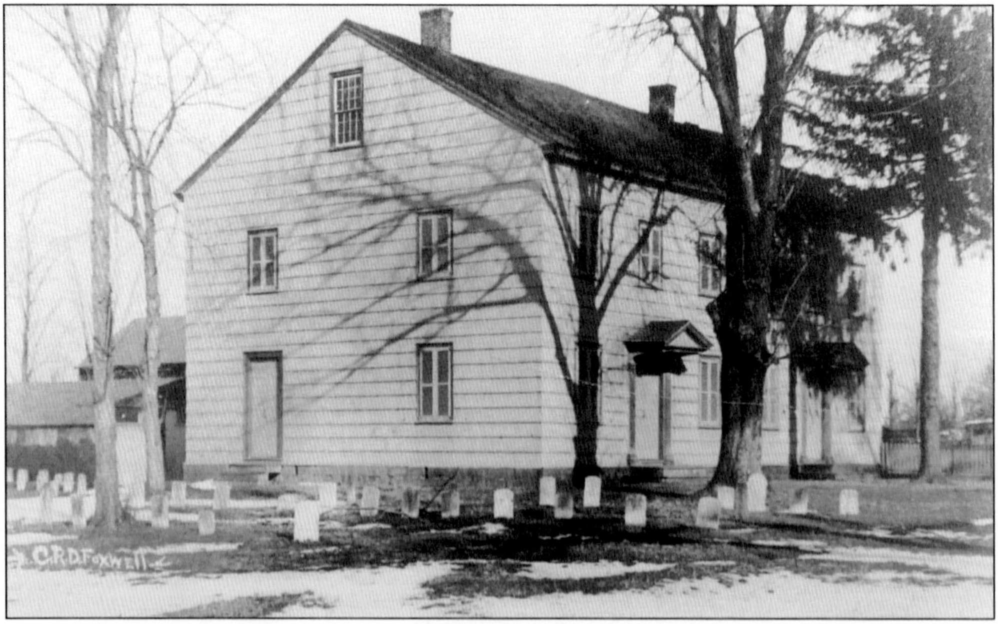

The Religious Society of Friends at Shrewsbury dates from the 1665 settlement of the area, with an early meetinghouse built by 1672 about a mile from the present house and later destroyed by fire. John Lippencott, an early Friend settler, sold the society one acre at its present site at the northeast corner of Broad Street and Sycamore Avenue, with a meetinghouse and cemetery existing by 1701. It, too, burned, as did a replacement brick house. The present meetinghouse was built in 1816 and is shown in this *c.* 1905 postcard. (John Rhody Collection.)

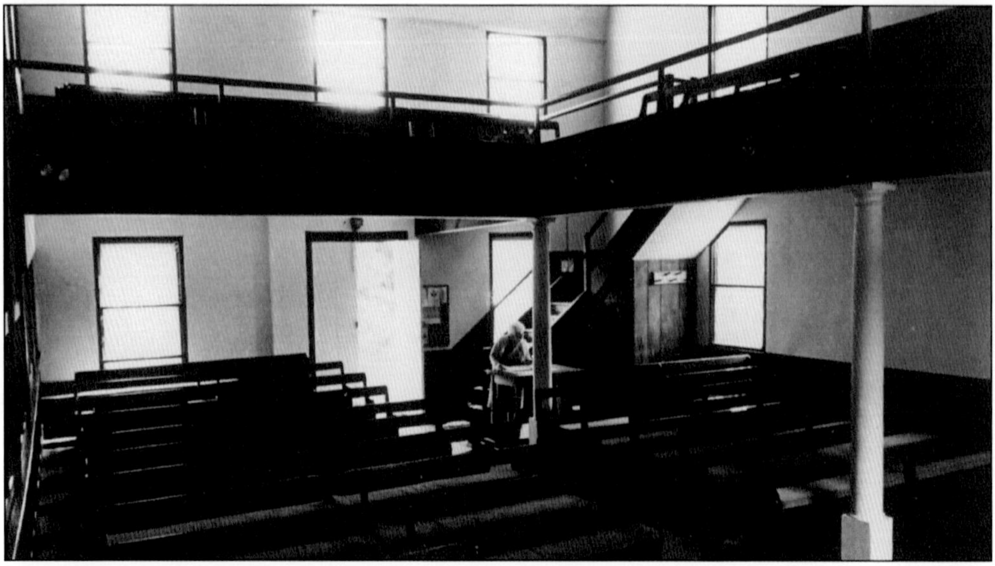

The gallery of the Quaker Meeting House has benches extending around three sides of the room. The building is divided in two sections, with men and women once occupying separate spaces. When the Quakers were divided by theological differences, the liberal Hixites, followers of Elias Hicks, occupied the old meetinghouse with the orthodox Quakers meeting elsewhere. The meeting became inactive in 1907, but was officially re-instituted in 1942 and has been active continuously since.

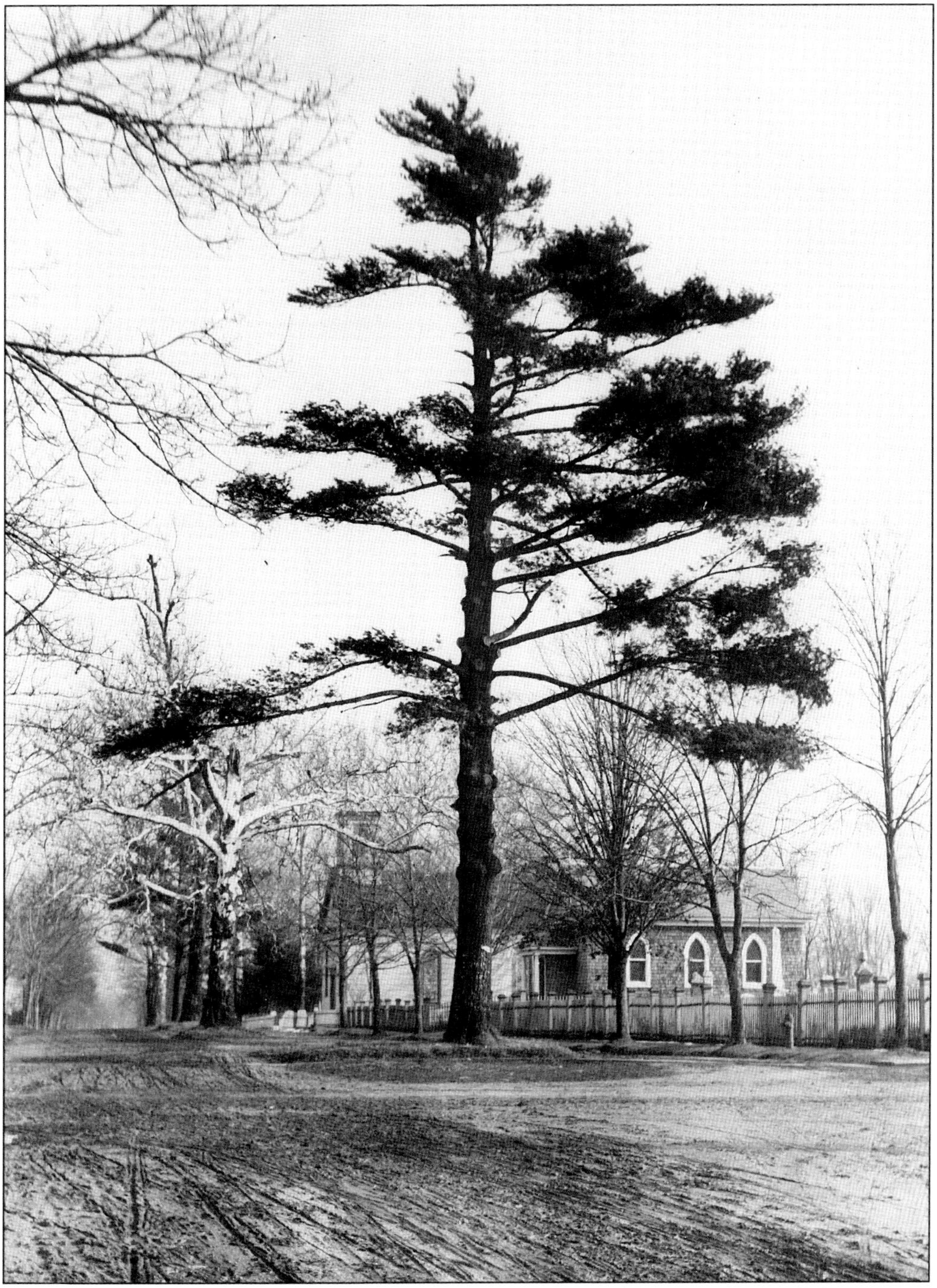

On September 14, 1910, the *Register* reflected on the history of the Council Pine while reporting on a poem written by Mrs. Walter Kimball about the tree. They noted it was believed to have been planted *c.* 1835 by Peter Haddon and was once a general meeting place for political orations. Her son, the noted lawyer and New Jersey attorney general Edmund Wilson, was said to have made his first speech under the tree. It was in poor condition when removed *c.* 1924. Its memory is preserved in the borough's seal (see p. 126). This is a 1920s photograph.

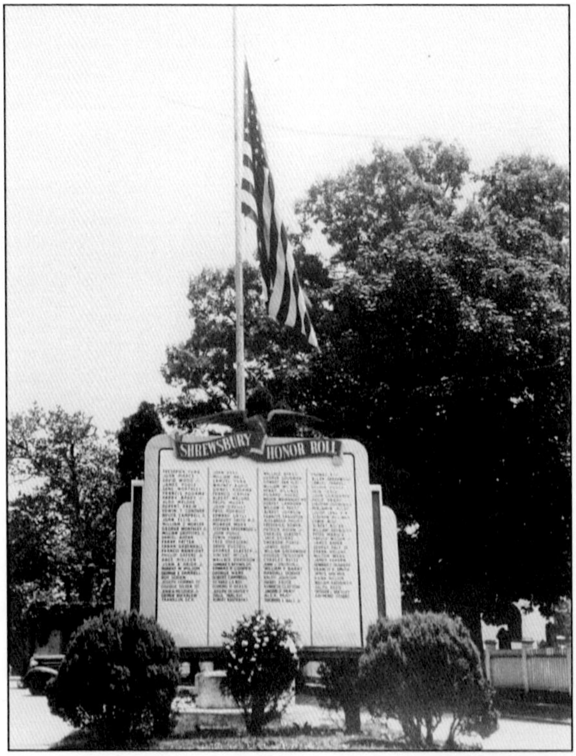

A temporary wood honor roll, typical of those many towns erected during World War II to denote local military participation, was placed in the island between Christ Church and the Quaker Meeting House. A memorial tablet now on the flagpole honors the veterans, including George L. Atkinson and Robert R. Campbell, the borough's two battle deaths. The dates of erection and destruction have proved elusive.

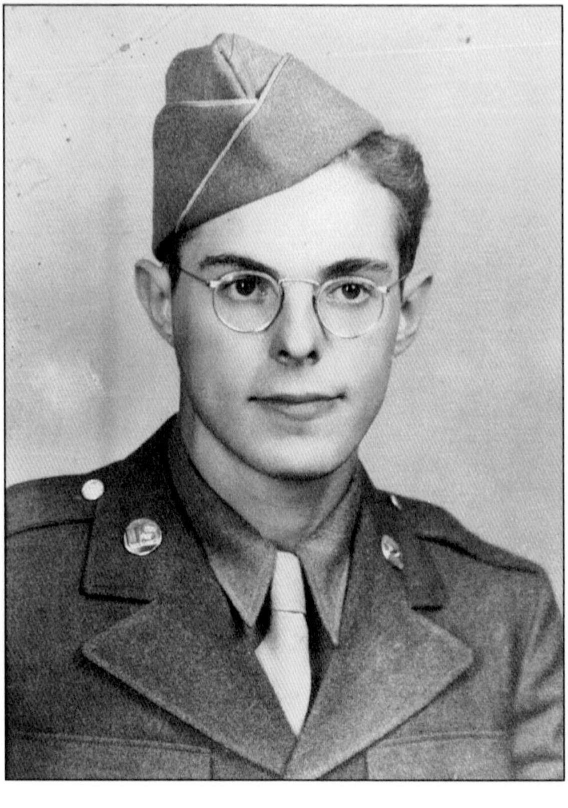

Pvt. Robert R. Campbell, the son of Bruce and Margaret Rue Campbell, and a member of the Red Bank High School Class of 1944, entered the army in August 1943 under an early release program. He left for North Africa around February 1944 and was killed in action in Italy, the borough's first World War II death. His memory is commemorated by the annual Robert Rue Campbell Award, the highest honor presented to a member of the Shrewsbury Borough School's graduating class. The students choose the designee who best exemplifies the twelve personal qualities used as the award's criteria. The 1996 designee is Theodore Blair Fetter, son of Robin Blair and Frank Fetter, and grandson of Dorothy Blair Manson (see p. 110).

Philip K. Dorn, known as "Tinker" to all, was a 1969 graduate of Red Bank High School, where he played football and baseball. He enlisted in the Marines in February 1965, becoming a member of a six-man assault team and initially serving on the aircraft carrier *Princeton*. While on patrol in 1966 guarding the airfield at Chu Li, Viet Nam, "Tinker" Dorn was killed by a sniper. The smile reflects the warmth of his personality. "Tinker" Dorn's memory is honored at Patriot Isle. This family memento was donated by Kathy Dorn Severini.

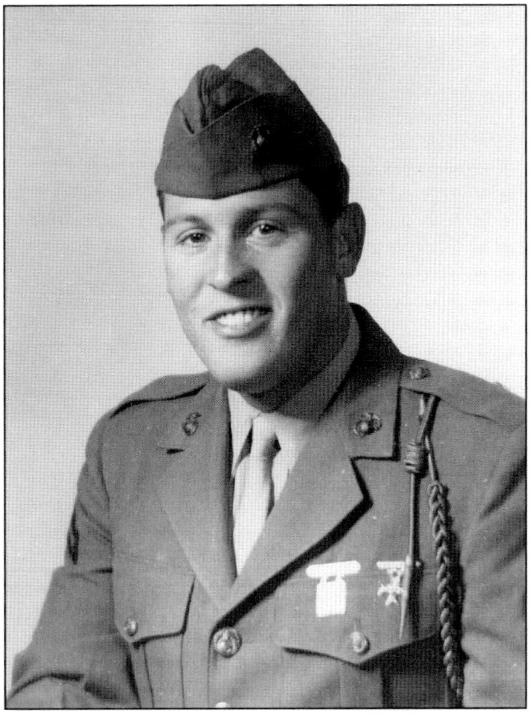

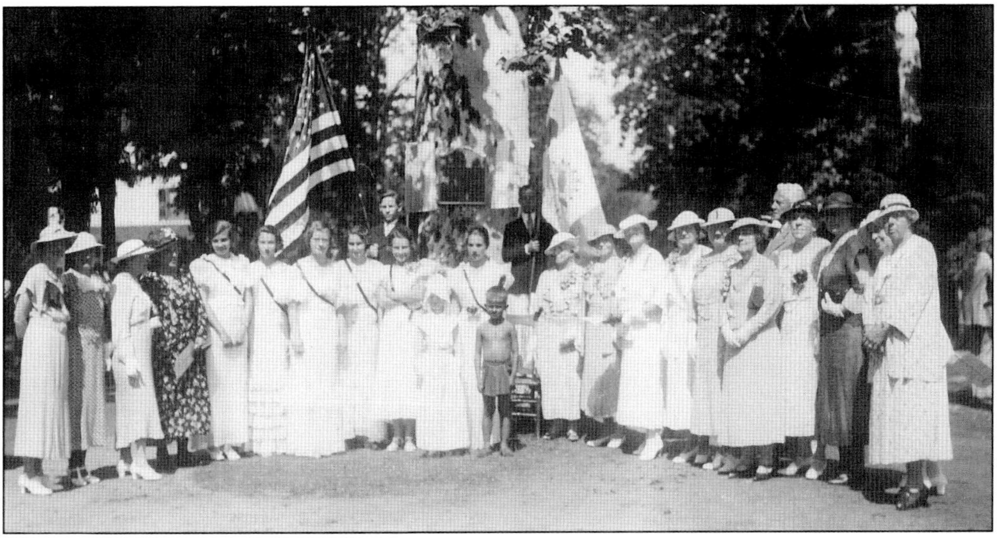

The Monmouth Chapter of the Daughters of the American Revolution placed a marker of what was believed to have been the oldest sycamore tree in Shrewsbury, celebrating their 35th anniversary and the 157th anniversary of the Battle of Monmouth. The inscription stated, "This sycamore planted by the early colonists of New Jersey marked the trail used by the Indians and later by Washington's troops on the Burlington path memorialized by Monmouth Chapter D.A.R., June 28, 1935." Mrs. Jacob B. Rue, Monmouth Chapter Regent, presented the plaque to Frederick W. Robinson, accepting for the borough. Rue is third to the right of the young boy dressed as an Indian, William C. Rue. His co-unveiler was Dorothy Parmly (in the Puritan costume, to his right). The picture was lent by Anna Louise Campbell Rudner (fifth from the left, Mrs. Rue's granddaughter).

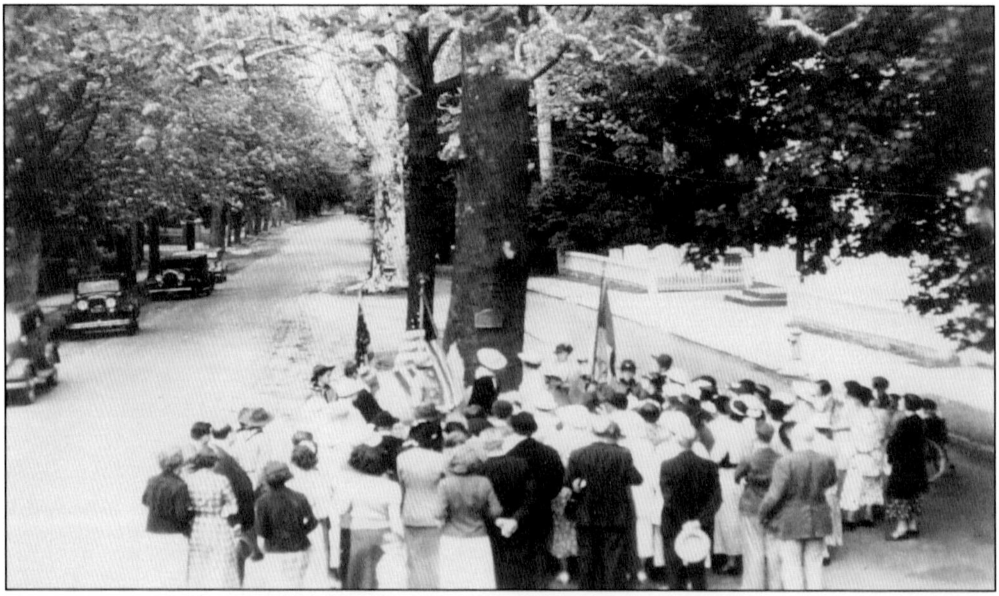

The Shrewsbury Towne Chapter of the Daughters of the American Revolution, the newer of two local DAR groups, placed a plaque on June 11, 1935, on one of Shrewsbury's old sycamore trees on a Sycamore Avenue island between Christ Church and the Quaker Meeting House. The celebration opened with a lunch for sixty people at the Allen House, then known as the Blue Door Tea House. Participants included Mayor George Silver, other Shrewsbury officials, and Boy Scout Troop No. 50, in addition to state and local DAR officers.

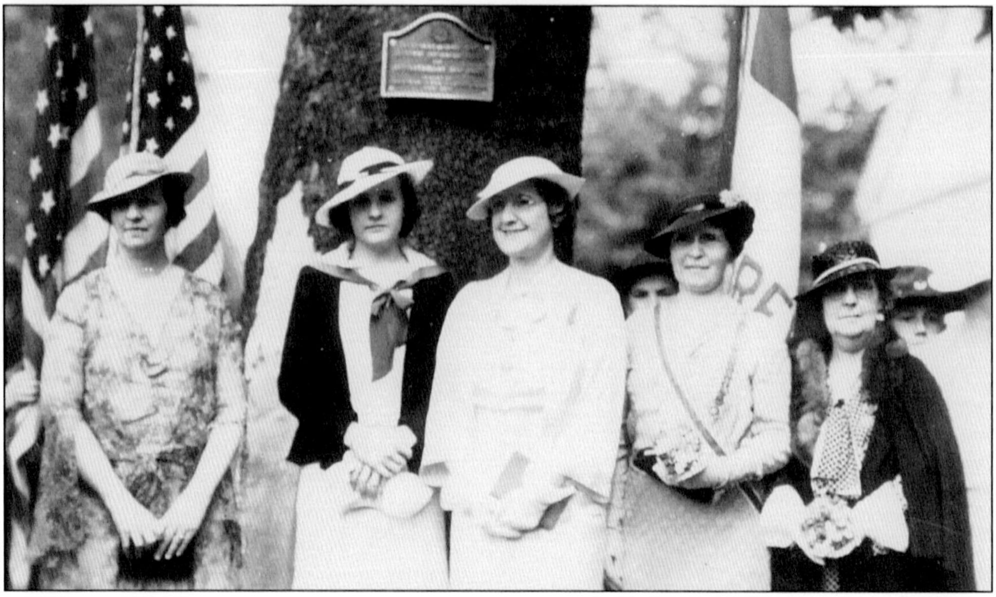

The inscription reads, "To commemorate the Historic Trees of Revolutionary Fame. Placed by the Shrewsbury Towne Chapter, D.A.R." The trees no longer stand and it is likely they did not originate at or prior to the Revolution, but let us not spoil a good story. The five women, who would appear at home in a Grant Wood painting, are not identified. A news account indicated that corsages were presented to State Regent Miss Mabel Clay and to State Historian Mrs. Samuel Johnson. Thus, they are likely the two on the right, but not necessarily in that order.

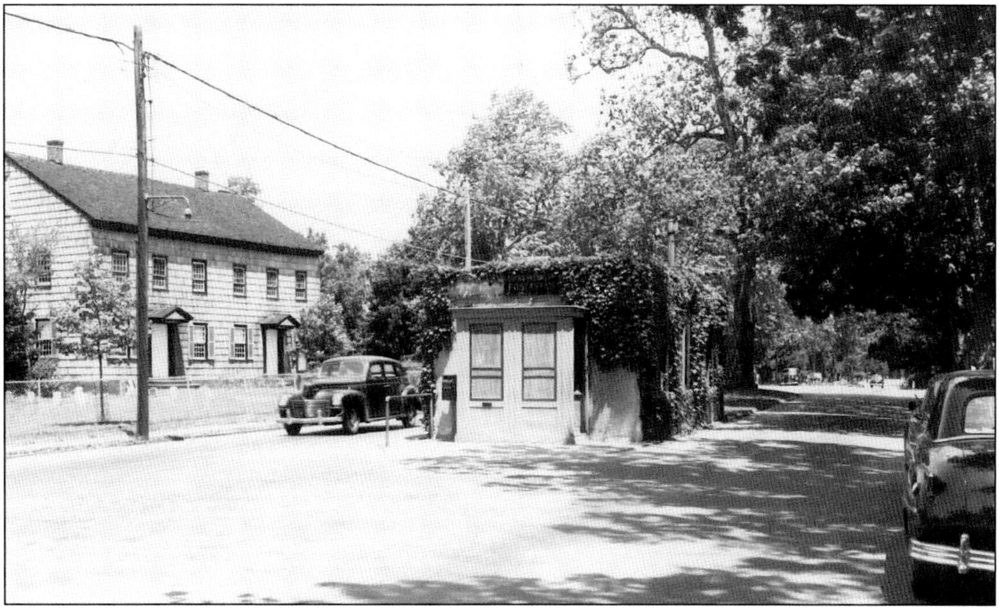

The Quakers wished to regain use of the lot leased for the Borden store (p. 29), requiring relocation of the post office. Freeholder Harry G. Borden suggested erecting a post office structure on a publicly owned island in the middle of Sycamore Avenue, opposite the then-current office. This small structure was built by Borden, opened in 1926, and soon became a curiosity as the post office in the middle of a street. It is shown here in the late 1940s. Lower traffic levels and a smaller customer base permitted its successful operation for about thirty years. See p. 9 for an aerial perspective. (Dorn's Collection.)

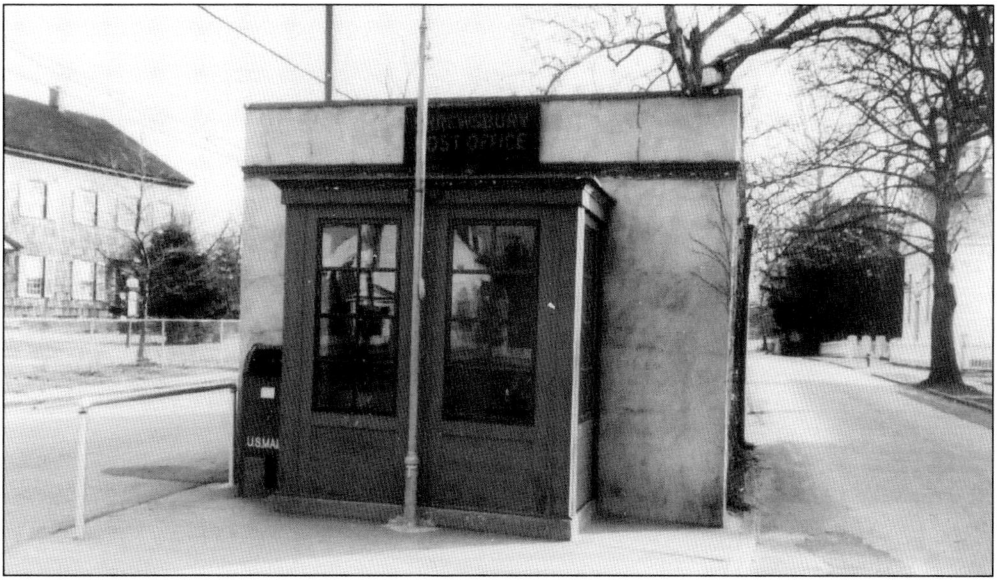

A growing Shrewsbury required modern postal facilities and a new post office opened on Broad Street in 1957. The borough's police used the building for several years, but the force found the space inadequate. The Daughters of the American Revolution had considered, then rejected, a proposal that the tiny, deteriorating building be used as a museum. Absent a use and user, the former middle-of-the-road post office was demolished in May 1966.

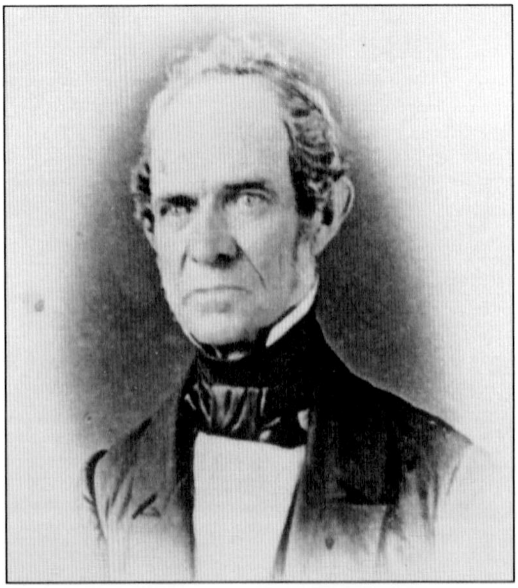 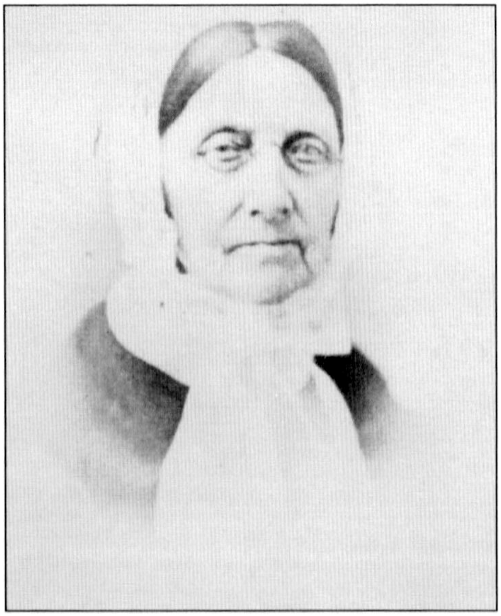

During his time, Dr. Edmund W. Allen (1788–1867) was better known as a Shrewsbury-area physician than as the 1814 co-purchaser of the ancient former tavern at the northwest corner of Broad Street and Sycamore Avenue. The tavern was built by Judah Allen in the late seventeenth century. There is no apparent familial tie among these Allens and another Judah Allen who bought the place in 1775. Dr. Allen's time probably saw changes better-adapting the large structure to private residential use. His wife's maiden name was Sarah Throckmorton (1790–1875). (Both images from the Shrewsbury Historical Society Collection.)

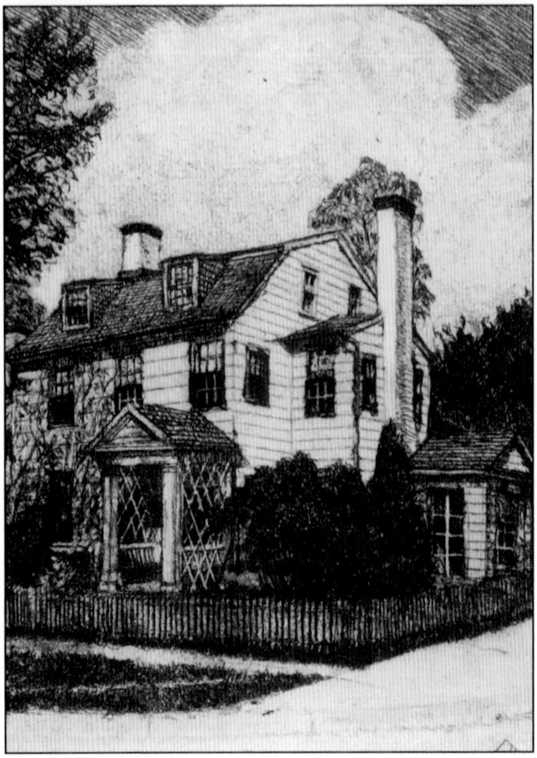

The Allen House's period of greatest notoriety was likely during the time of Josiah Halstead, a local carpenter who bought the place in 1754, when he was licensed to operate a tavern. He continued to run the tavern for some while after he lost it by foreclosure in 1773. The building, known as the Blue Ball Tavern, was a virtual town center, typical of colonial-era taverns. The house was expanded in stages, likely starting as a small one or one-and-one-half-story building. A kitchen, not visible on the west (left) was a likely addition. This relatively recent 1945 etching post-dates the store. (Shrewsbury Historical Society Collection.)

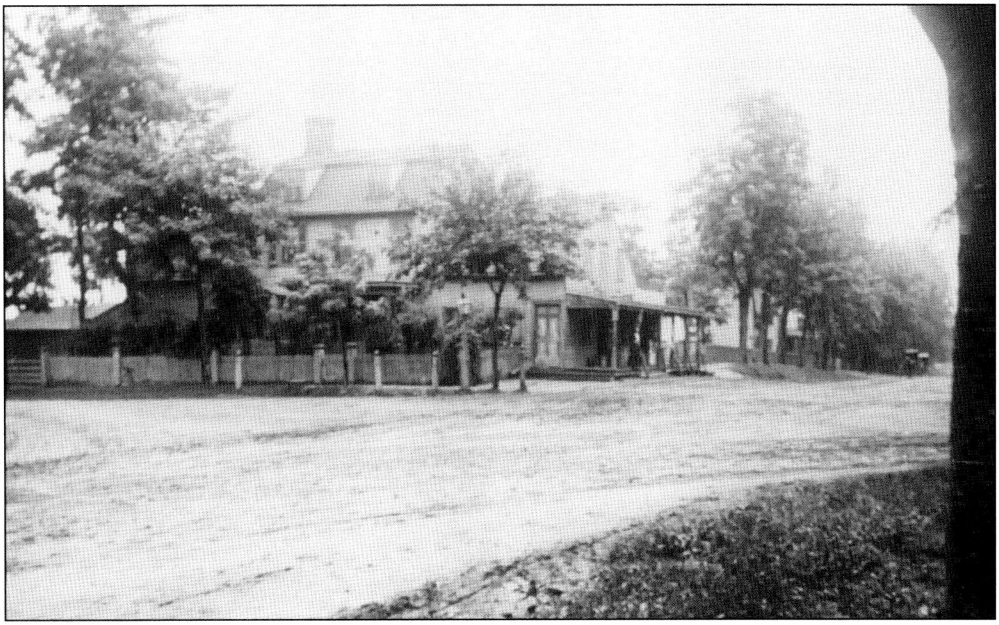

Shrewsbury's historic Four Corners (seen here looking north) form at the intersection of Broad Street (long a major north-south route, part of the King's Highway) and Sycamore Avenue (part of the old Burlington Path, a route to the shore). This view shows the addition of the store on the east (or right) built *c.* 1814, when Jacob Corlies was co-owner with Dr. Edmund Allen. The store was initially known as Corlies and Allen, the doctor's son, Joseph, being the Allen member of the firm.

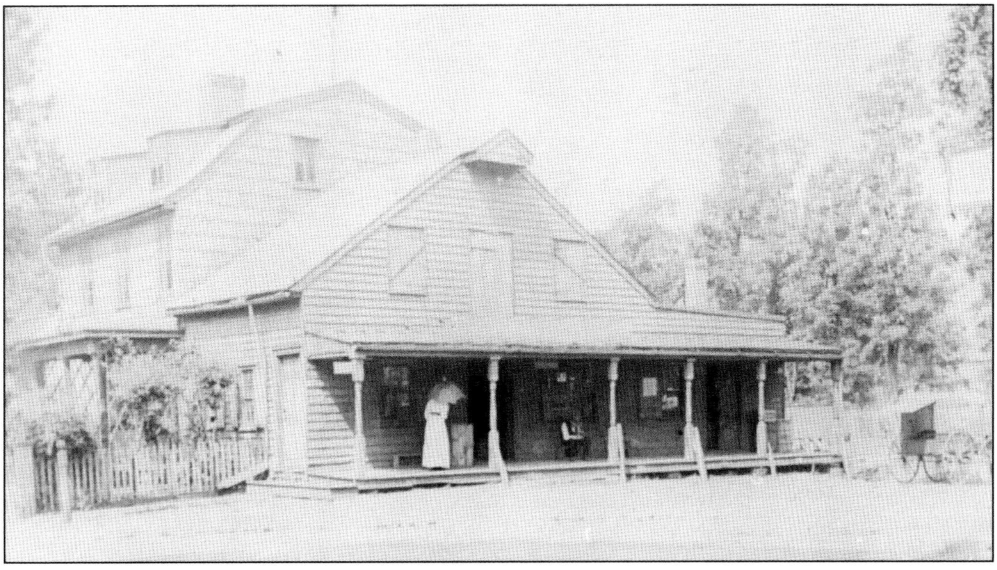

A. Holmes Borden, who had clerked in the general store of George Bradford and Charles Price near the Shrewsbury railroad station, bought Joseph T. Allen's store at the Allen House in 1883. Although Allen had a general mercantile establishment, Borden specialized in general groceries, flour, canned goods, and country produce. The store's interior was about 30-by-60 feet. The place continued the tavern's traditional role of community center and long contained Shrewsbury's post office. This is a late-nineteenth-century photograph.

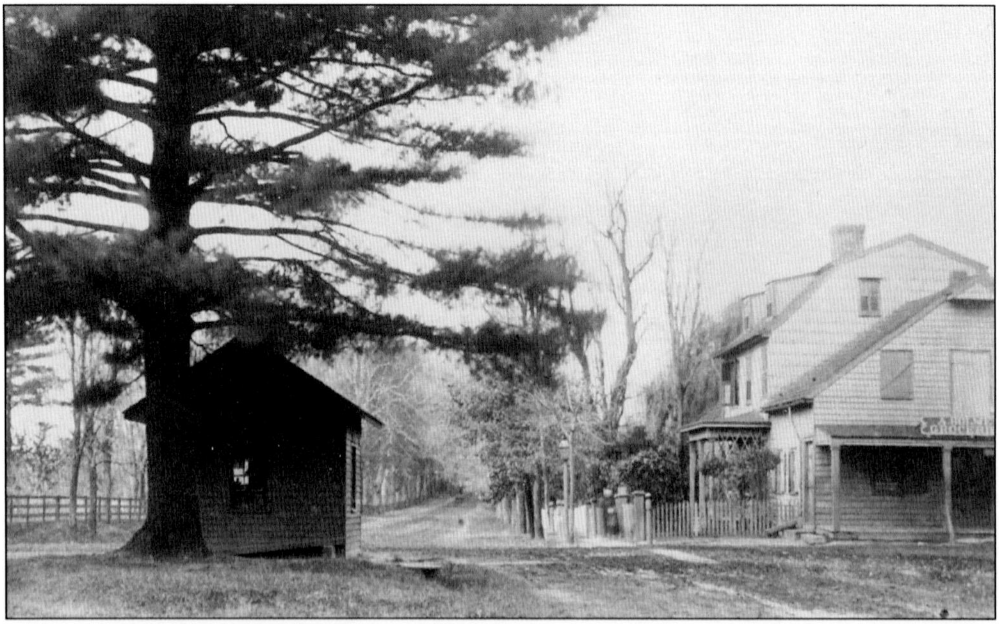

This unusual view looking west on Sycamore Avenue shows the Allen House from the perspective behind the Council Pine and the former tollhouse. The addition of the porch expanded the appearance of the store's size, but removed the apparent former hoisting capability for second-story storage. The porch was subject to heavy wear, as it was replaced in March 1892. This is an 1890s photograph by W.H. Richardson. (Special Collections and Archives, Rutgers University Libraries.)

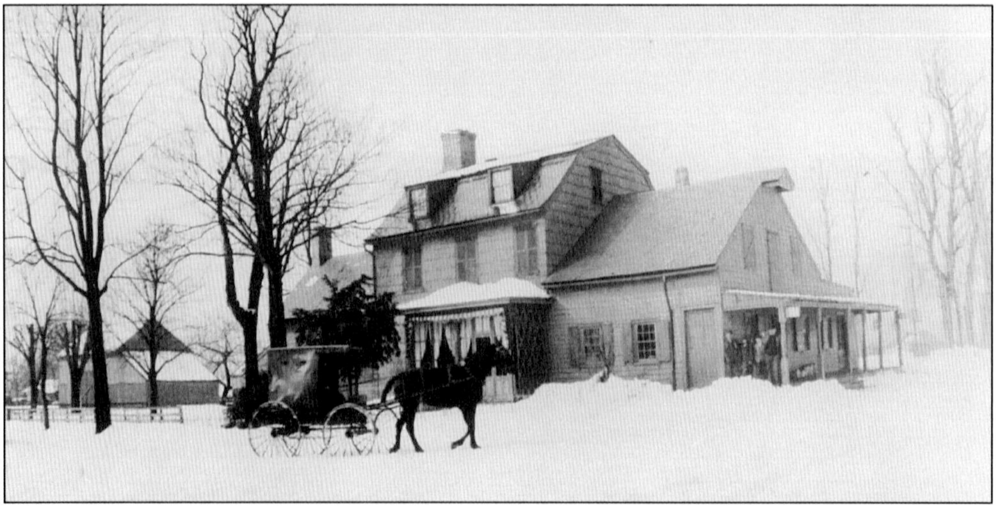

The Allen House (seen here in the 1890s) has a lengthy history that does not fit caption space. For greater depth, see Margaret K. Hofer's *A Tavern for the Town: Josiah Halstead's Tavern and Community Life in Eighteenth Century Shrewsbury*, presented at the 1992 meeting of the Monmouth County Historical Association. It recounts Revolutionary War bloodshed, including the 1779 "Allen House massacre," first reported in a March 25, 1846 letter by Lyttleton White to Daniel Veach McLean, D.D., of Freehold and the Executive Committee of the New Jersey Historical Society. A contemporary account was told to him years later by Joseph Price, the leader of the assailing Tory forces.

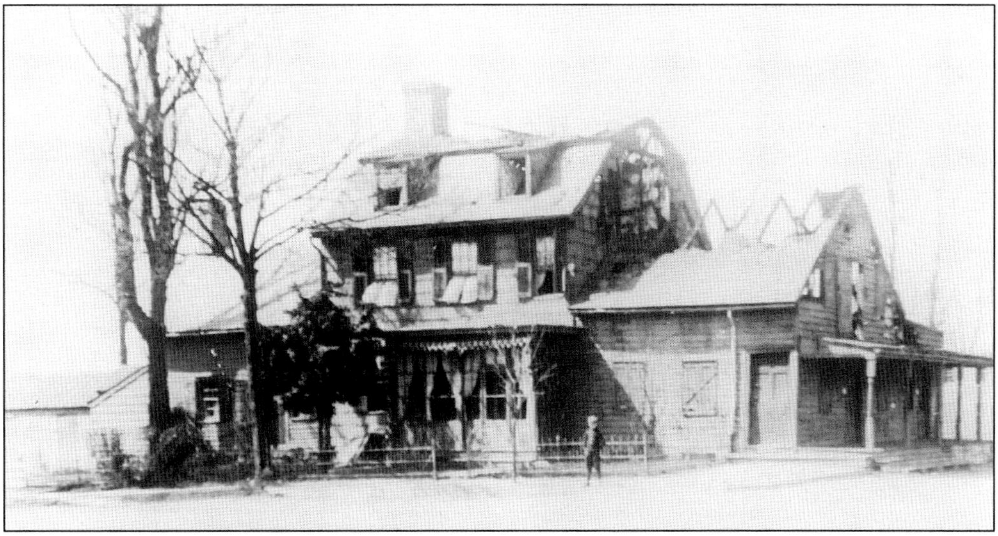

A fire on April 17, 1914, destroyed A. Holmes Borden's grocery business and seriously damaged the residence of Dr. William C. and Mrs. Sarah Nicholas (a daughter of Dr. Edward Allen). The fire apparently started in an upper story and spread downward, threatening the entire building, which was saved through the exertions of three fire companies. Much effort was spent removing contents, with Borden and Michael Sagurton crawling inside to rescue the store's account books. John Hawkins, a fireman overcome by smoke, was revived in fresh air and returned to firefighting duties. The house was repaired; the store moved.

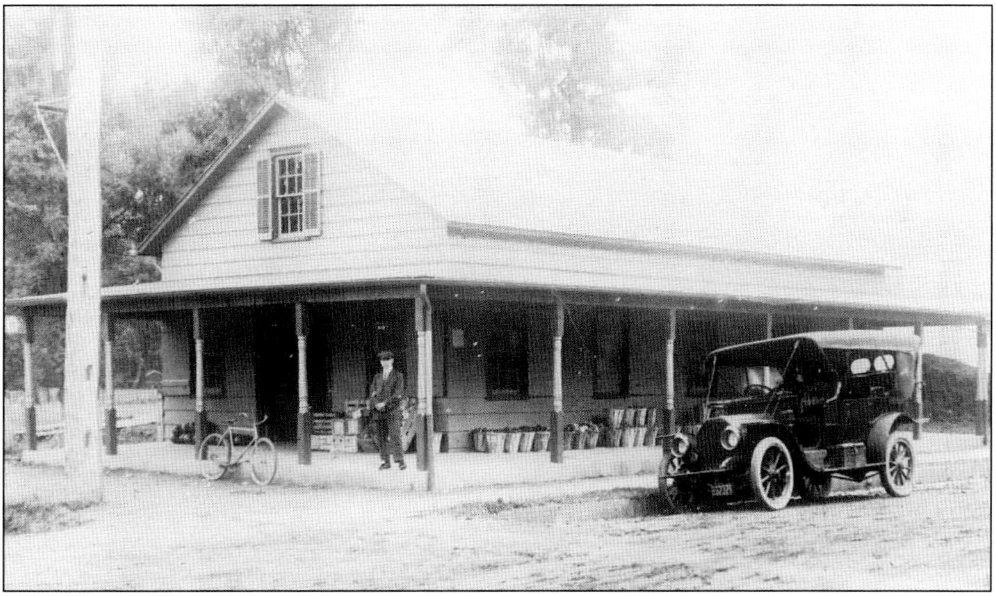

A. Holmes Borden secured a ten-year lease on the grounds of the Quaker Meeting House on the northeast corner of Broad and Sycamore and erected this building. The photograph accompanied a c. 1914 article in *The New Jersey Trade Review* which indicated Borden, paying cash, enjoyed a wide following among county farmers and had customers from a long stretch of the shore. On September 20, 1916, the *Register* reported that President and Mrs. Wilson, motoring with Senator James E. Martine, stopped here. The store was removed to Apple Street, Tinton Falls, remodeled to a residence, and was destroyed by a crashing airplane.

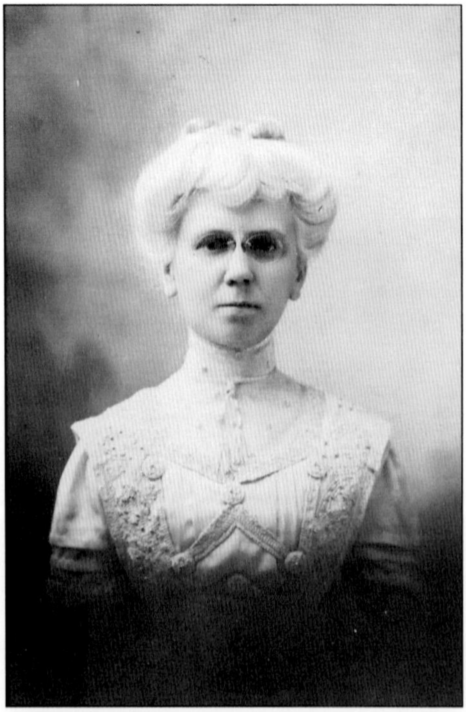

Margaret Allen (1860–1959), daughter of Dr. Edmund Allen, was the last Allen to occupy the house, using it in summers during the 1920s. In 1927 she sold the house to George Silver, Shrewsbury's second mayor. Silver, who did not occupy the place, was motivated by preservation interests, following reports that an oil company desired the site for a gas station. The Shrewsbury Towne Chapter of the Daughters of the American Revolution urged unsuccessfully that the National Parks Service purchase the Allen House. (Shrewsbury Historical Society Collection.)

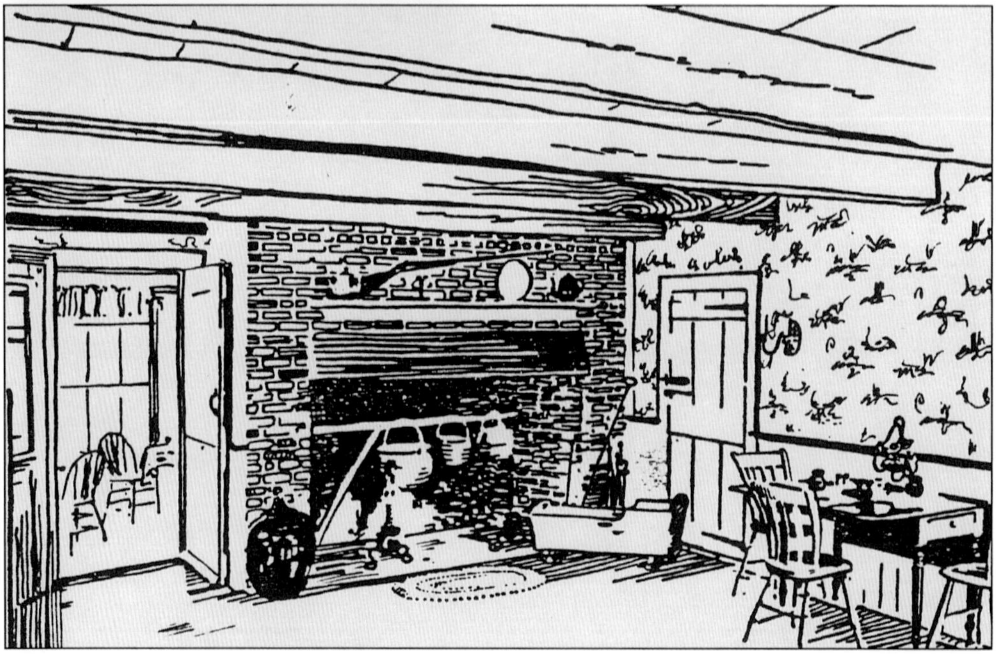

The 1930s saw a number of rented occupancies of the Allen House, usually involving art, antiques, or tea. Homer K. Secor operated the Colonial Tea Rom in 1933–34, and sold his homemade ice cream here. This view, from his trade card, reflects his dining room. In 1937, owner Silver proposed to sell it to the borough for use as a municipal hall, but economy-minded voters rejected the idea. A 1942 fire gutted the third floor, destroying drawings of architect Robert C. Edwards, son of lessee Ethel M. Edwards.

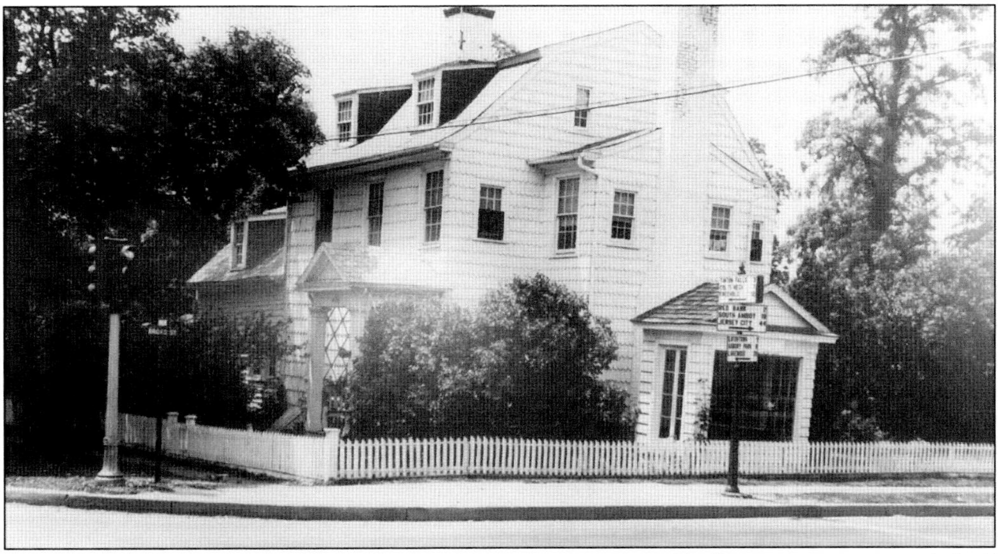

George and Jessie Silver sold the Allen House to Mary McDonald of Bayonne, acting on behalf of Henry H. and Nellie Reid Holmes of Jersey City, who rented it out for some years. The house, shown here in the 1950s, was later occupied by Lillie Huelsen, a friend of Mrs. Holmes, who was at first reluctant to follow the latter's suggestion to occupy, but who later enjoyed the place. Mrs. Holmes willed the house to the Monmouth County Historical Association, who accepted it after Miss Huelsen's tenancy. (Shrewsbury Historical Society Collection.)

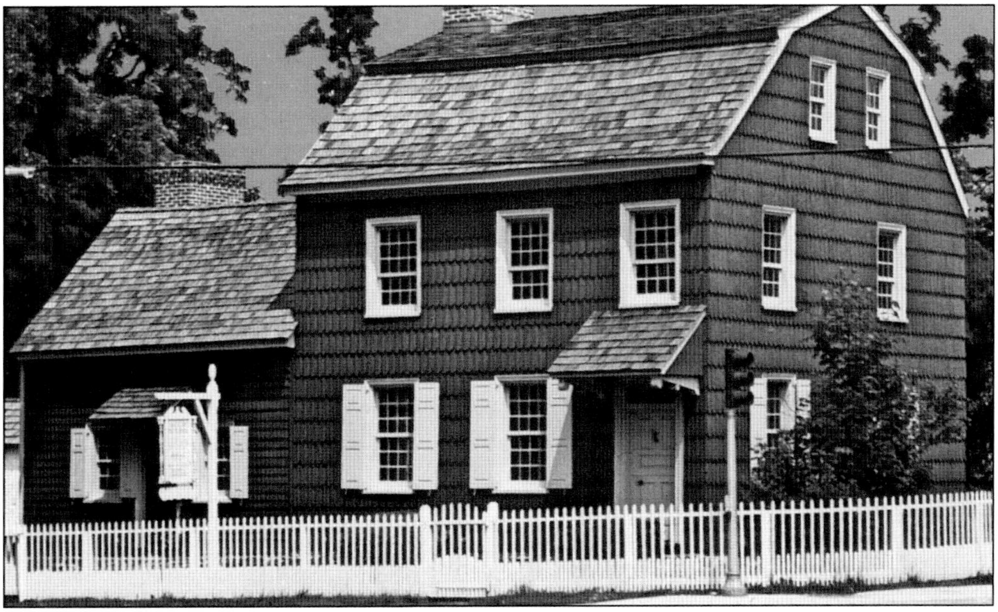

The Monmouth County Historical Association undertook restoration of the Allen House in the early 1970s. Fund-raising was aided by a local group, the Shrewsbury Association for the Restoration of the Allen House, better known by its acronym, SARAH. The project's goal was to return the house to its late-eighteenth-century appearance. This is a 1970s postcard of the home after the project was completed. A sale advertisement of 1770 described the house as two stories. One wonders if the dormers, present in the early nineteenth century (see p. 32), were part of the upper story's construction.

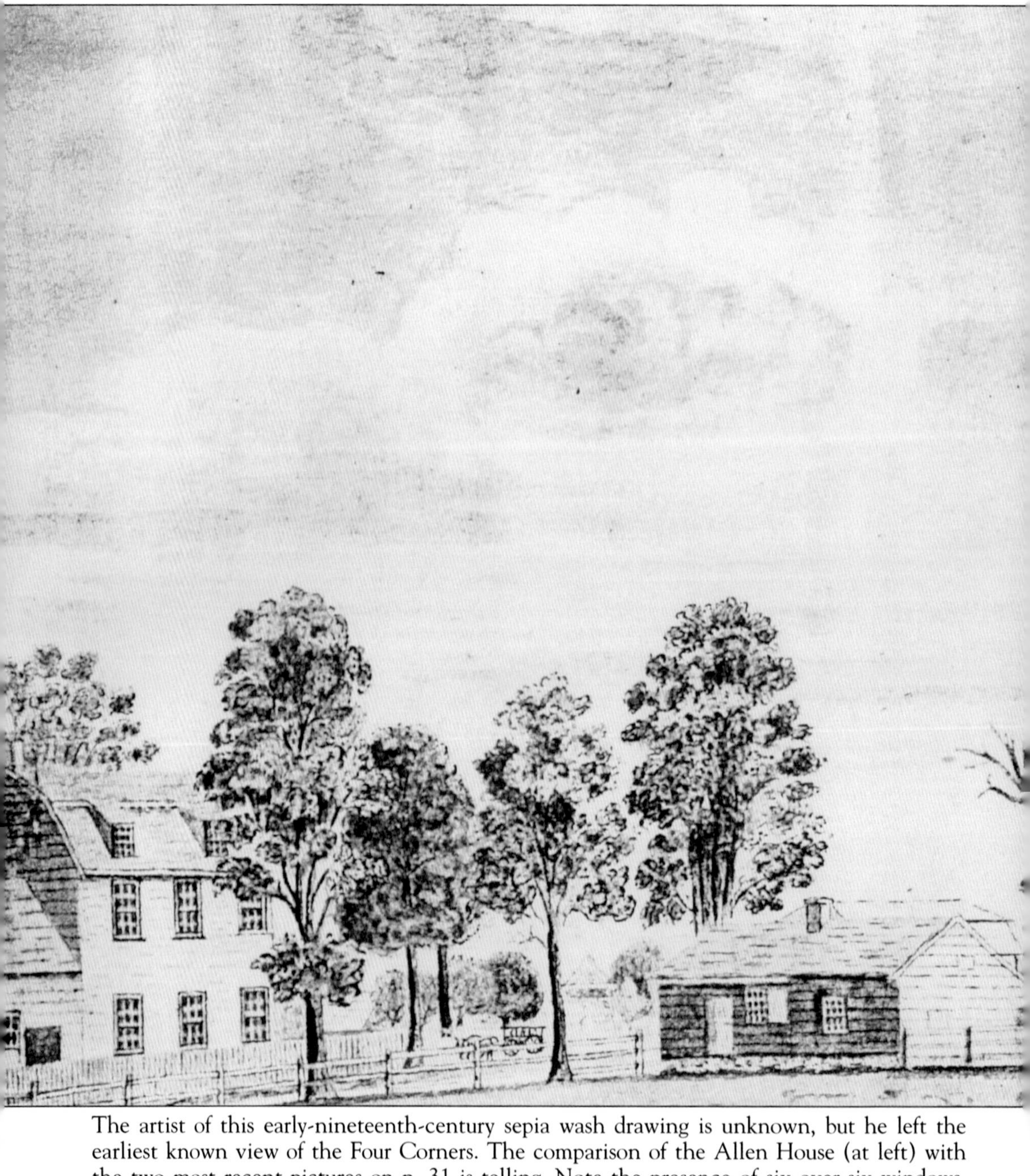

The artist of this early-nineteenth-century sepia wash drawing is unknown, but he left the earliest known view of the Four Corners. The comparison of the Allen House (at left) with the two most recent pictures on p. 31 is telling. Note the presence of six-over-six windows, and the pre-restoration fenestration as opposed to the twelve-over-eights installed now. The dormers were, perhaps, built when the third floor was raised. Also note the absence of a door on the south facade. The blacksmith-wheelwright shop, outlined on the 1860 map (p. 92), was removed by 1889 (p. 93). Behind it is a corner of the Quaker Meeting House. Pre-remodeling

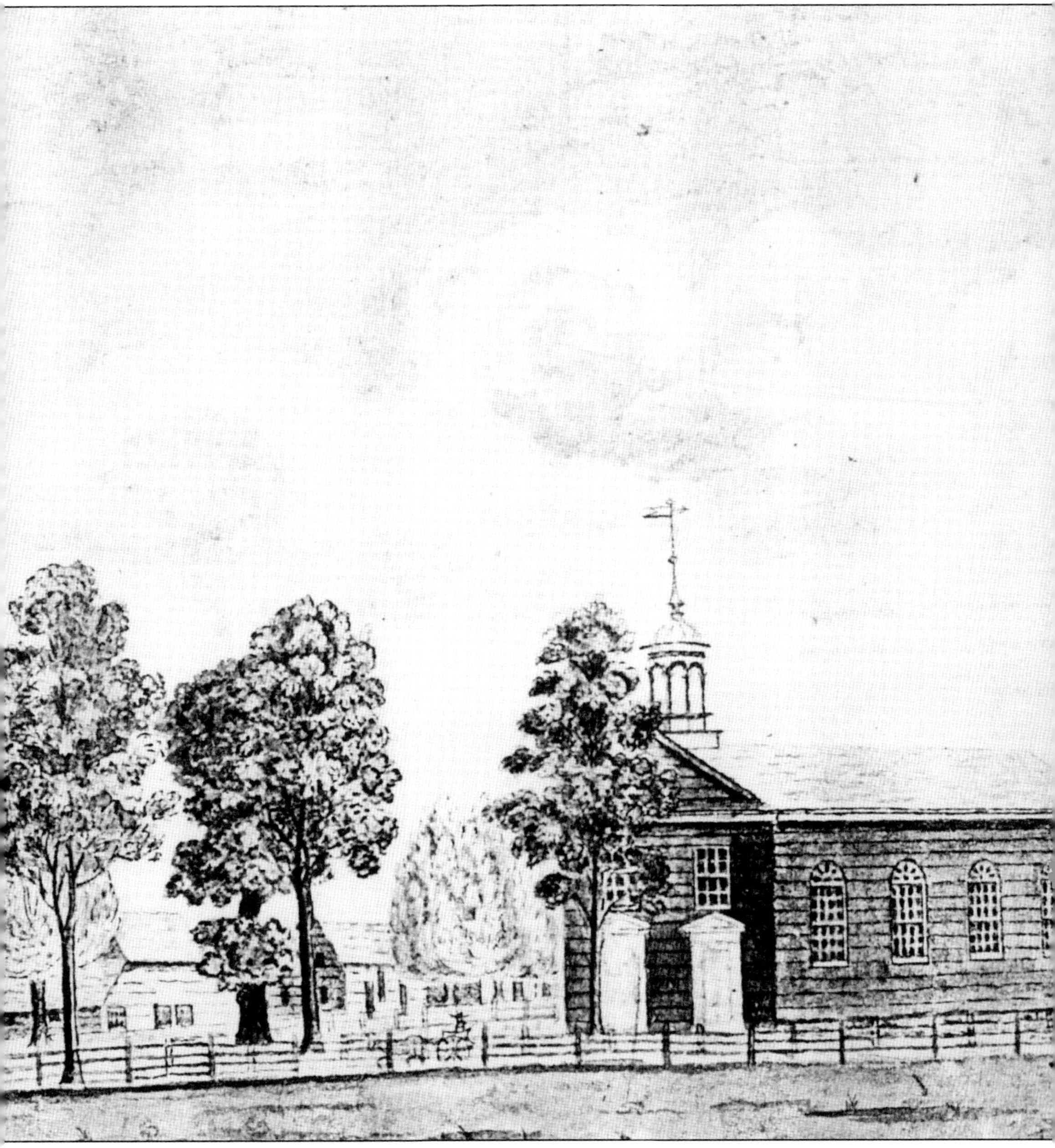

Christ Church has the same appearance as in the p. 10 photograph. This view likely pre-dates the 1822 erection of the present Presbyterian edifice and may date from the time they were without a church. Although the perspective could have the Presbyterian site obscured by Christ Church, one suspects the artist would have changed the view to make a nearby church visible. The original drawing is owned by the Monmouth County Historical Association, publisher of the print from which this image was made.

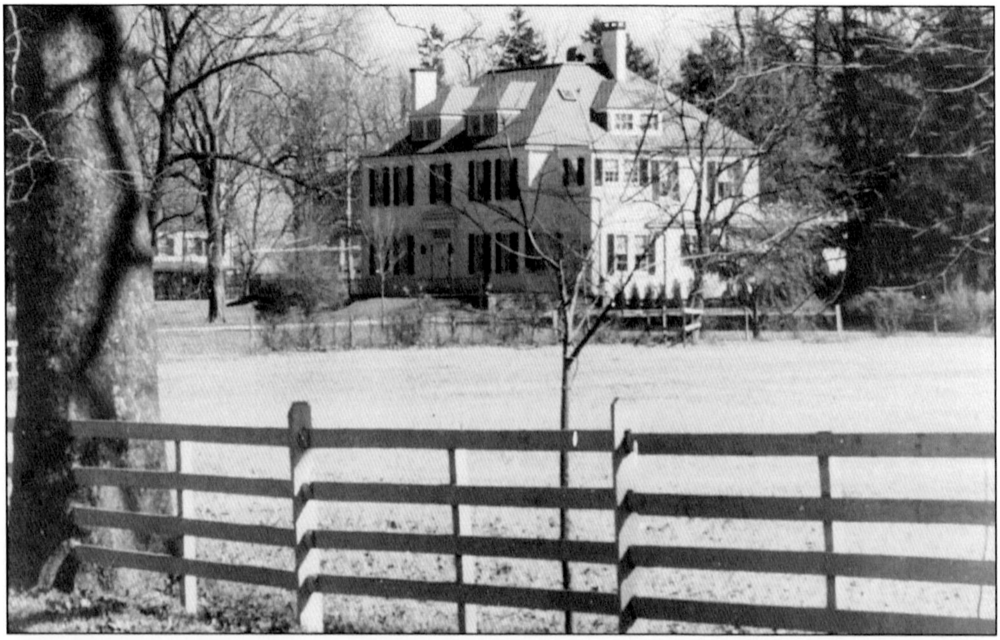

This is the Shrewsbury Borough Hall, at 419 Sycamore Avenue at the southwest corner of Broad Street, as seen *c.* 1940. The structure was built *c.* 1825 by Seth Lippincott, probably as a three-bay house with a side hall. Commonly known as the Wardell House, it is also known as the Meacham House for the last private owners, and the Tallman House for a late-nineteenth-century owner. It was later owned by Edward Kemp, James Loeb, and L.L. White in succession. (Shrewsbury Historical Society Collection.)

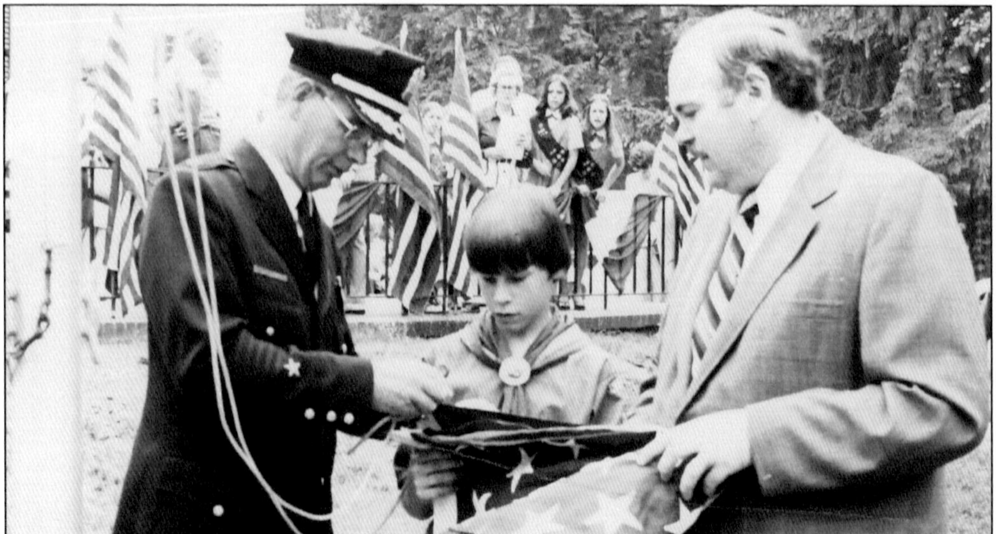

The Wardell, or Lippincott, House was occupied by the borough offices in 1975 and dedicated May 15, 1976, in ceremonies conducted by one Boy Scout and two Girl Scout troops. Scout Kevin Calandriello is receiving assistance with a flag from Police Chief Raymond "Bucky" Mass (who would later be mayor) and Mayor Joseph F. Dennis. Preserving this fine building is one of the borough's significant current public issues.

Two

Shadowbrook

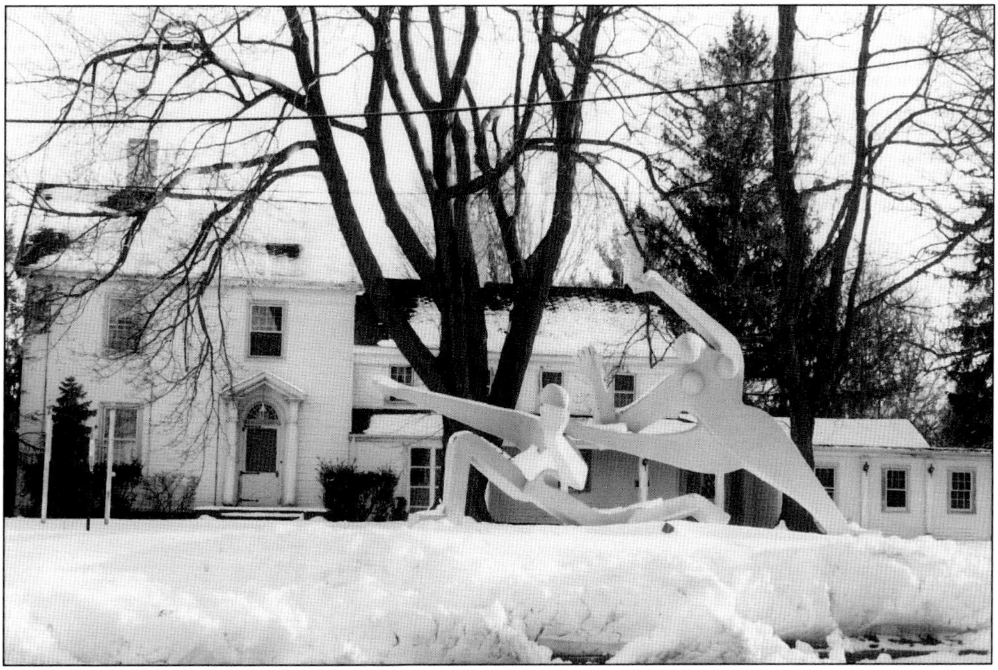

Sculptor Sid Martin's *The Dancers* has enlivened a busy commercial stretch of Broad Street during 1995 and 1996. A career which embraced many styles of painted and sculpted work culminated in a specialty of large, fiberglass figures in action or contemplative poses. Sid enjoyed the public's reaction to his work, as much as he enjoyed the creative process. He died unexpectedly on April 26, 1996. May this image of his work, overlooking the Stillwell House, the superintendent's cottage of Shadow Brook, serve as a memorial to a rich career and a fine gentleman.

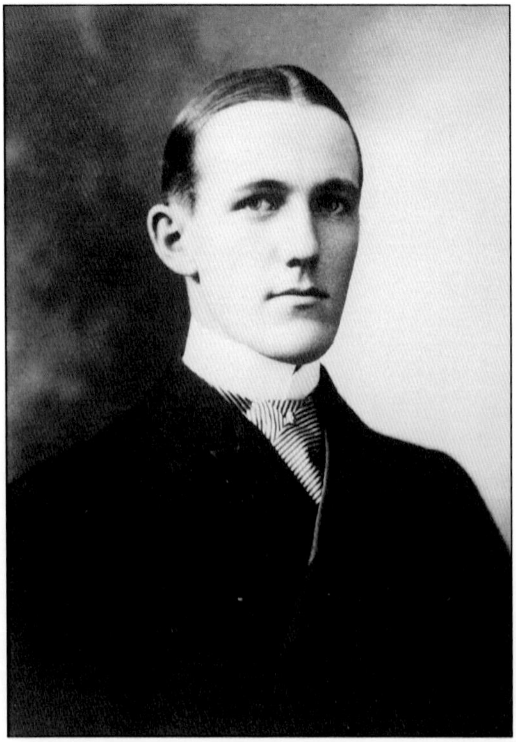

Ernest Fahnestock was born in New York City on January 27, 1876, the son of Harris and Margaret Antoinette (McKinley) Fahnestock, who summered at Elberon, Long Branch. His father was a noted financier, enjoying a close relationship with the federal government during the Civil War. Ernest, shown here *c.* 1900, received his pre-medical education at Harvard and studied medicine at Columbia, graduating in 1900 in the same class as his brother Clarence. Fahnestock was a surgeon and a patron of varied medical and welfare organizations, including the predecessor of Monmouth Medical Center. (Shrewsbury Historical Society Collection.)

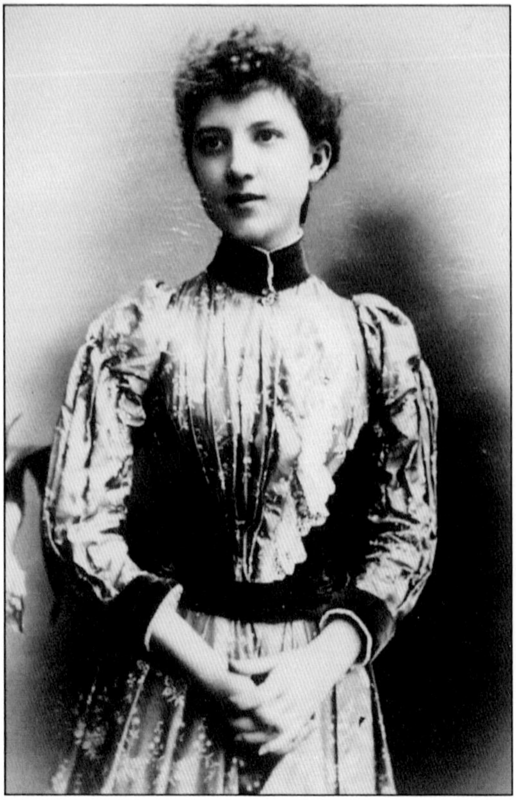

Georgette (De Grove) Perry was born in Paris in 1873, daughter of New York lawyer Edward Ritzema De Grove. Shown here *c.* 1900, she was the widow of Edward Perry, with two children, when she married Ernest Fahnestock on February 15, 1905, in New York. They had two daughters, Mildred Helen and Evelyn. The family pronounced the first syllable of their name "fan." (Collection of the Shrewsbury Historical Society.)

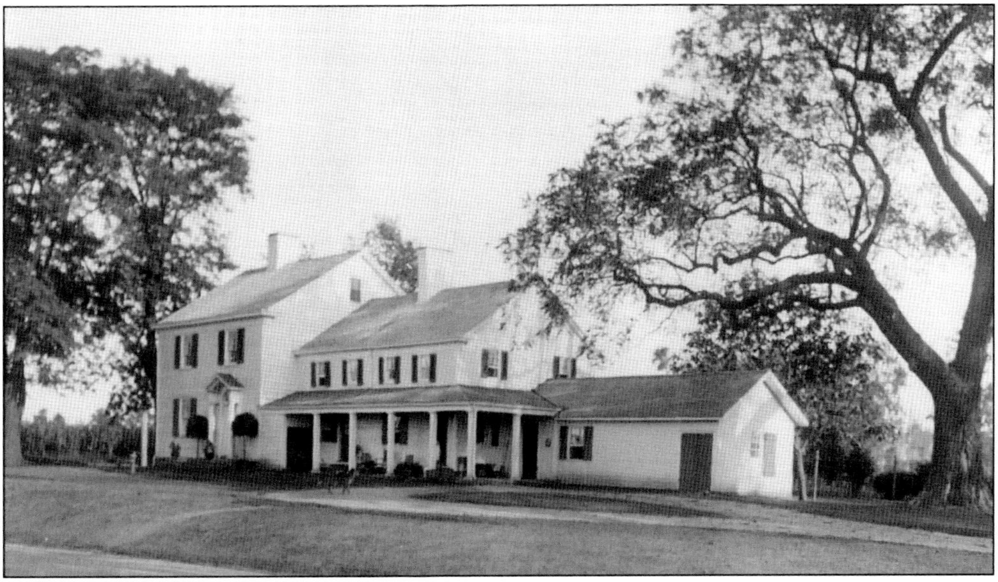

Fahnestock bought the 115-acre George W. Stillwell farm from his estate in 1908. Stillwell operated a profitable farm, invested in real estate, and was an expert cattle dealer and butcher. Fahnestock remodeled the house, using it as a superintendent's residence. His farm spanned Broad Street. An unnamed brook marked the northern boundary of the section east of Broad Street. It, and the shadows cast by the many plantings on the estate, gave rise to its name: Shadow Brook, long spelled as two words. This is a *c.* 1912 photograph.

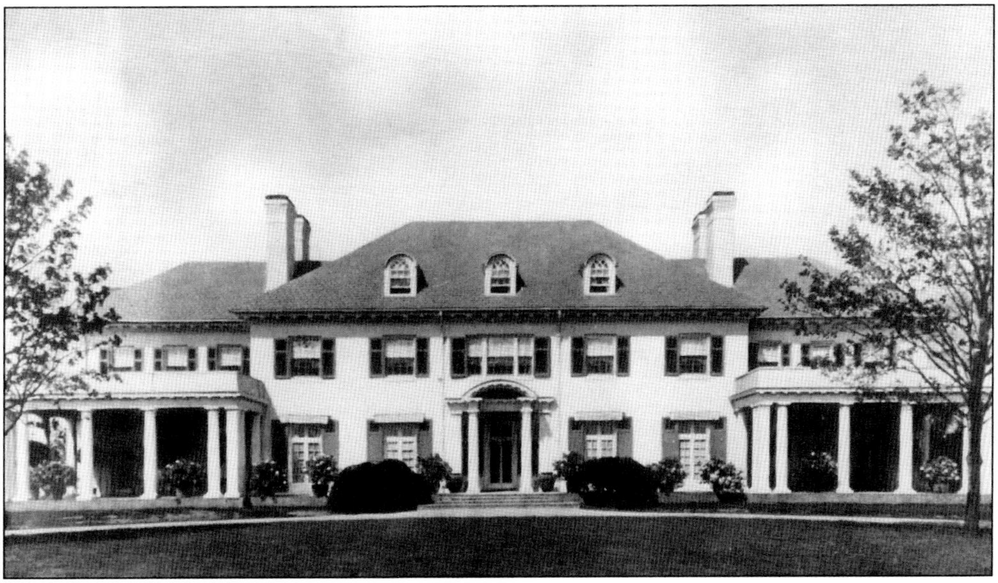

The main house was a five-bay, hipped-roof Colonial Revival, with segmental arches over the door and third-story dormers. Wings on each side were fronted by open piazzas, which were enclosed after the Fahnestocks' time. Three large rooms made up the principal first-floor living quarters: the living room on the east of the main block, the library in the east wing, and a dining room in the west. Bedrooms and guest room made up the second story, while staff room and storage space occupied the upper story. This is a *c.* 1912 photograph taken not long after the house was completed in the summer of 1910.

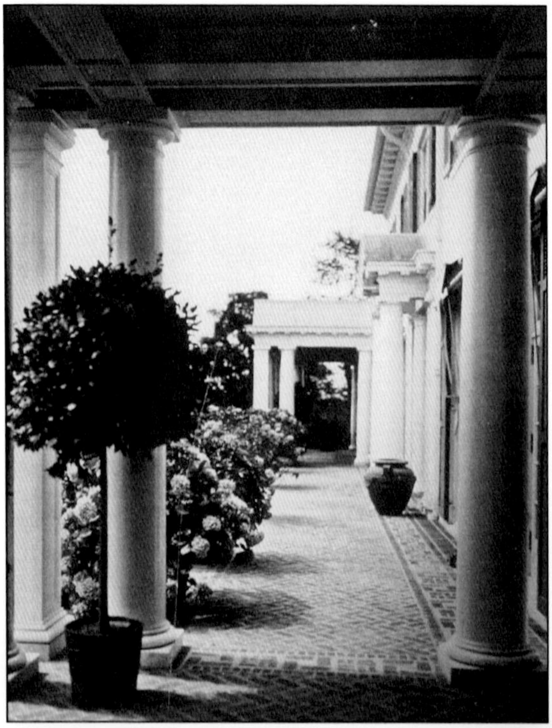

Shadow Brook was produced during the 1906–14 partnership of Lewis Colt Albro and Harrie T. Lindeberg. It was likely a collaborative effort, perhaps more the work of the lesser-known Albro, who maintained the Fahnestock family tie, a relationship recalled by architect Edward Ritzema Perry, Dr. Fahnestock's stepson. Albro also designed a farm group of French Norman influence, built for brother Clarence in Putnam County, New York, which Ernest Fahnestock gave to the state after the former's death in France during World War I. This is a *c.* 1912 photograph.

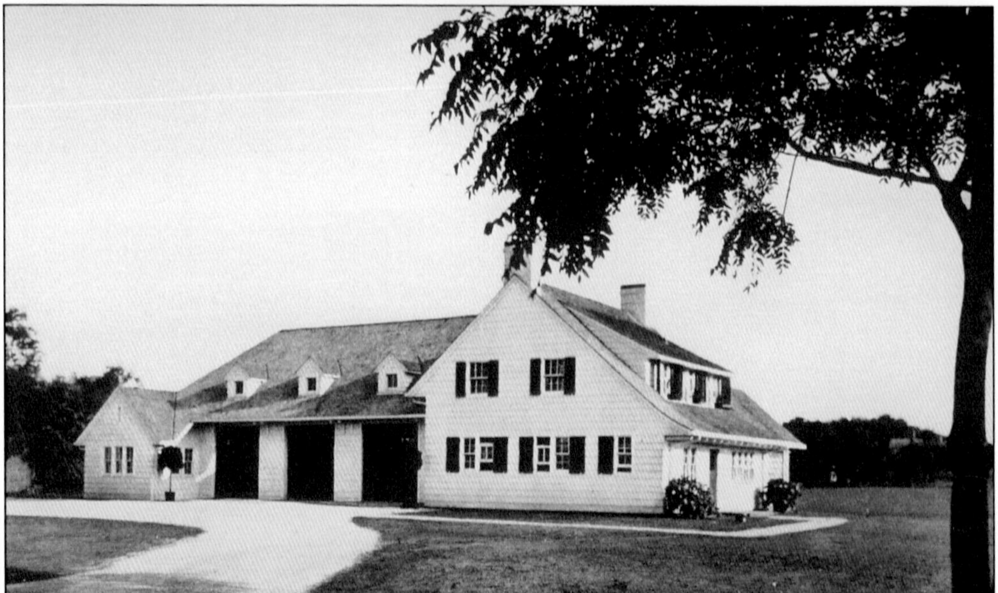

Fahnestock's combination automobile garage and chauffeur's residence was begun in the spring of 1910, built by Ashbel W. Borden. The frame structure was about 30-by-90 feet. Catherine Attridge, daughter of John Ellis, Fahnestock's chauffeur, recalls, "We lived most of the year in New York, but came to Shadow Brook for three months each summer. My father lived in the garage apartment." The farm buildings were designed as a unified group with the main house. The building, shown here *c.* 1912, was remodeled as a private residence.

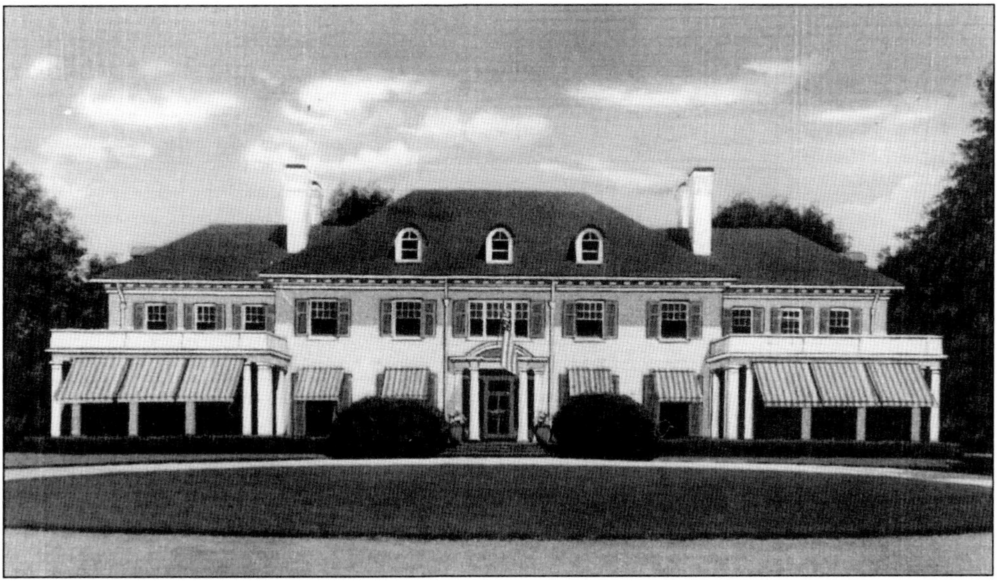

Fred Thorngreen, a noted restaurateur in southern Monmouth County, lost his Squankum Inn to fire on March 9, 1942. He bought the Fahnestock house and about 10 acres from Ray Stillman in August 1943. In 1944 he opened a restaurant here called the Shadow Brook Inn. The war years were not opportune for new restaurants, with Thorngreen claiming he was compelled to close for a time in 1944 due to inadequate meat supplies. This *c.* 1940s postcard shows the restaurant looking little changed from the house. (John Rhody Collection.)

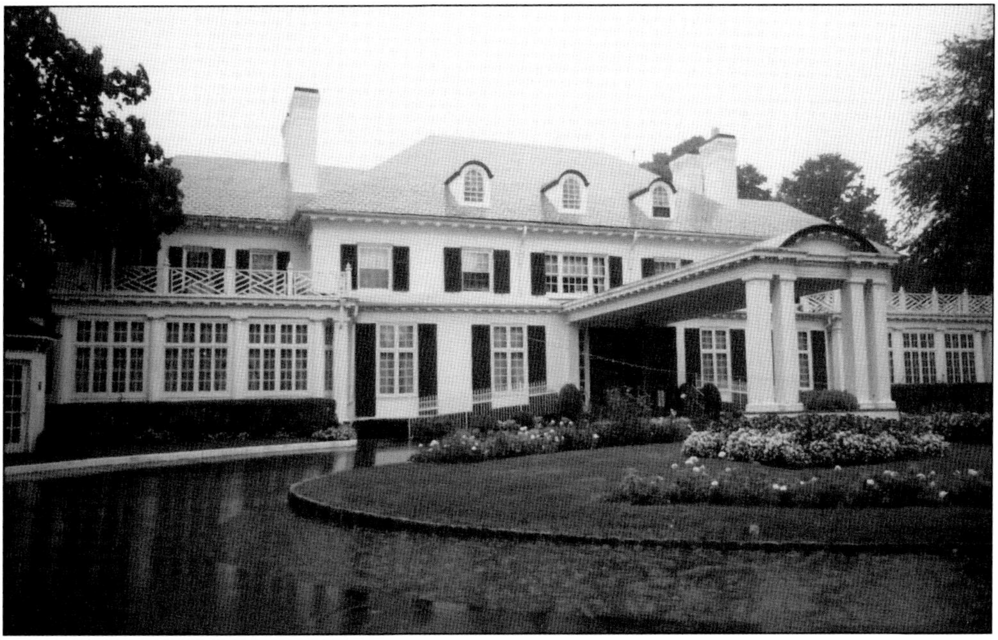

The Shadowbrook as it appears today, physically and with its one-word spelling. The earliest known occurence of the name as one word is an October 31,1946 *Register* ad—it not known if the words were linked by forethought, typesetter's error, or the need to fit a space. The open piazzas were enclosed and a canopied entrance built out, the latter retaining the segmental arch and square columns of the front door.

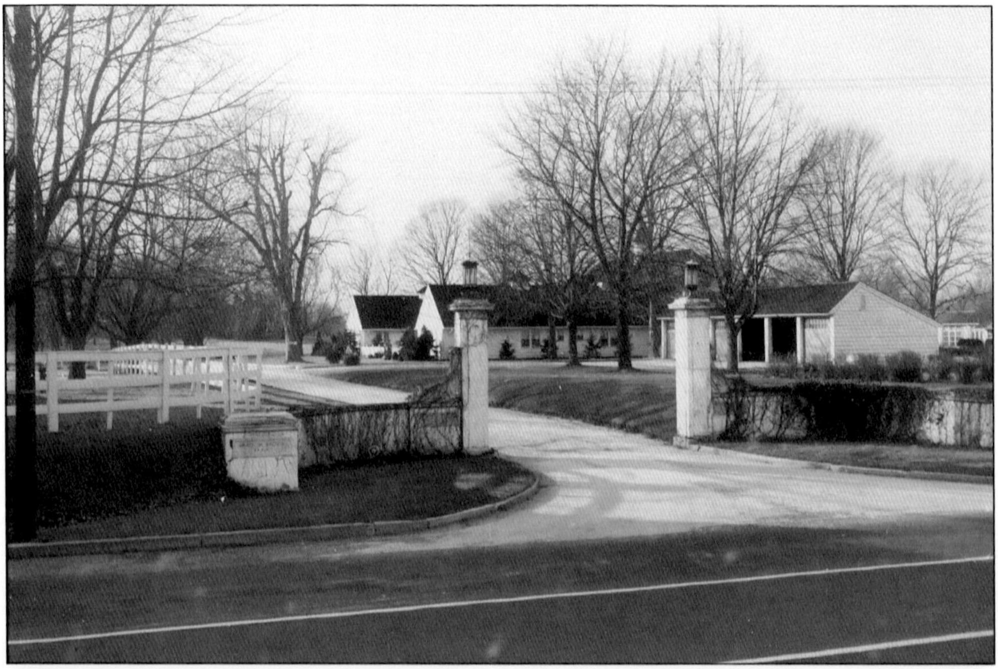

Today's Shadowbrook Drive was one entrance to the estate. This early 1950s view shows the former carriage house in the background and a narrow path between the gate posts. The posts proved an irresistible target for a delivery truck *c.* 1960, and they no longer stand. The street has since been widened significantly. (Dorn's Collection.)

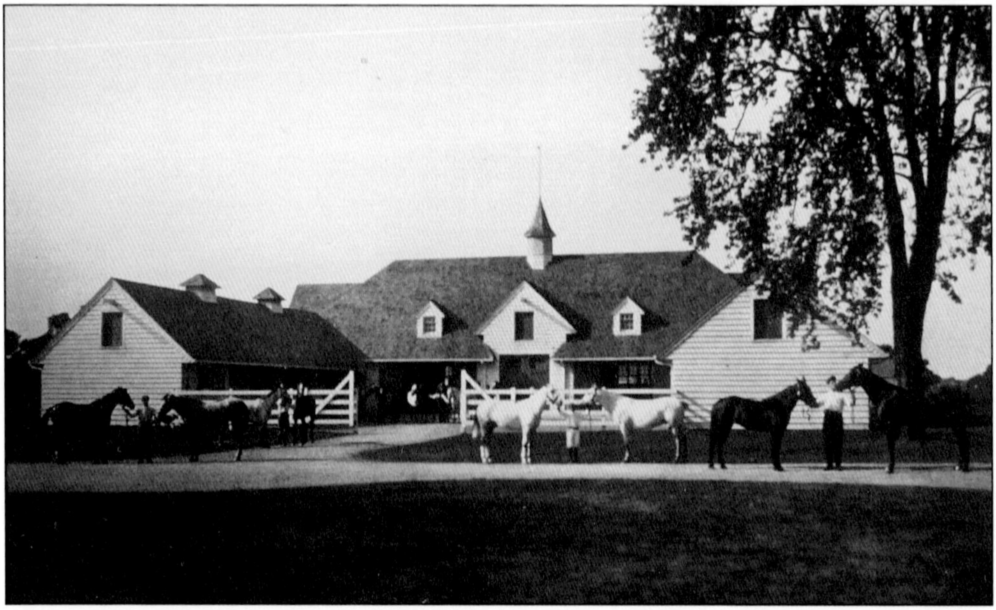

The carriage house, shown here *c.* 1912, was designed in a U-shape, with the massive carriage storage room at the base of the U. Horses were stabled in the wings, one side for farm horses, the other for saddle horses. Dr. Fahnestock liked to ride "in the back country," often traveling with his groom, a former jockey. He was not known to be a member of the organized equestrian circles so popular in his day.

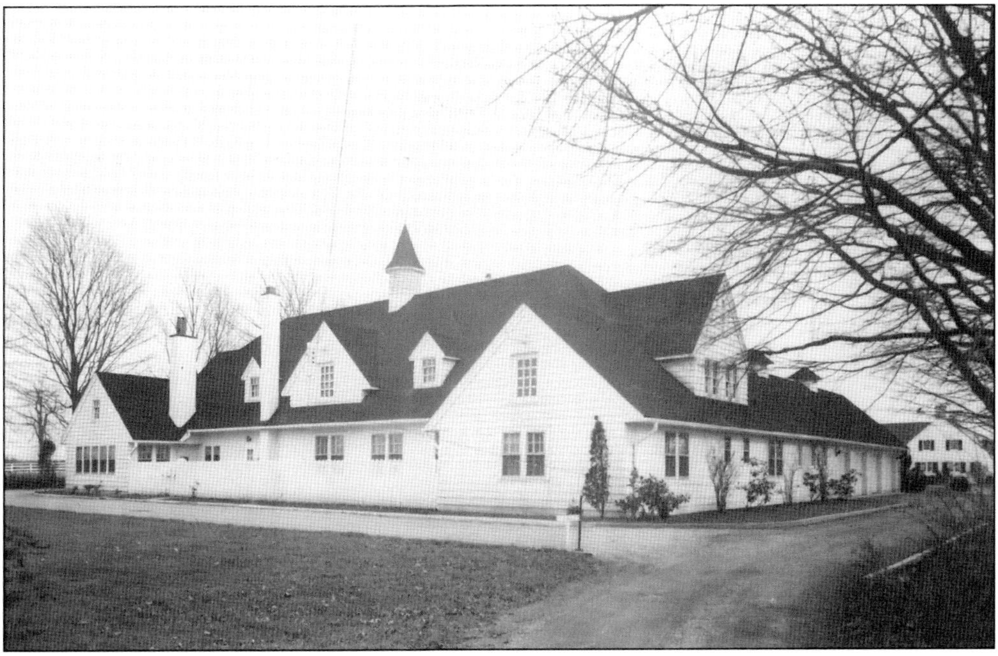

This is the rear of the carriage house in the early 1950s, with the large center dormer the entrance to the hay storage area. The living quarters for hired help were also on the second floor. (Dorn's Collection.)

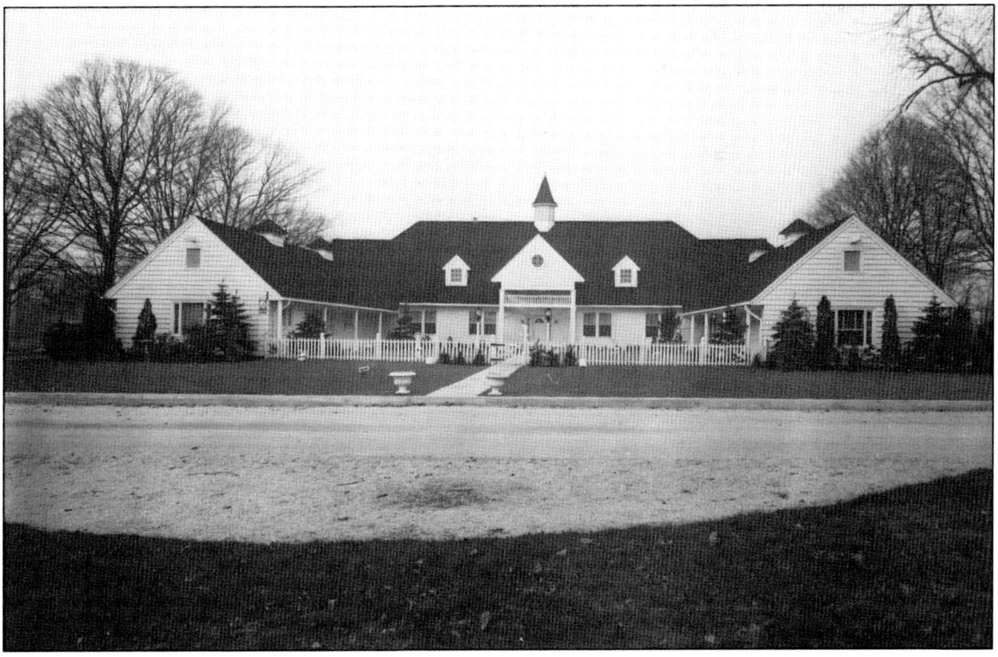

The carriage house at 25 Shadow Brook Drive has been remodeled into a private residence, and is shown here in an early 1950s view. The former carriage storage area is a 30-by-40-foot living room, whose 1,200 square feet could contain a modest house. A guest suite and office are in the east wing of the U, while the west wing is largely garage and storage space, and a pool room. (Dorn's Collection.)

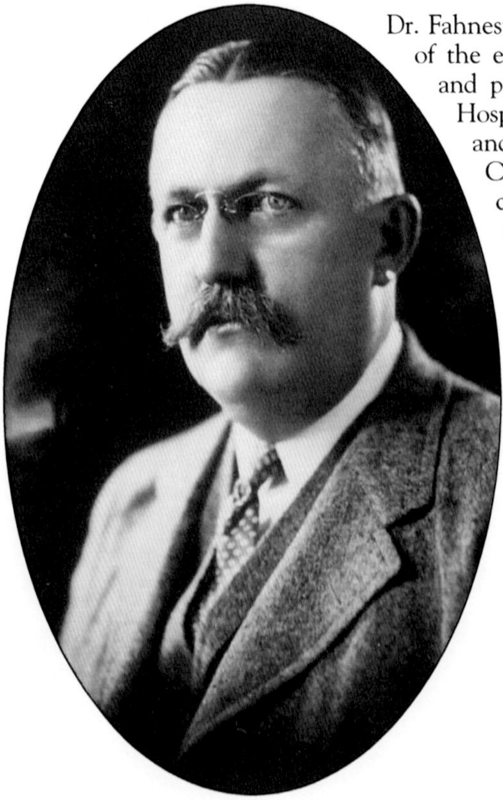

Dr. Fahnestock's rise in medicine included chairmanship of the executive committee of Misericordia Hospital and positions at St. Vincent's and the Foundling Hospital in New York. He was a contributor and honorary member of the Shrewsbury Fire Company and served on the borough's zoning committee. Fahnestock was a vestryman at St. Thomas' (P.E.) Church in New York, while locally he supported not only Episcopal churches, but a Catholic church in Long Branch. He endowed a medal for bravery for the New York Police Department and was an honorary member of the Red Bank police. Fahnestock died of a self-inflicted gunshot wound on April 5, 1937, in New York. This is a 1930s photograph. (Shrewsbury Historical Society Collection.)

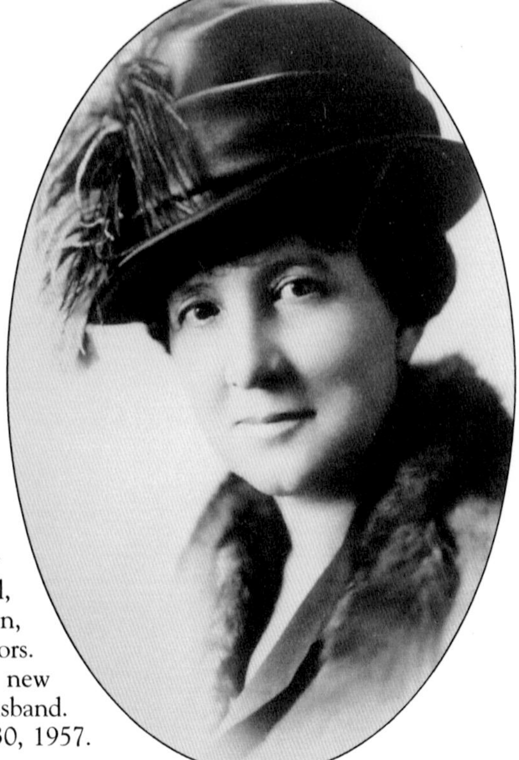

Georgette stayed at Shadow Brook for five years after her husband's death. This photograph was taken in the 1930s. There was little demand for country estates during the Depression and Shadow Brook was sold for a mere $25,000 in 1942. Mrs. Fahnestock moved to Rumson, and continued family service to Monmouth Memorial Hospital, as the Medical Center was then known, taking a position on the board of governors. In 1949, through a major donation for new rooms, she honored the memory of her husband. Mrs. Fahnestock died in Rumson on April 30, 1957. (Shrewsbury Historical Society Collection.)

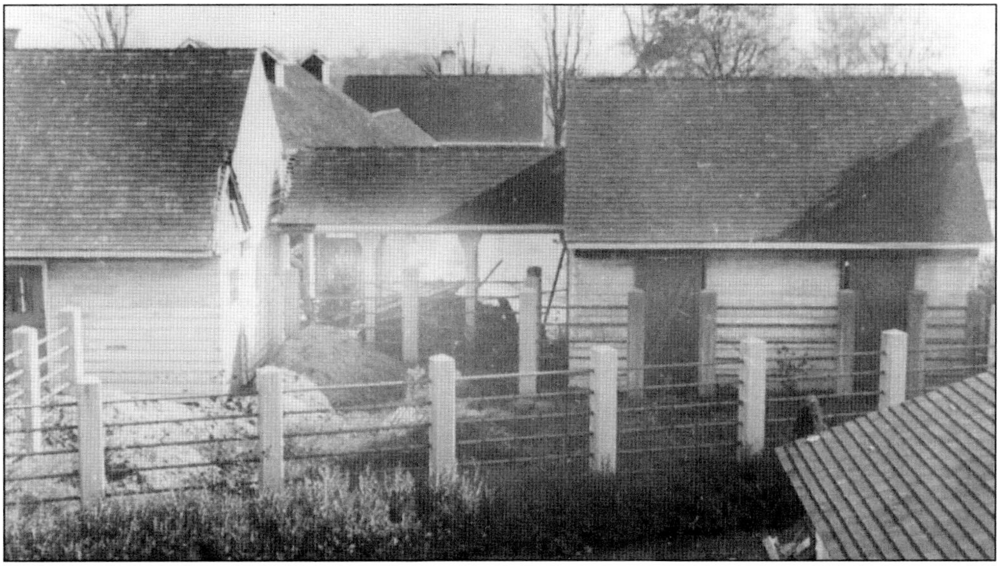

Harry Borden, local contractor, built this dairy barn in 1911. The 1911 *Register* reported that it was provided with every facility known to those times for the care of cattle. Gentlemen farmers made significant contributions toward advancing the cause of sanitary dairy practices in a then under-regulated industry. The Fahnestocks had milk shipped to their New York City residence via the local train. The farm was remodeled to a house in 1945. The bull barn on the right was converted to a garage. The breezeway was enclosed and a library built there. (Shrewsbury Historical Society Collection.)

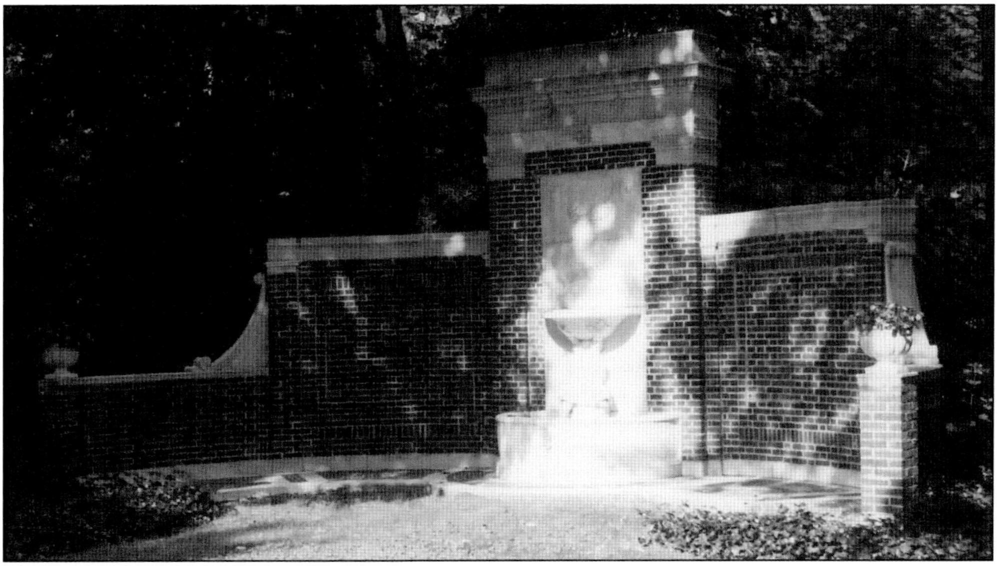

One of Shadow Brook's splendors was covered for years, not discovered until after the land was sub-divided for residential construction. The wall fountain terminal to the rose garden had been published in Lewis Colt Albro's office monograph for the period from 1914 to 1924. It was hidden by a tent-like structure when Edd Patterson was building his California contemporary ranch house at 67 Shadow Drive in the early 1960s. Its fountain origins were not clear until piping was discovered. The fountain was retained in the backyard plan. Today his daughter Donna maintains it as one reminder of the splendor of Shadow Brook.

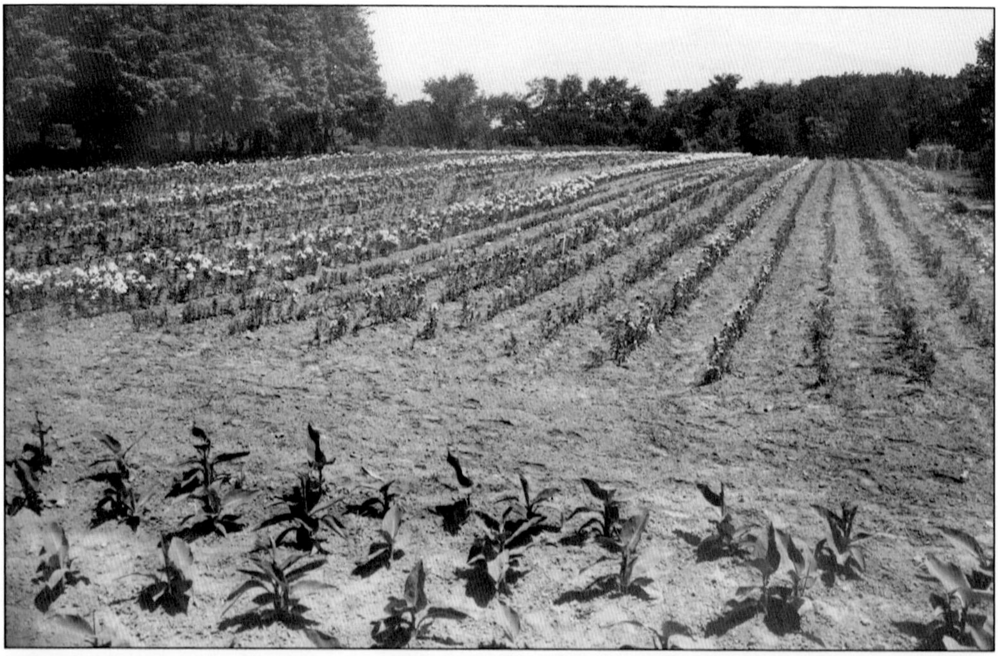

Lovett's Nursery of Little Silver bought 61 acres of Shadow Brook's east side of Broad Street property in July 1942. Lester C. Lovett had drawn plans for the gardens in 1911. Their field is the site of The Grove shopping center today. This photograph was likely taken in the 1950s. (Dorn's Collection.)

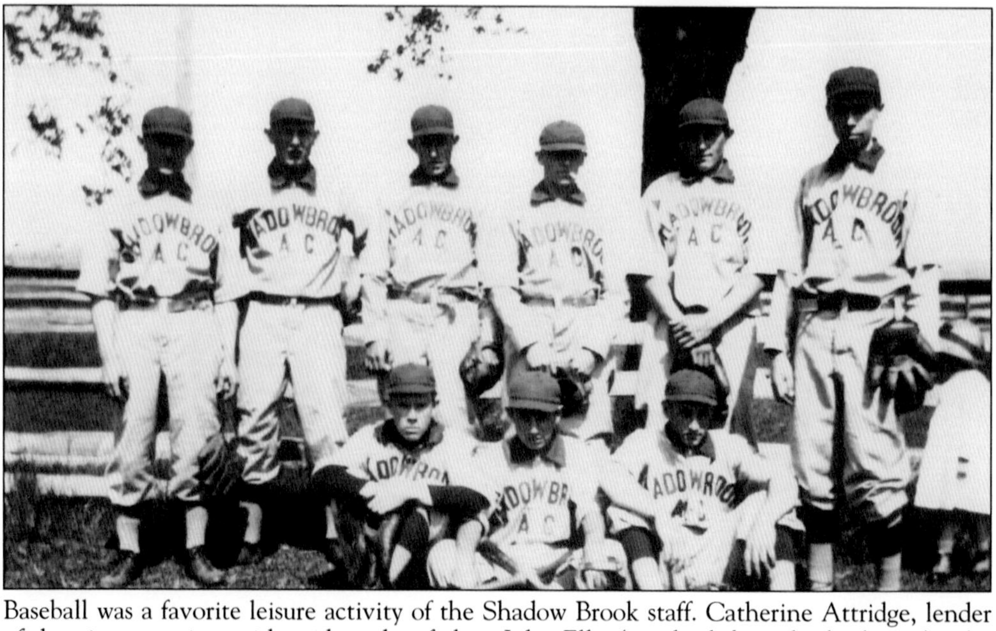

Baseball was a favorite leisure activity of the Shadow Brook staff. Catherine Attridge, lender of the picture, points with pride to her father, John Ellis (on the left in the back row). The others are, from left to right: (front row) Paul Parker, Frank Callahan, and Les "Spider" Hayes (who must have been a sure-handed infielder); (back row) Walt Anderson (to Ellis' left), J. McGarrity, Ed Hounihan, Jim Anderson, and Frank Lawes. The two-year-old girl at the far right is Elsie Hounihan, later Elsie Dorick.

Three

Broad Street

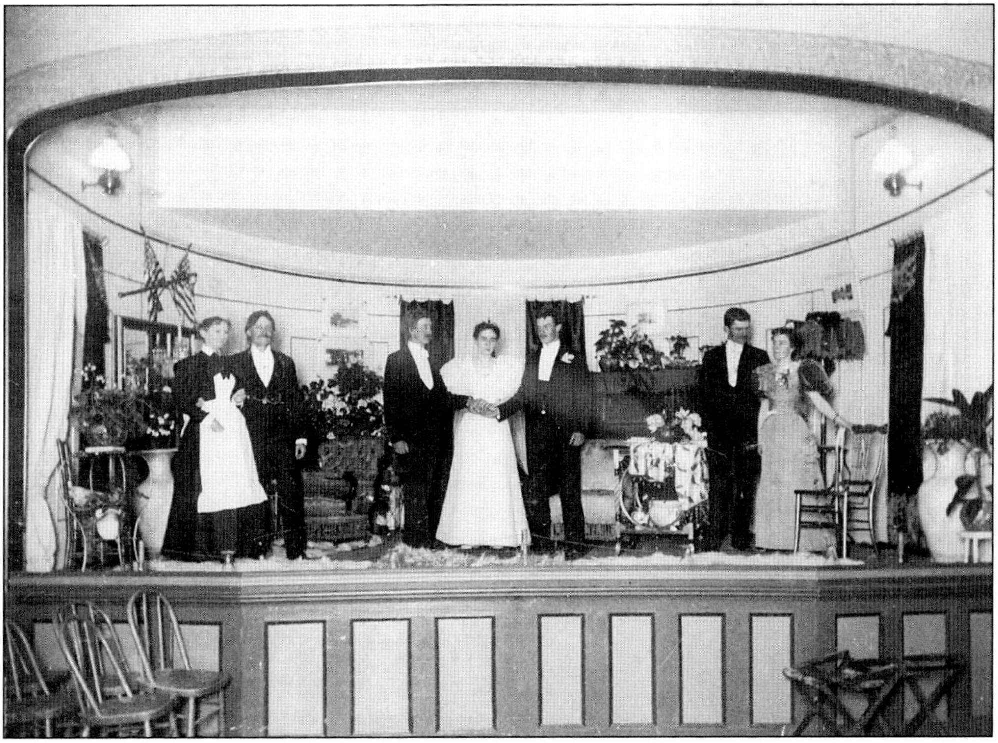

Shrewsbury can claim the earliest public library in the county, albeit one with varied incarnations. A Shrewsbury Reading Club was organized in 1877. A library association was formed in 1879 and a library built *c.* 1881 on a lot on the east side of Broad Street donated by Robert H. White. This *c.* 1890 photograph of a theatrical play at the hall exemplifies one of its uses. A borough library was disbanded in the 1970s as Shrewsbury is home to a major branch of the Monmouth County Library. (Shrewsbury Historical Society Collection.)

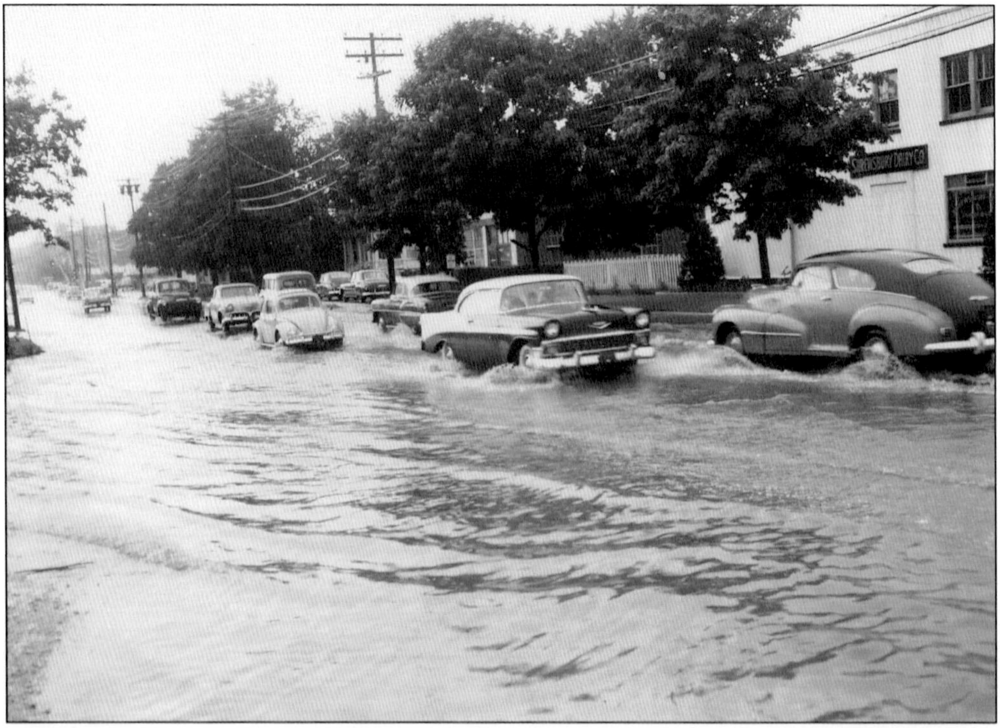

Poor drainage caused repeated highway flooding, as can be seen here at the northern stem of Broad Street at White Street in the late 1950s. The problem was reportedly remedied with larger drain pipes. (Dorn's Collection.)

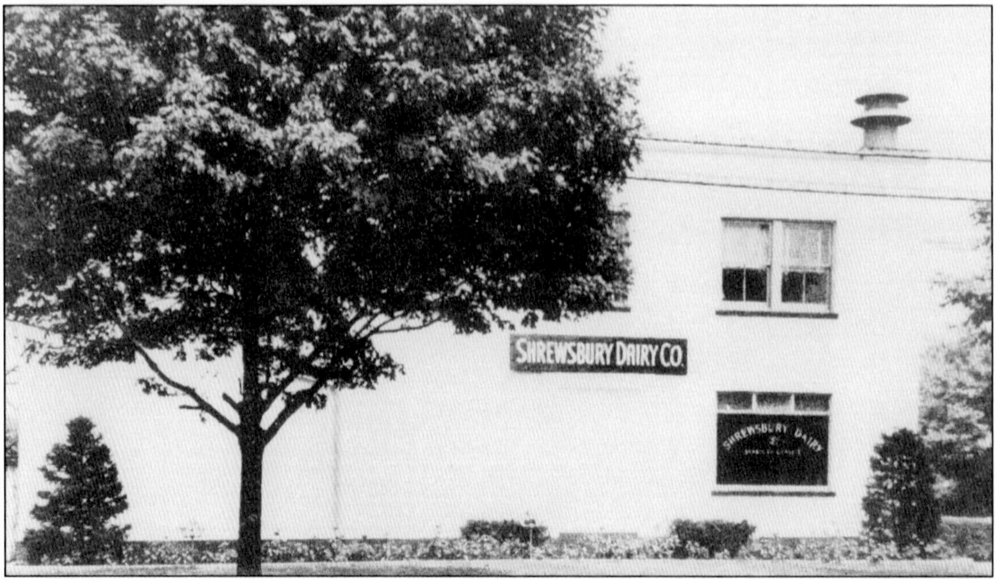

The antecedent of the Shrewsbury Dairy Company was the Sycamore Avenue dairy owned by Albert Grover. It was purchased in 1919 and organized under the former name. The Shrewsbury Improvement Company built the structure shown in this 1950s photograph at Broad Street and White Road in the 1920s. Mary Sutphen Starks, an owner, coined the slogan: "The Bluebird for Happiness, Shrewsbury Milk for Health." The Shrewsbury State Bank is now on the site.

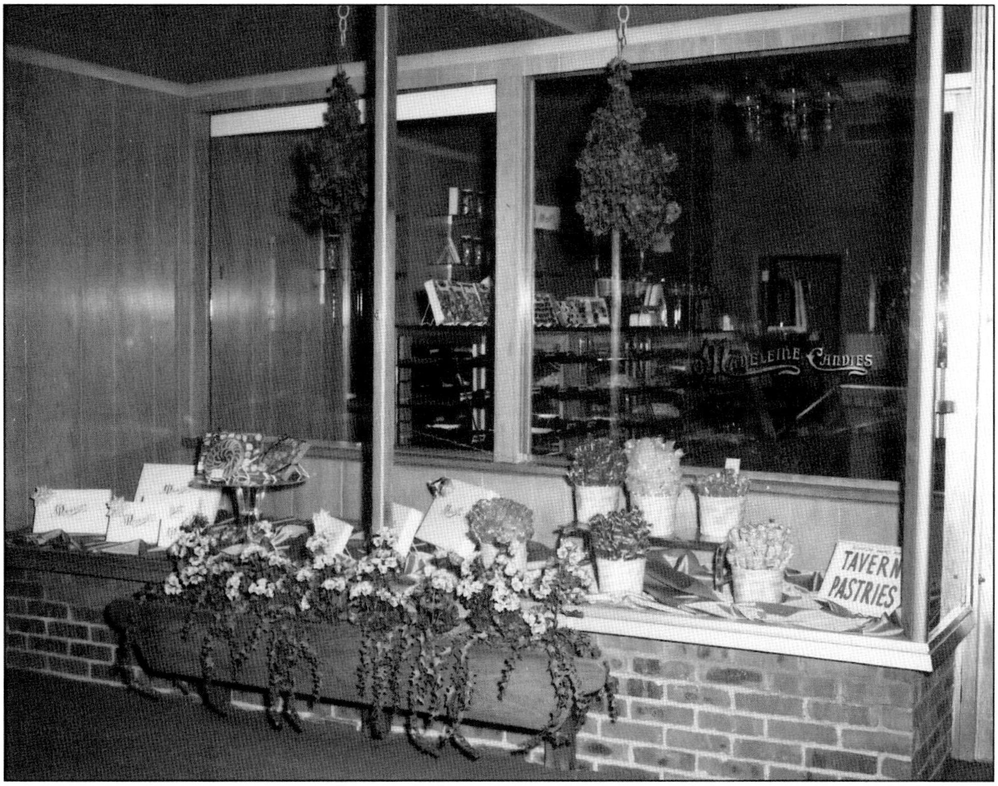

Madeline Candies in the Shrewsbury Shops, Broad Street and Meadow Lane, had strong eye appeal for their fancy candies. Note the attractive spiral arrangement of the fruit slices at left. They were a registered agency for Tavern Pastries, which will make more than one observer wonder, "Who went to taverns for pastries?" This is a late 1950s photograph. (Dorn's Collection.)

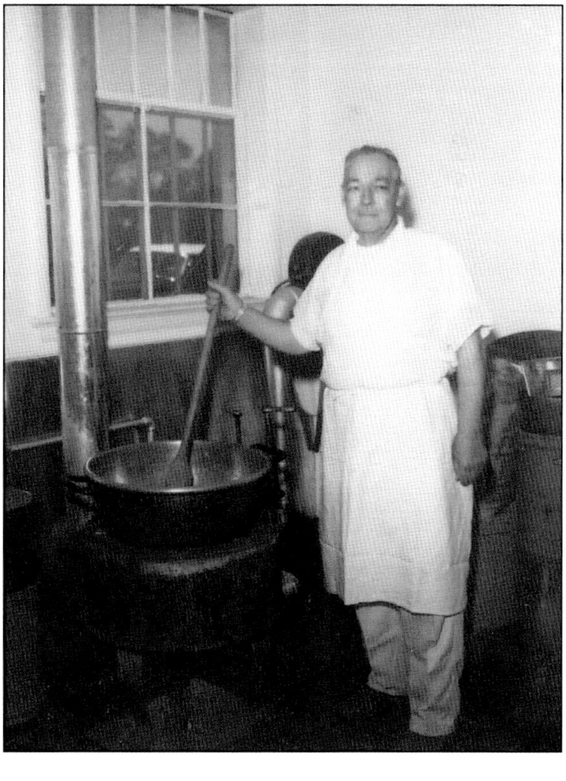

Yes, the candy at Madeline's was fresh and handmade, as attested to by the unidentified "Candy Man," shown here in the late 1950s. (Dorn's Collection.)

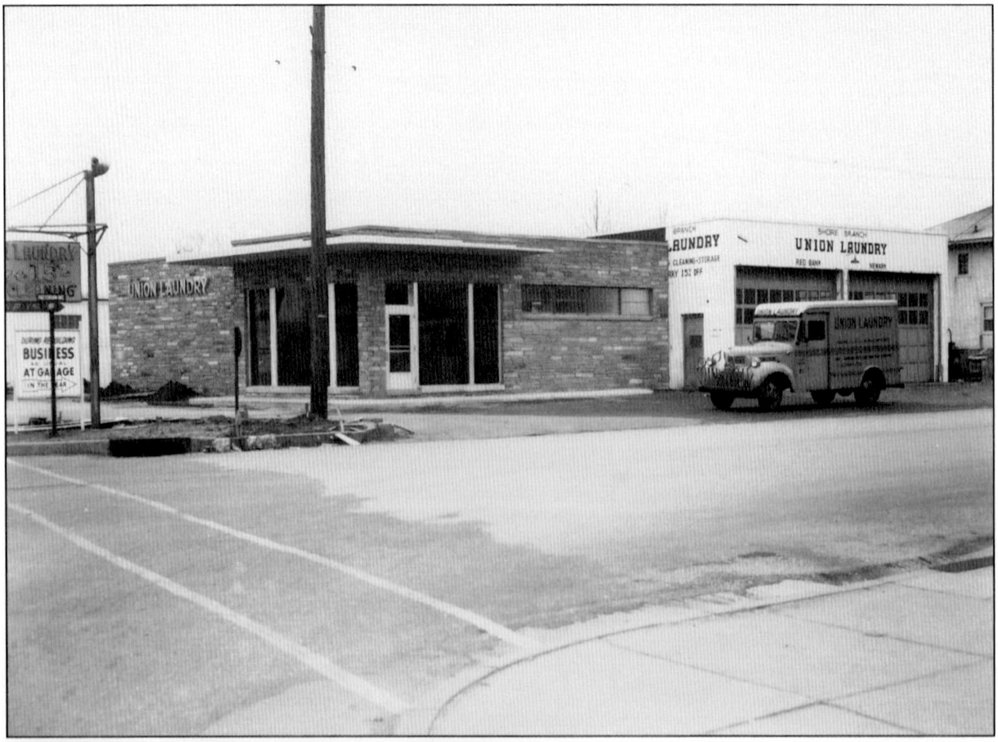

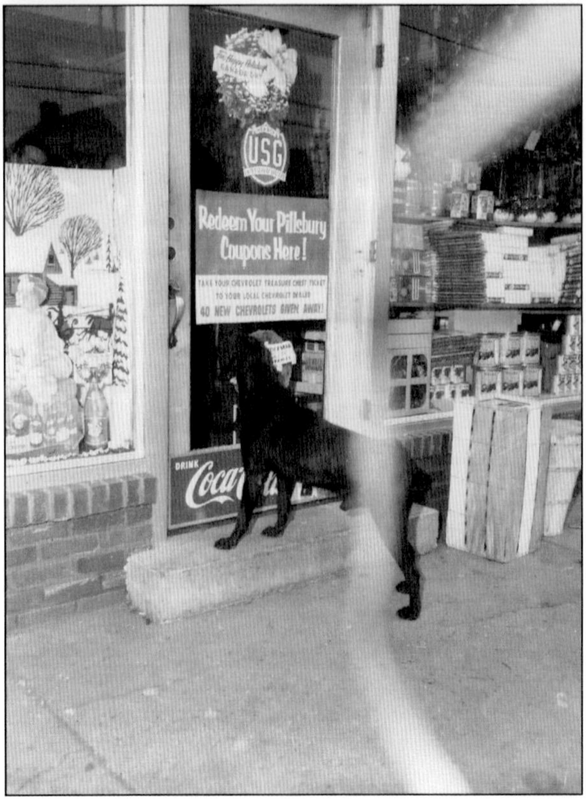

The Union Laundry building at Broad Street and Monroe Avenue is typical of northern Broad Street's transition from a residential to a commercial street in the post-World War II period. The Judge Wainright House is in partial view at right. It is now occupied by a tire dealer. (Dorn's Collection.)

Seeing a dog approach the Shrewsbury Market, on the west side of Broad Street, north of Obre Place, one expects he is looking for a handout. But, no! This appears to be a working dog. This and the two following pictures were taken in the early 1950s. (Dorn's Collection.)

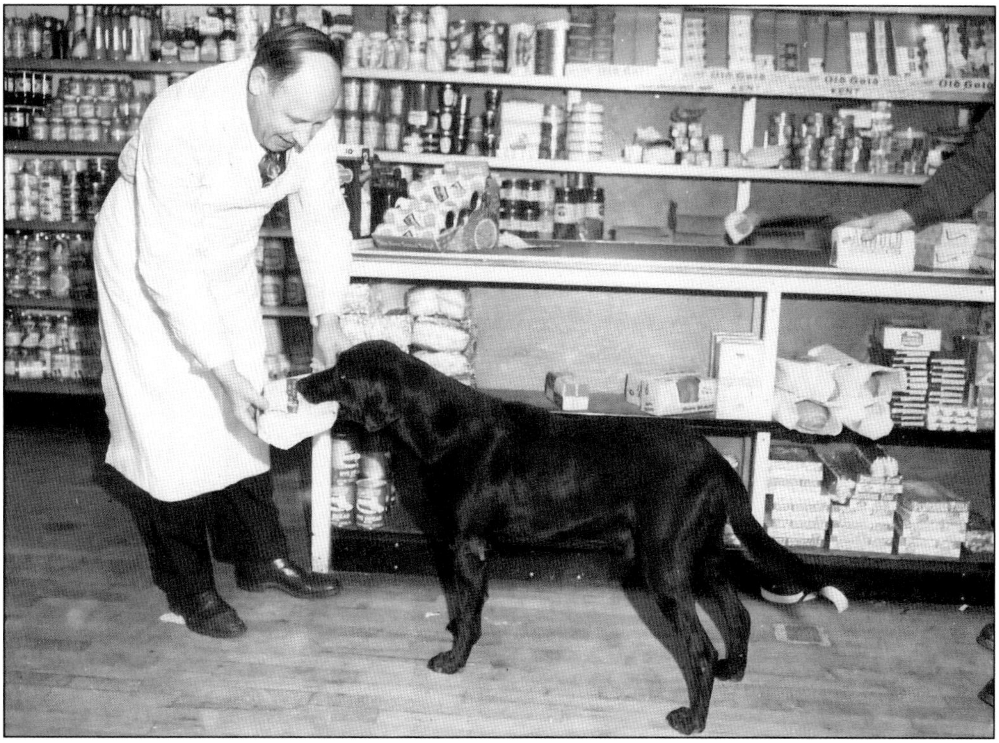

How about this—Eric Hecker is giving the dog a package to deliver. Look how neat the store is, with hardly a can missing or out of place. Hecker must have enjoyed a large clientele, as one customer recalled the floor was worn uneven by traffic. (Dorn's Collection.)

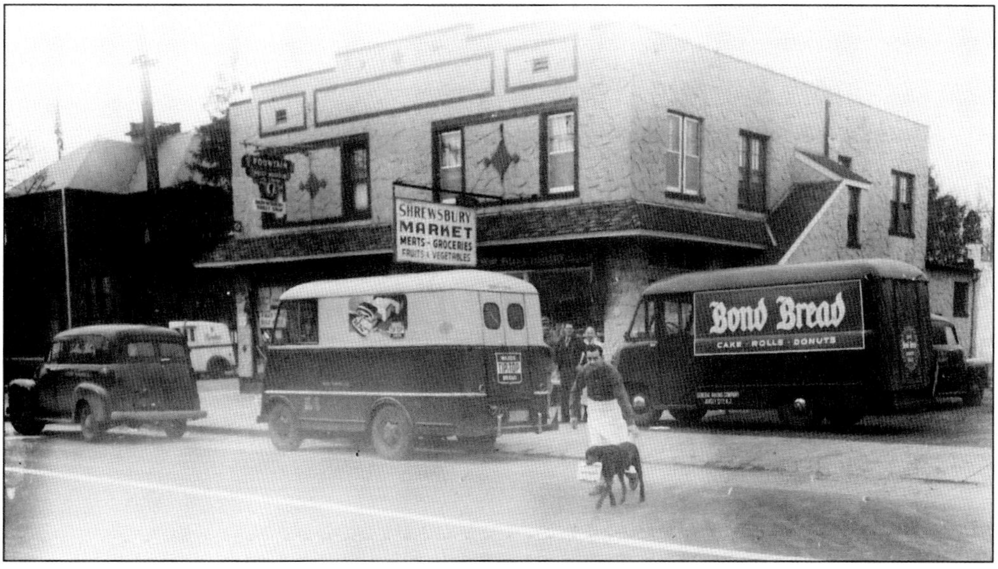

So, maybe this dog is not such a big deal. It needs help crossing the street and one could not trust him with meat. The Sweet Shop on the left brings instant nostalgia to all who remember it. It had a mirrored ice cream parlor on the right, with the fountain and parlor stools one would expect for the time. The room on the left contained penny candy, magazines, and "great comics!" as Kathy Dorn Severini recalled. (Dorn's Collection.)

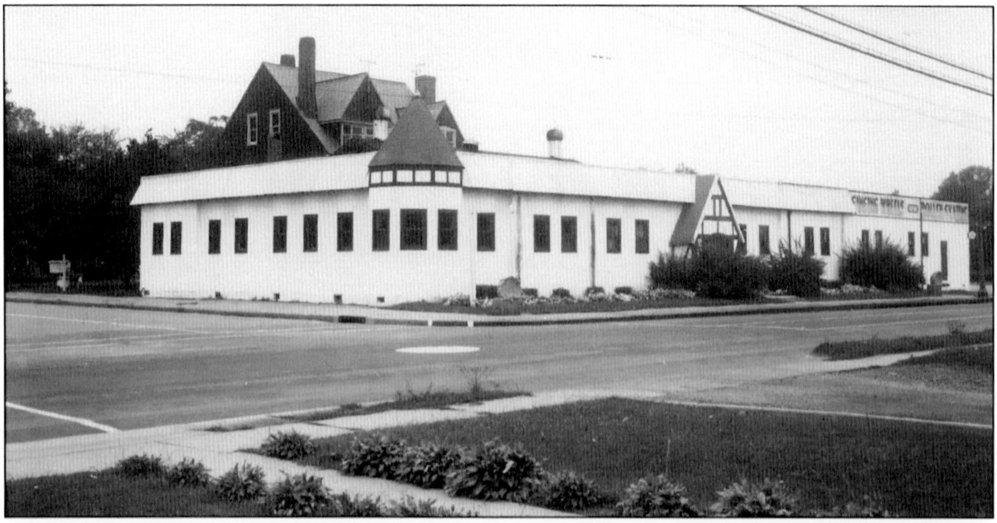

Sarah McClees bought the Alexander Denis House on the northwest corner of Broad Street and Patterson Avenue and opened the Smoke Shop Tavern *c.* 1926. The night club could serve hundreds, featured live music, and was a site of 1930s marathons. It was reopened by Felix and Rockly Santangelo as La Conga in 1939. Those looking for an area souvenir might keep their eyes open for a "Dinner Is Ready" bronze bell given to diners. This picture was taken in the 1950s (after remodeling). (Dorn's Collection.)

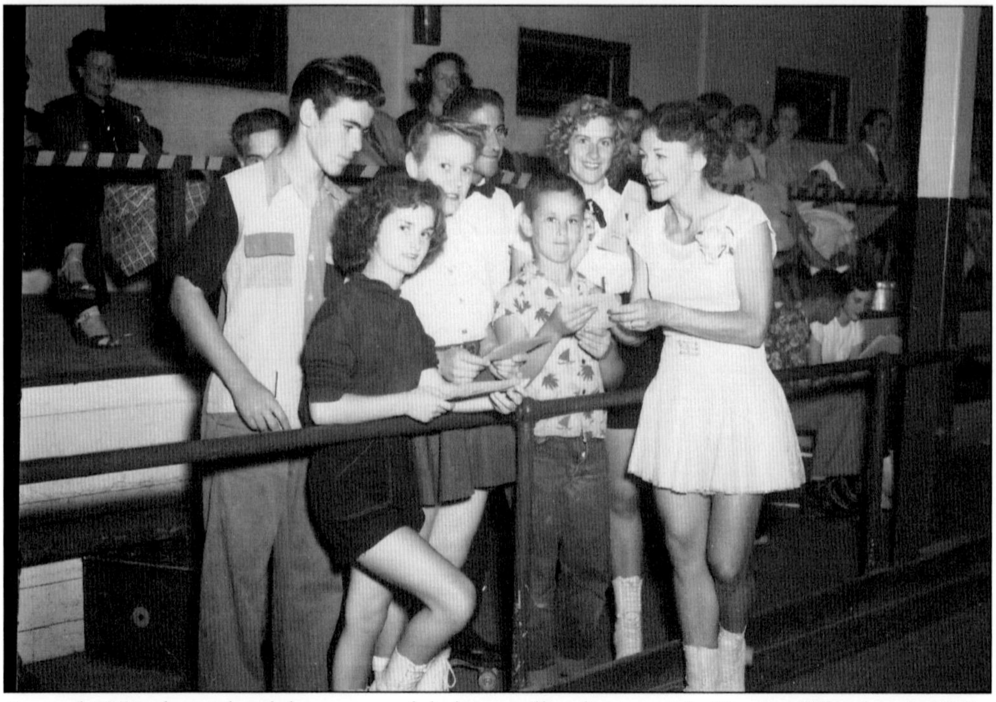

Around 1950, the night club was remodeled as a roller skating rink, Singing Wheels, which for ten years enjoyed a large following, finally closing *c.* 1960. This skilled 1950s instructor could dance on the rear wheels of her skates. The house in the rear was demolished, and the place was remodeled for mercantile use, with the one-story building doubling in size. It remains a store. A Singing Wheels skate box would be another prize find from the past. (Dorn's Collection.)

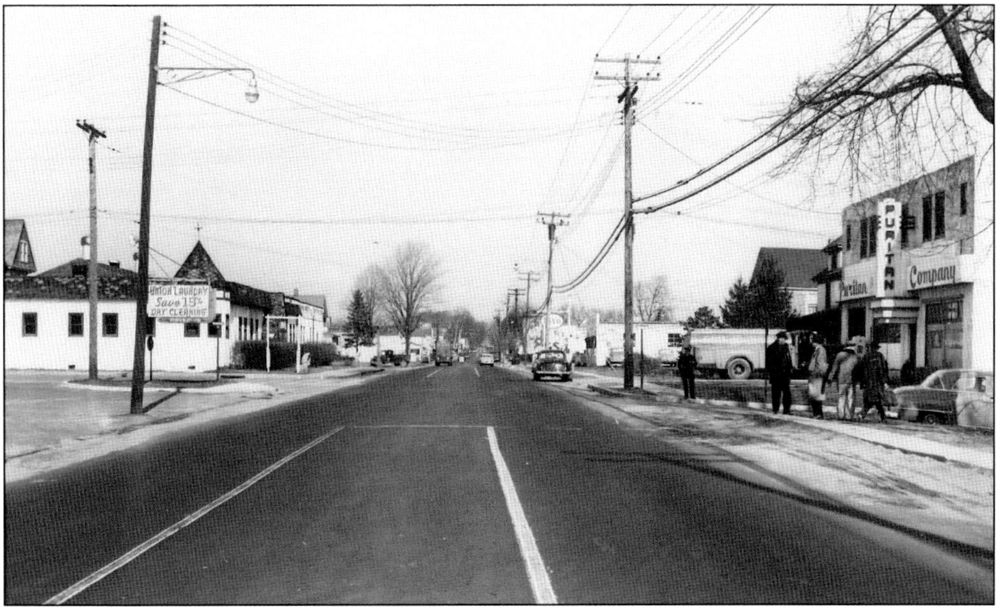

The narrow Broad Street of the early 1950s seems hardly recognizable to those familiar with 1990s traffic. The view is north, near Patterson Avenue, with Singing Wheels on the left. The Puritan Dairy (right) was a convenience in an era when most stores closed for the night. Its outdoor vending machine provided a handy source when the milk ran out after hours. (Dorn's Collection.)

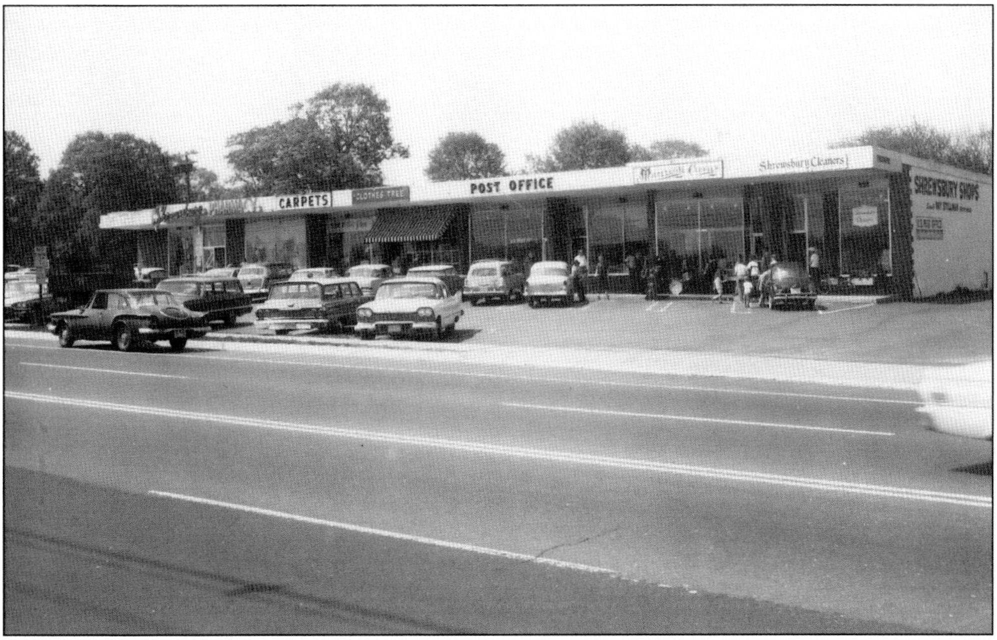

The Shrewsbury Shops, shown here in the late 1950s, were built on Ray Stillman property at Broad Street and Meadow Lane in 1956 following borough-made suggestions to increase the set-back and parking spaces. The post office moved from its Sycamore Avenue island (p. 25). The Shrewsbury Pharmacy was a long-term tenant until a 1994 fire. The store is now Thrift Drug. (Dorn's Collection.)

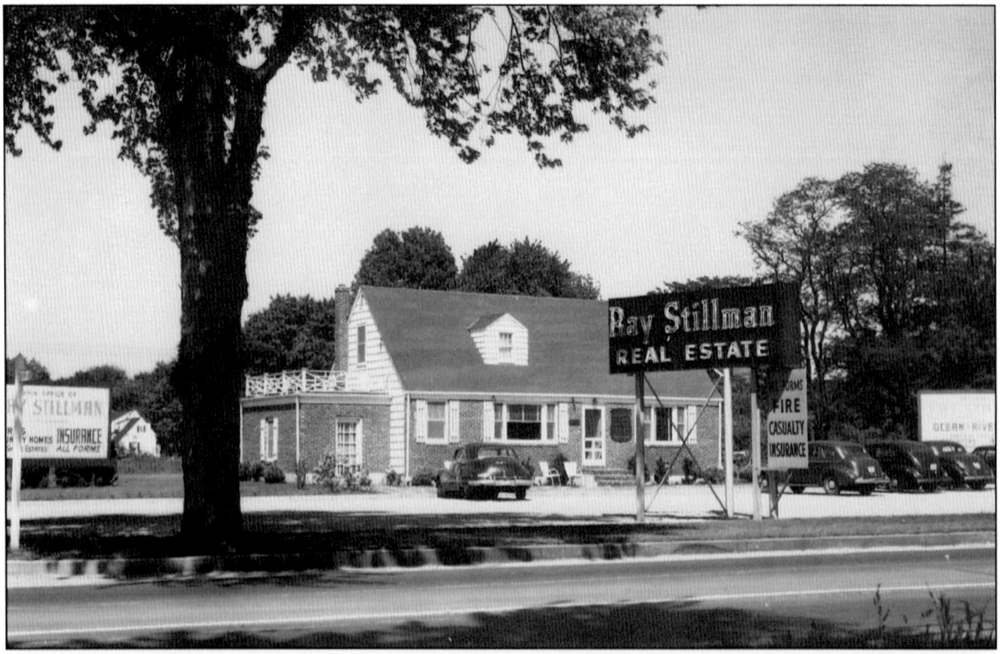

Raymond H. Stillman began his career as a farmer in Eatontown, starting a real estate business in 1923 as a sideline. He engaged in real estate full-time in 1926, opening a new office in 1928, and specialized in country farms and estates. His greatest coup was the purchase of Shadow Brook for $25,000, a minute sum, even in view of the depressed market for country estates. He promptly demonstrated that the sum of the parts was far greater than the whole. The main house was sold for a restaurant (p. 39) and the farm buildings were remodeled as residences. Stillman built this office south of Shadowbrook Drive in the late 1940s. (Dorn's Collection.)

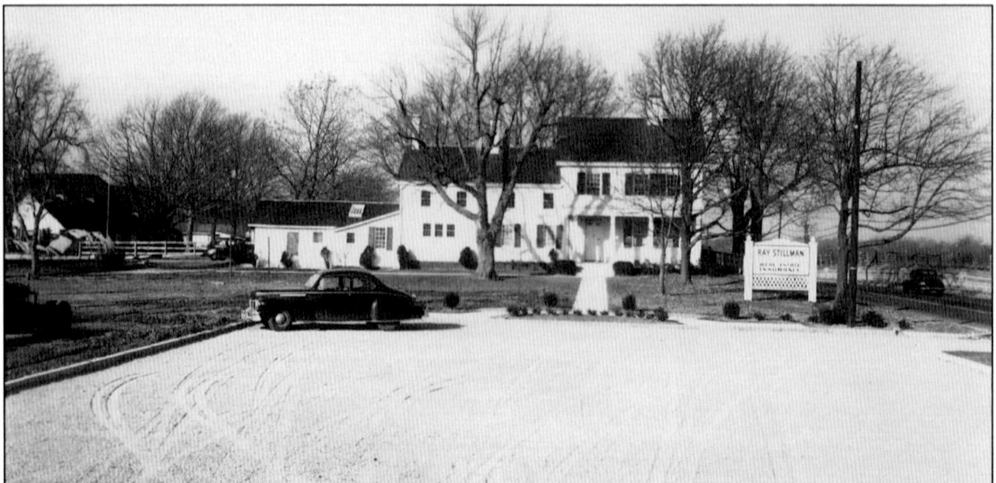

Earlier, Stillman had occupied Fahnestock's superintendent's house (seen in the background). This picture contrasts older and newer Shrewsbury: a large house close to a road, narrow and little traveled when the house was built, but now a modern highway, with its new construction necessarily set back from the road. Stillman also carved about twenty-five building lots from the farm, now filled with 1950s houses. (Dorn's Collection.)

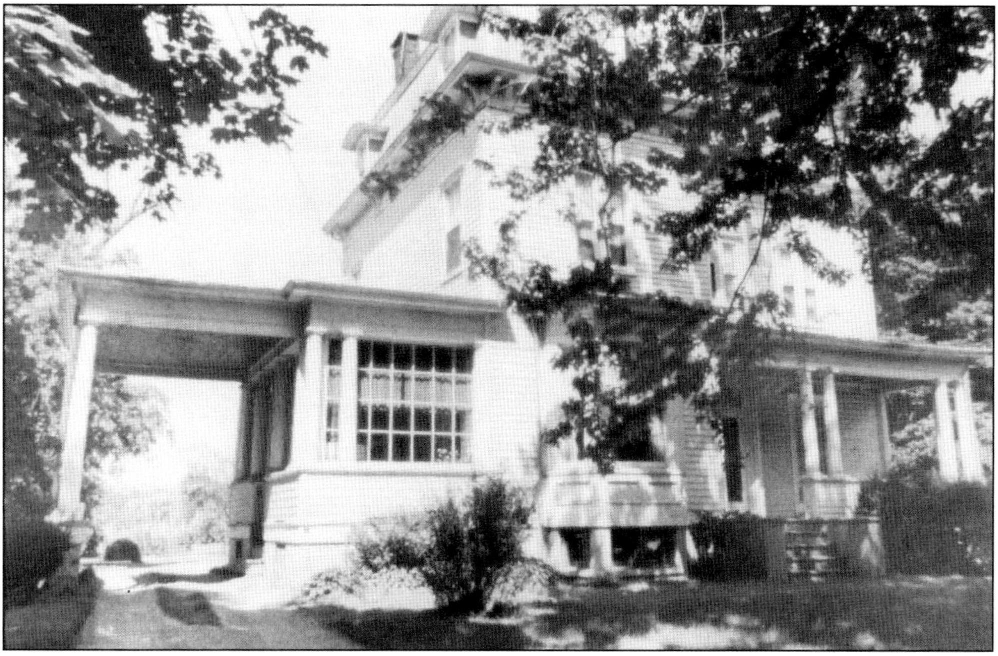

In 1910, Henry Classen bought the Daniel Vanderveer house at 746 Broad Street, about 350 feet south of the Shrewsbury Borough School, He remodeled it into one of the town's finest residences. He stayed only three years, finding travel to his Farmingdale ketchup factory difficult, and sold the late-1800s home to James McCue in 1913. Vincent McCue Sr., a Shrewsbury attorney, was the last private owner, living there sixty-four years and selling to a builder in December 1977. The house was destroyed by fire in 1978, and was replaced by a modest office. The office was demolished in 1996, with the site under construction as this book is being completed.

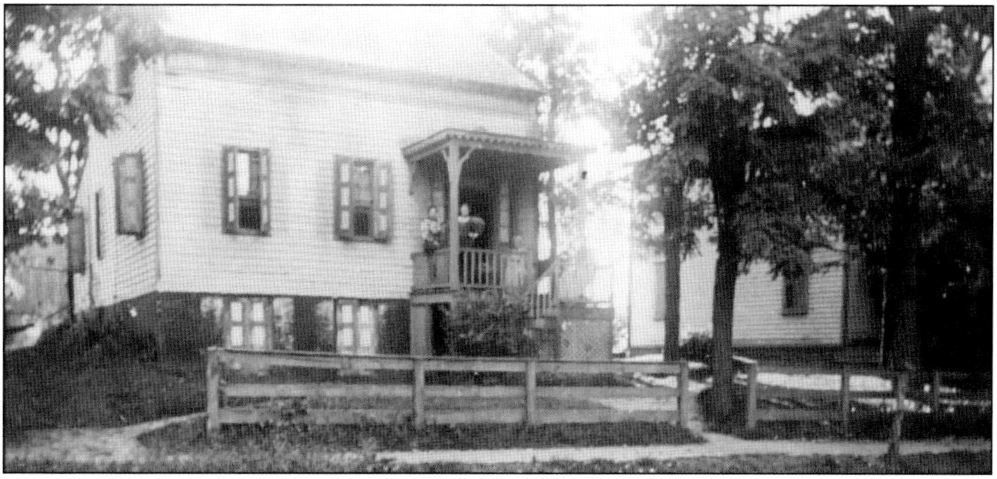

A tall brick foundation that exposes a full story at near grade level is a distinctive feature of 800 Broad Street, featured here *c.* 1900. A plaque claims it was built in 1834 by Edward Bowne (not confirmed by the author). If true, the foundation would be a replacement. This former residence was owned in the late nineteenth century by Mrs. Sleeper, relative to Samuel Sleeper, who was killed during the Civil War. The home is now an office. Its early origins are concealed on the exterior with vinyl siding, but are suggested inside by exposed beams.

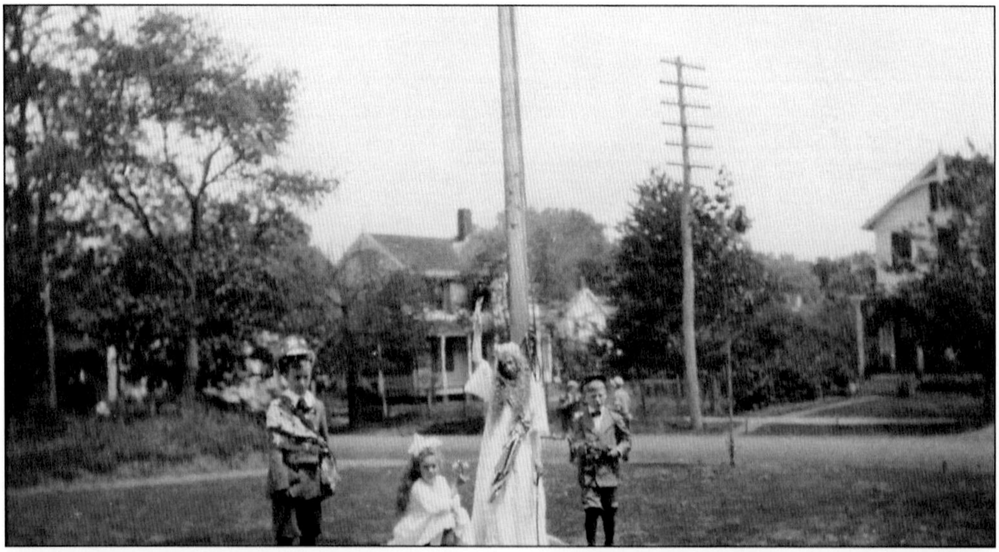

Four unidentified youngsters are engaged in an unspecified celebration, with Goldilocks apparently portraying Miss Liberty. The elder boy is probably Uncle Sam. One hopes the younger boy and girl were not so overdressed as to stifle them. This photograph was probably taken c. 1910 on Broad Street. (Shrewsbury Historical Society Collection.)

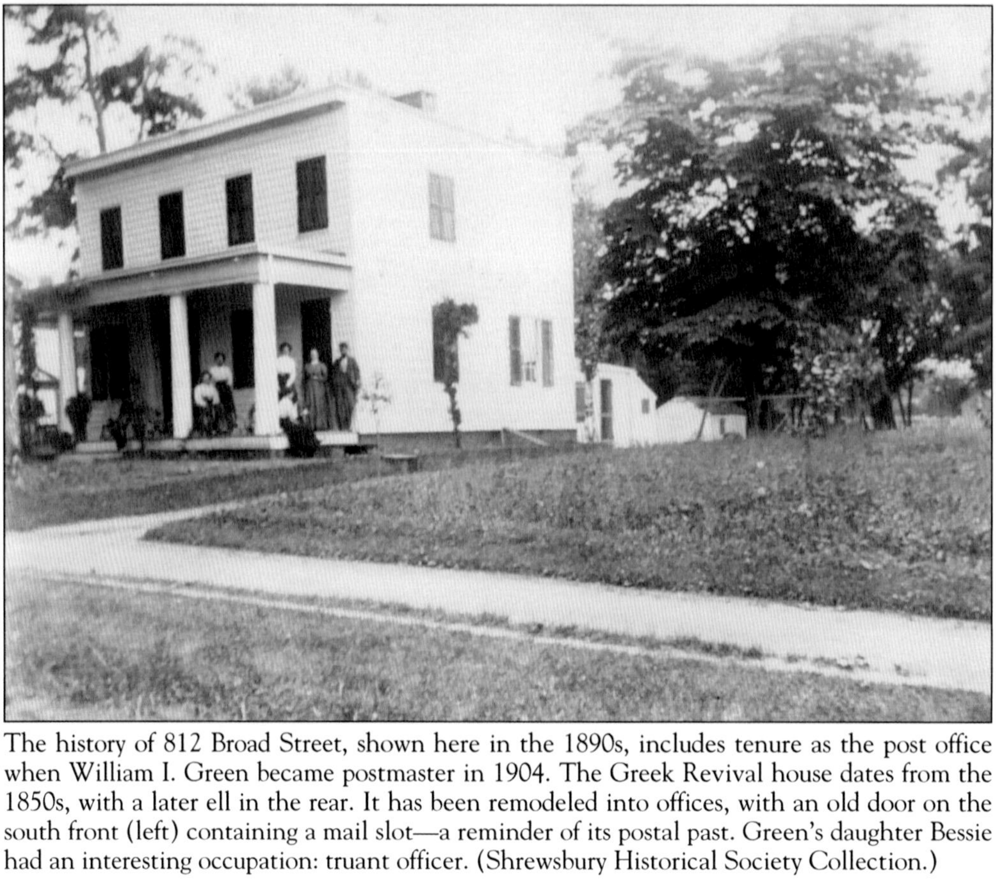

The history of 812 Broad Street, shown here in the 1890s, includes tenure as the post office when William I. Green became postmaster in 1904. The Greek Revival house dates from the 1850s, with a later ell in the rear. It has been remodeled into offices, with an old door on the south front (left) containing a mail slot—a reminder of its postal past. Green's daughter Bessie had an interesting occupation: truant officer. (Shrewsbury Historical Society Collection.)

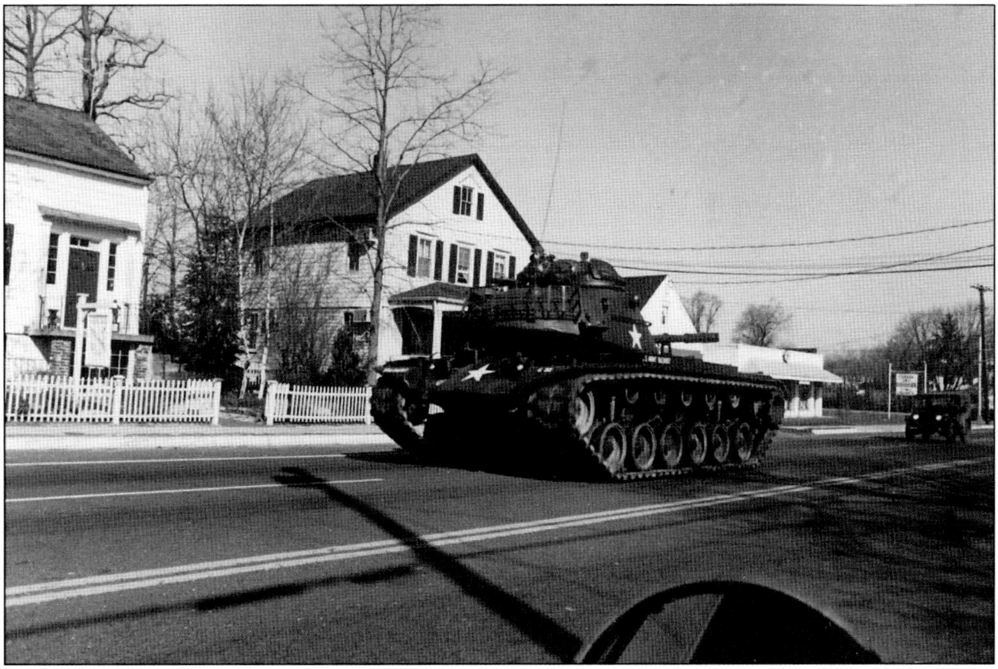

A brief moment of travel behind one of these two-lane-clogging, slow-moving vehicles may seem disruptive, but consider the home owners on this route. One of them recalls the house-shaking rumble of regularly passing tanks. These vehicles came from the Red Bank Armory and are traveling south during the mid-1970s on Broad, approaching Sycamore, on their way to a weekend drill.

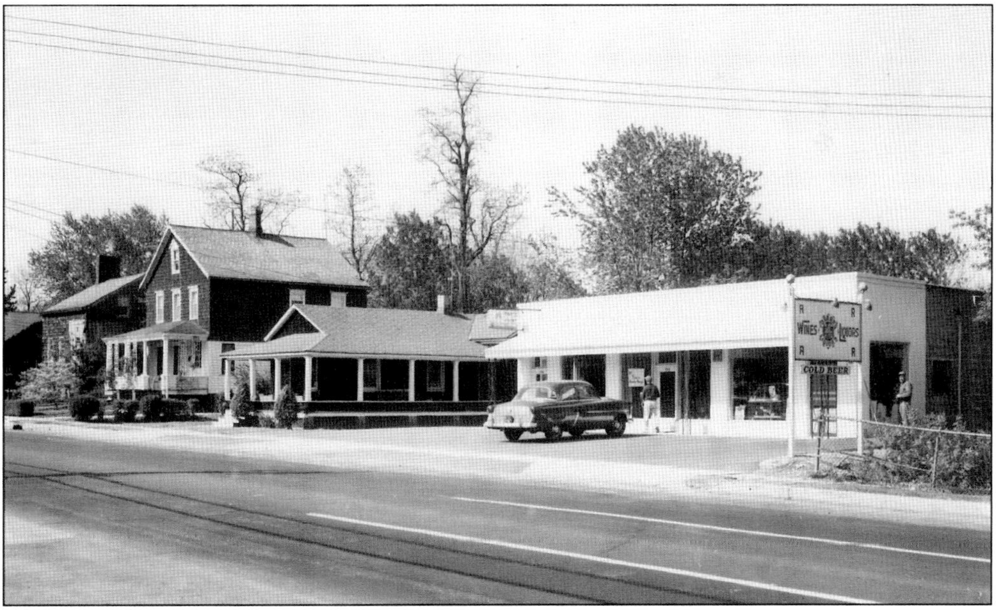

New shops and a still-narrow Broad Street, seen on the west side, north of Sycamore Avenue, provide another view of a changing thoroughfare in the mid-1950s. Ed Sagurton's two-story, front-gabled house was demolished and Chet Forrar's liquor store is gone, but the shops remain. (Dorn's Collection.)

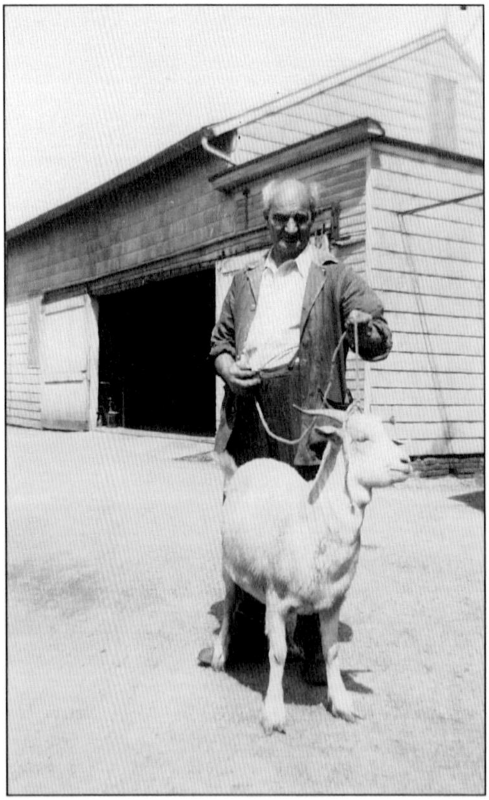

Nathan Marx stands in front of the old library used as a garage by the Marx Brothers in their wholesale meat business, *c.* 1940. The author attempts to find a goat for each book, typically pulling a cart, but, surprise! This one probably wound up on someone's table.

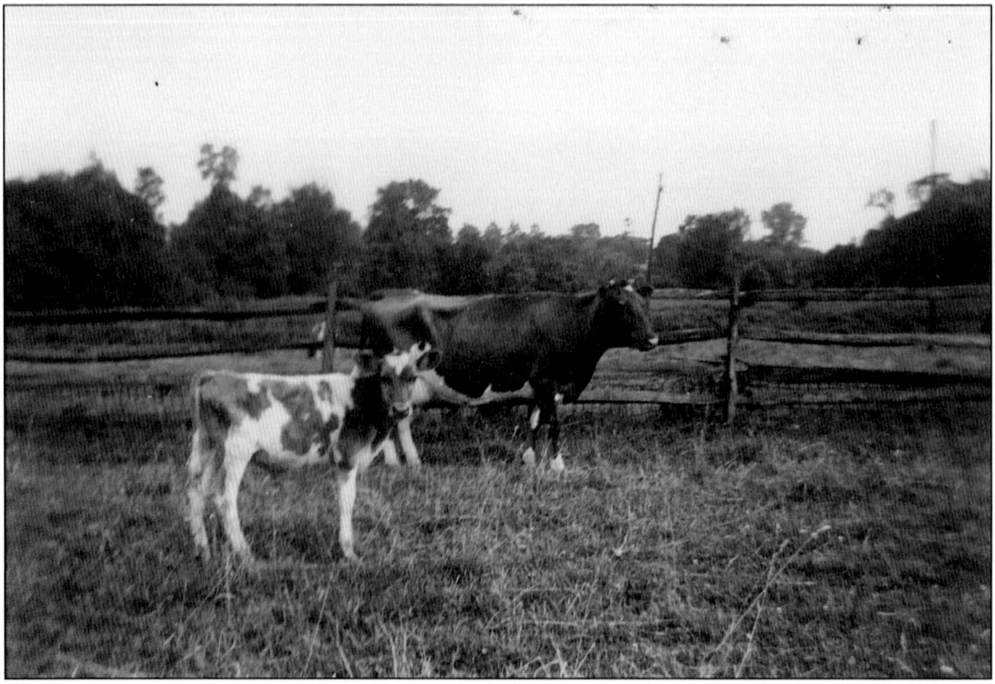

This 1940s cow and calf are representative of the Marx Brothers cattle that were pastured on a field west of Broad Street, now part of Shrewsbury Borough School property.

Shrewsbury Hose Company No. 1 was organized in 1908, with Benjamin Lane elected as first chief. Their first firehouse was built in 1909 on a 40-by-100-foot lot located just south of the present firehouse's driveway at 783 Broad Street. A bell donated by the First Presbyterian Church of Red Bank was installed on a tower paid for by Dr. Ernest Fahnestock in 1915. The firehouse was expanded that year by construction of an addition in its front. The building, shown here in a 1920s photograph, was demolished after the 1961 completion of the present firehouse, built adjacent to the earlier one.

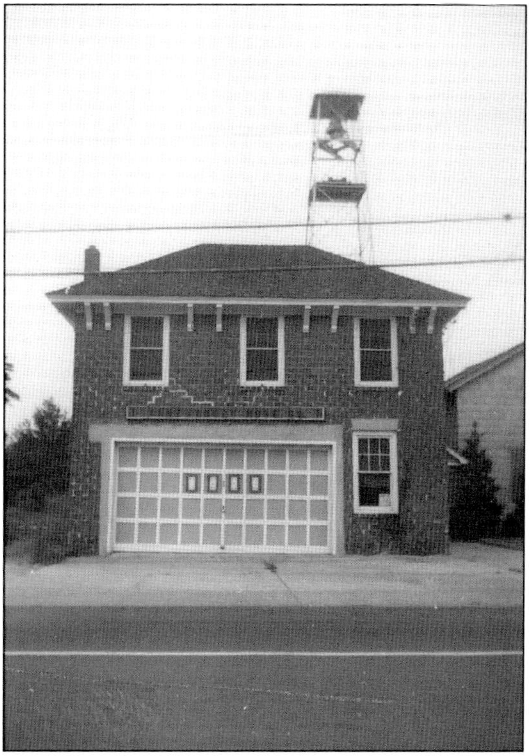

The field on the west side of Broad Street, north of Sycamore Avenue, about opposite the firehouse, is shown here in the 1950s. (Dorn's Collection.)

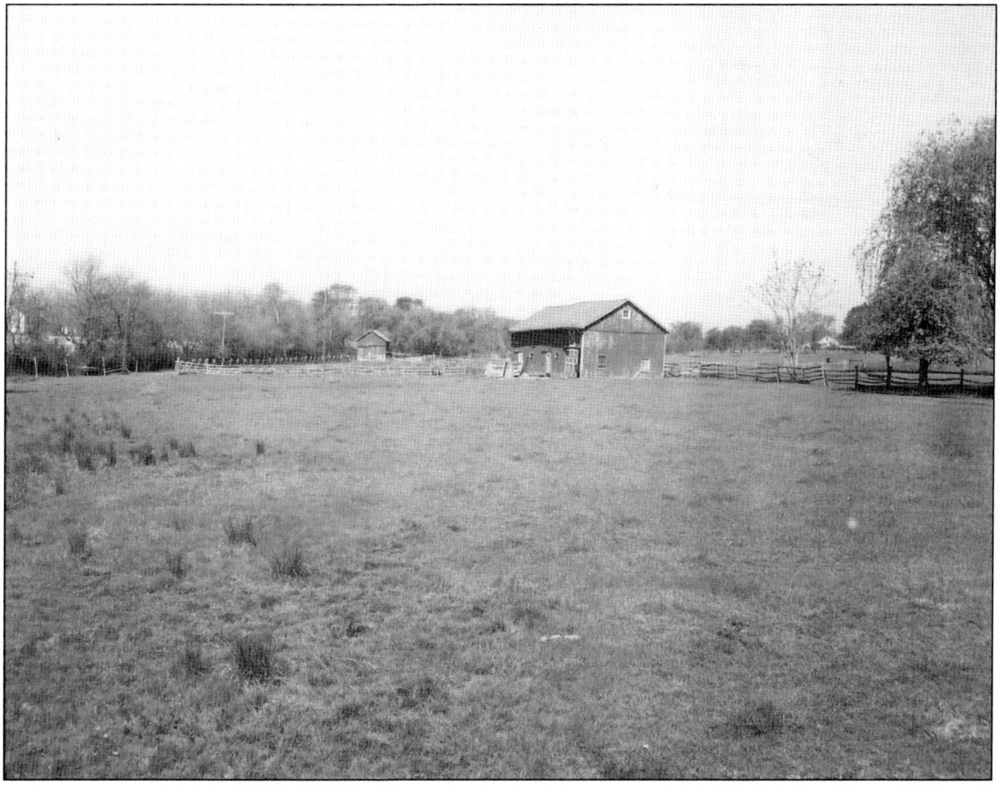

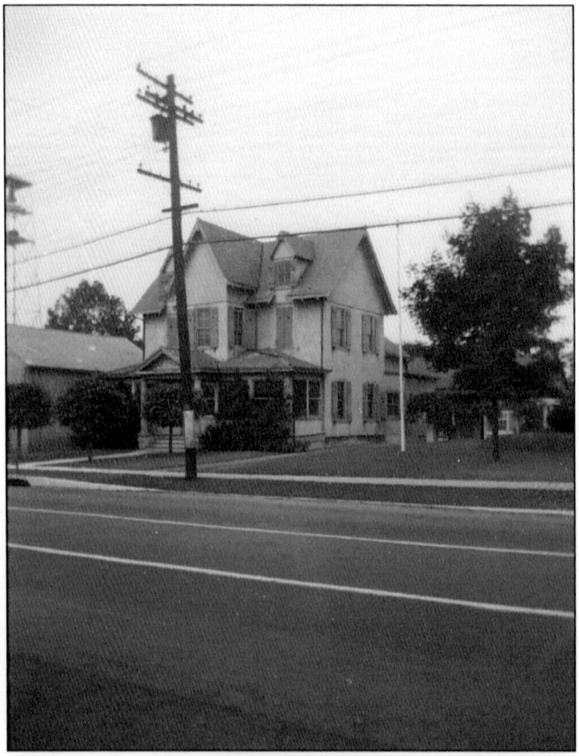

Frank and Fannie Marx built this house on Broad Street in the 1890s. It was demolished in the late 1940s and a retail store now occupies the site at 795 Broad.

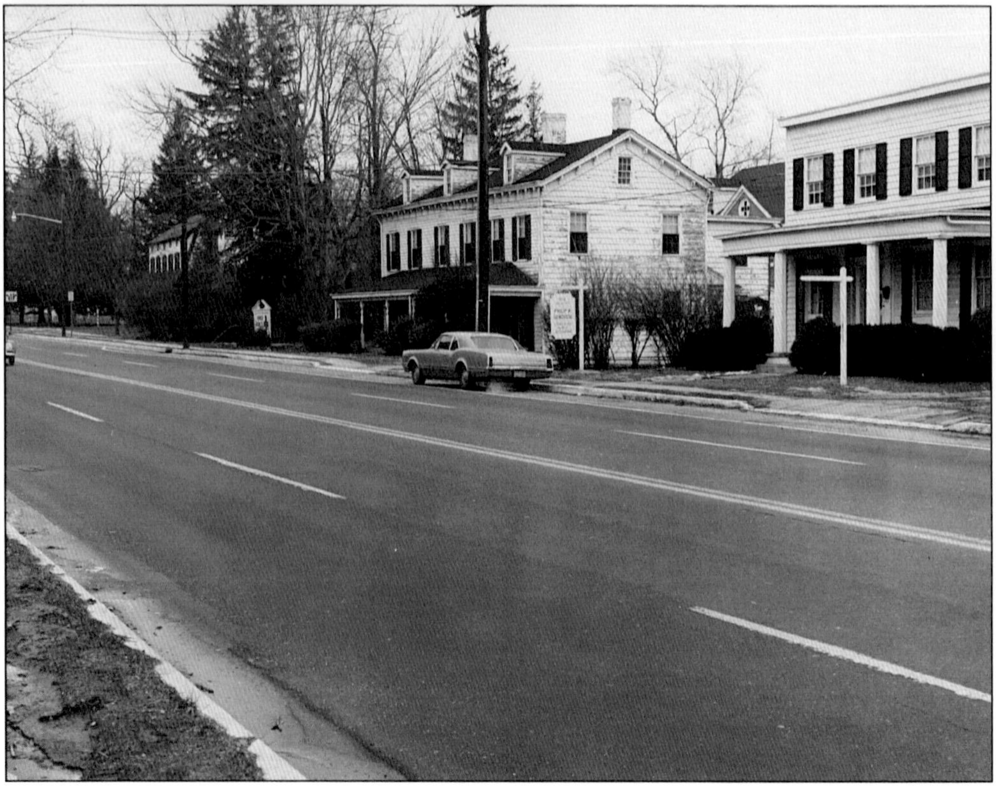

The house in the center was once the home and private school of Theodosia Finch. She sold it to George Stillwell in 1878, who sold it to George Silver in 1910. Silver was later a mayor of Shrewsbury. The house was remodeled for Red Cross use in 1944 and purchased by them in 1945. The place was long home to the Monmouth County Chapter (now Jersey Shore), but was in disrepair and inadequate to their needs in the late 1960s. The gable of the present building at 830 Broad Street, built in 1971, is barely visible between the two houses. The older building was demolished in 1972.

This Italian Renaissance Revival house was built *c.* 1920 by Martin Marx at 801 Broad Street. It was one of the last houses built on the stem of Broad north of Sycamore. It was later remodeled into medical offices.

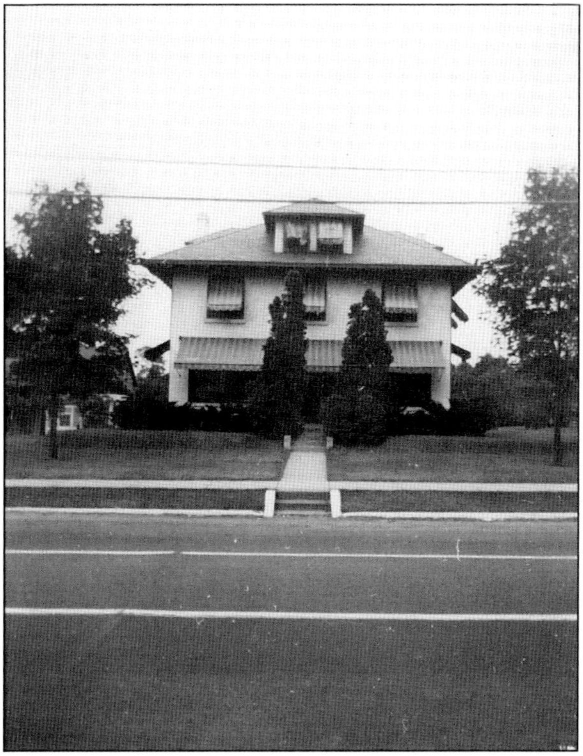

In the 1950s, the Ransonoff Memorial Fund presented this De Soto to the Red Cross, apparently for use as an ambulance. The event's disappearance from the memory and archives of the local Red Cross office is not unlike the De Soto's disappearance from our roads. (Dorn's Collection.)

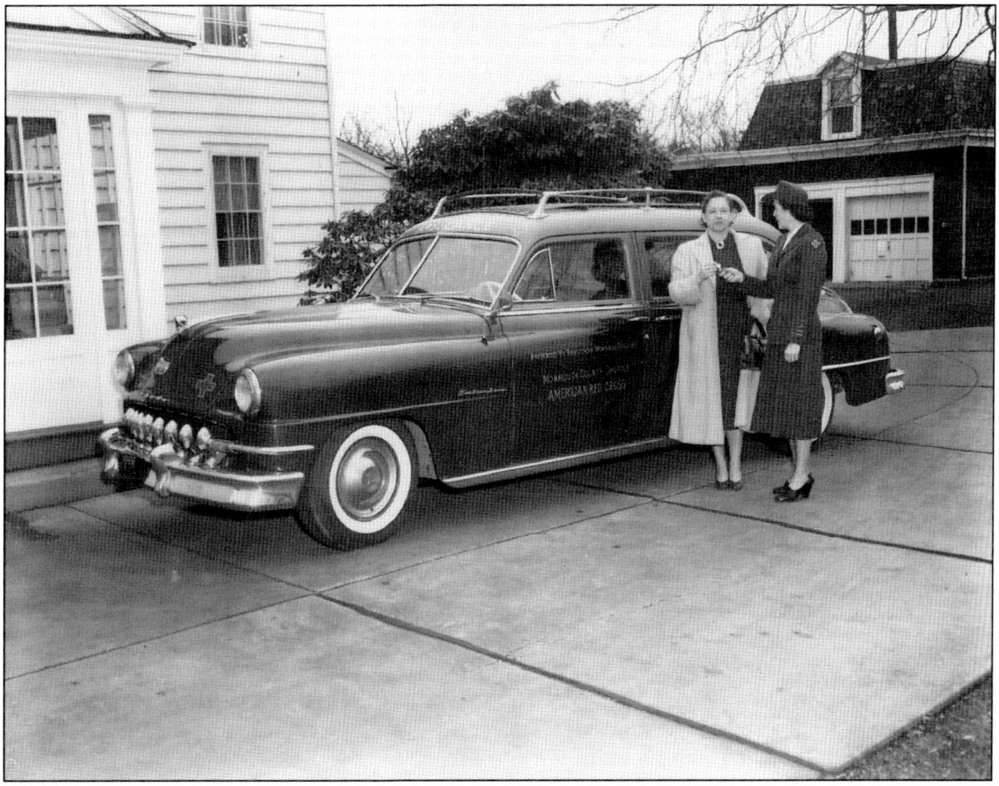

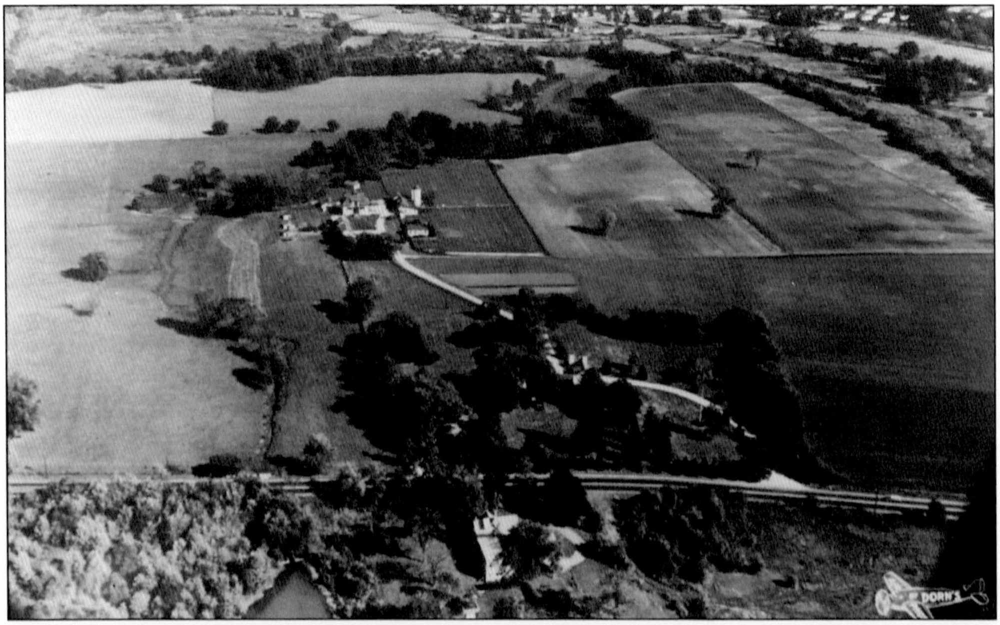

The Lafetra farm on the east side of Broad Street consisted of about 85 acres when it was sold in the early 1900s. Lafetras Brook, which empties into Parkers Creek, passes through, forming Shrewsbury's southeastern border with Eatontown. The stream can be seen running diagonally across this 1957 view. The farm changed hands several times early in this century. Visible in the foreground is the Broderson House, built by Charles Bunn and destroyed by fire in the late 1940s. An office is on that site now. (Shrewsbury Historical Society Collection.)

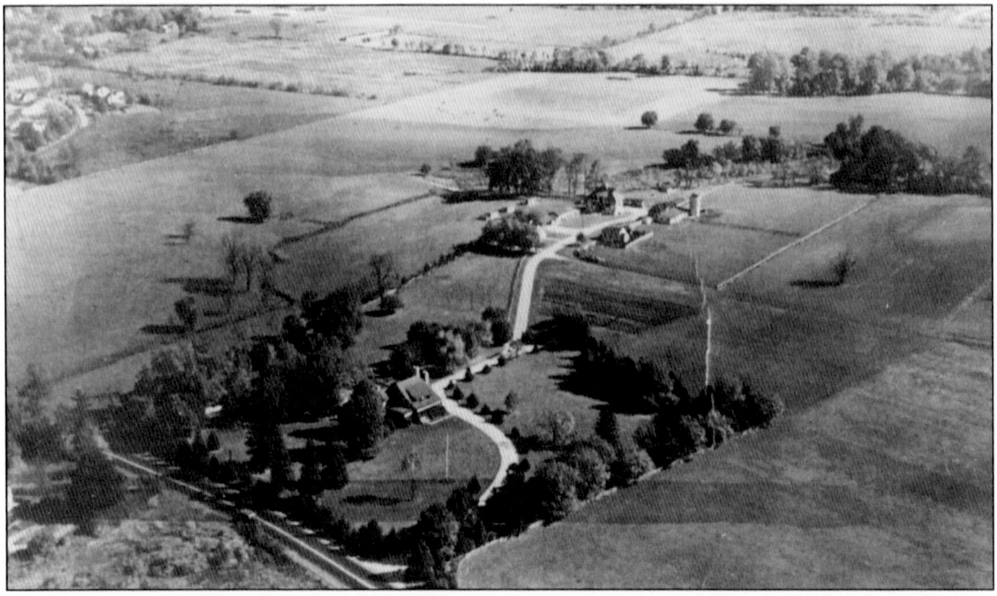

J. Preston Lafetra built a house in the mid-nineteenth century after being given a farm by his father Joseph. The house burned *c.* 1904 when occupied by the widowed Harriet Lafetra. This *c.* 1947 view looking northeast embraces property now occupied by the Eastern Branch of the Monmouth County Library and the strip shopping center to its south. (Shrewsbury Historical Society Collection.)

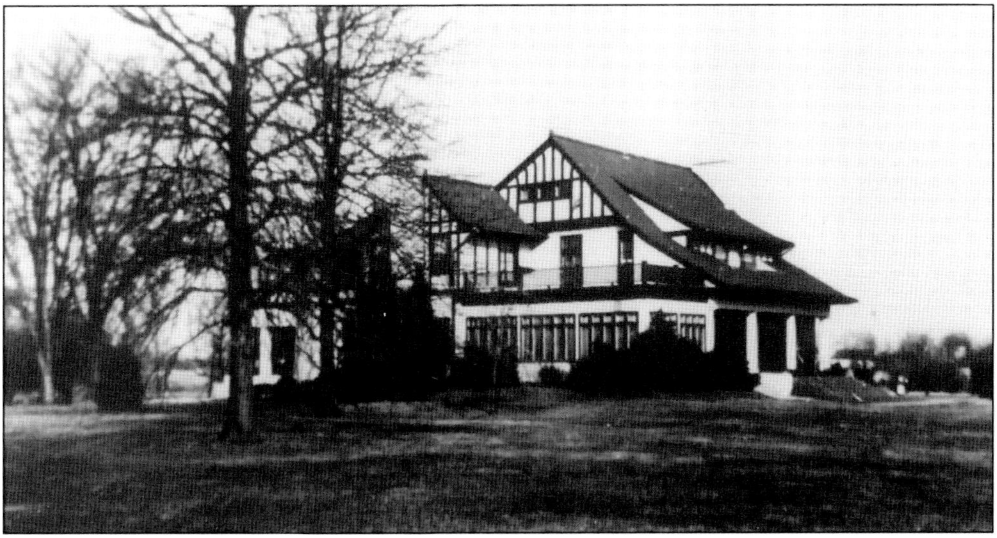

W. Del Wallbridge bought the Lafetra farm in 1911 and built a hollow-tile, stucco-clad Tudor Revival house with a red-shingled roof, designed by Gifford Slocum of New York. After interim ownership by the Hardings, Howard G. Strauss of New York bought the place in 1934, making various improvements, as can be seen in this 1950s photograph. (Shrewsbury Historical Society Collection.)

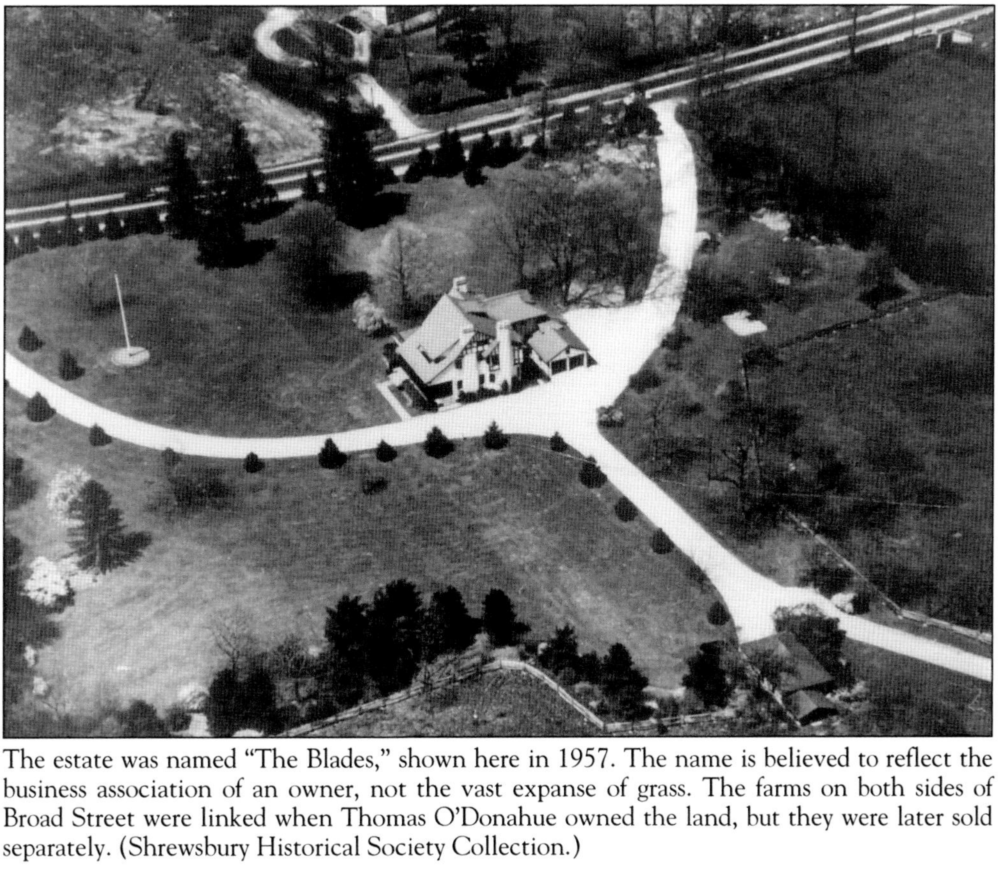

The estate was named "The Blades," shown here in 1957. The name is believed to reflect the business association of an owner, not the vast expanse of grass. The farms on both sides of Broad Street were linked when Thomas O'Donahue owned the land, but they were later sold separately. (Shrewsbury Historical Society Collection.)

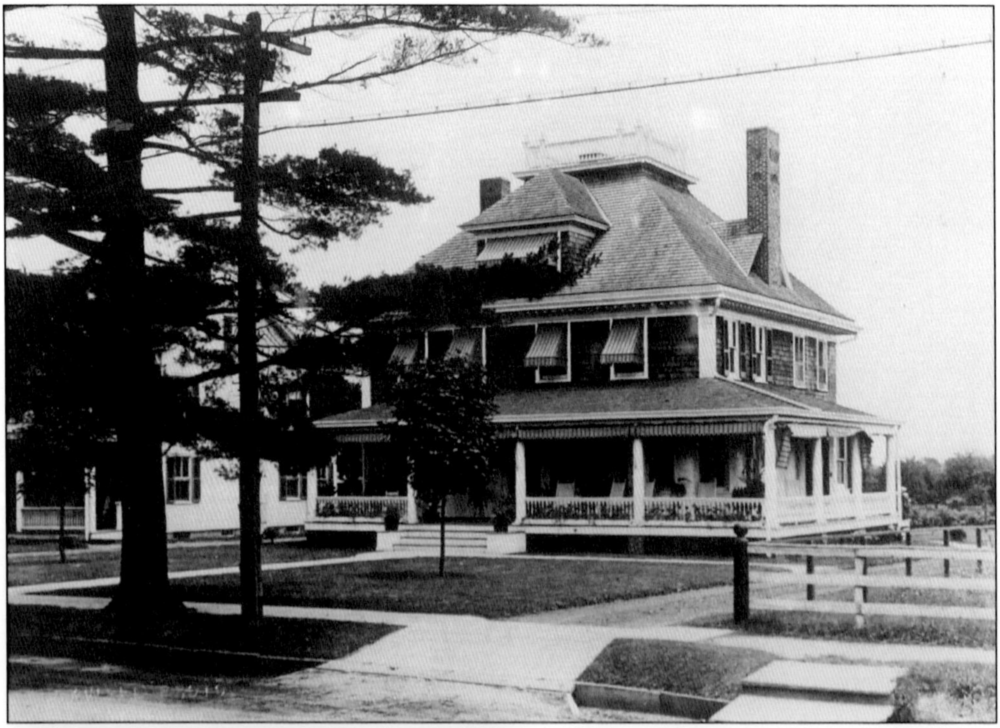

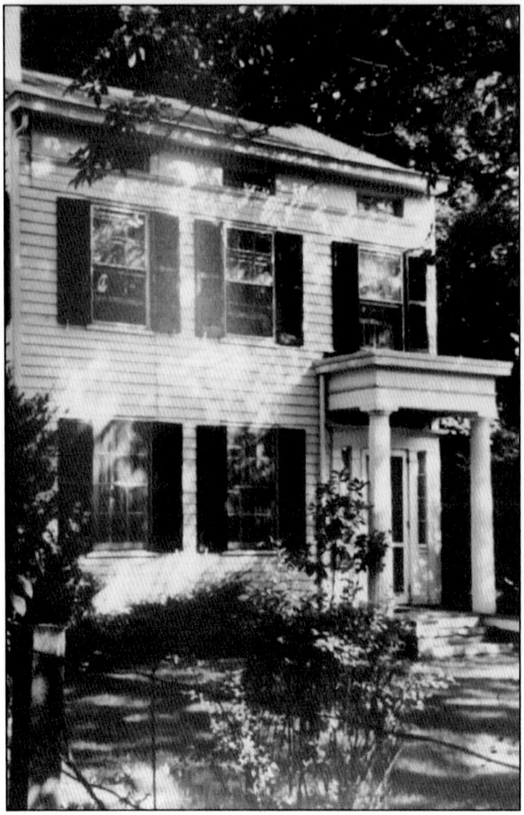

Harry Borden built this Four Square house at 909 Broad Street in 1905. The 38-by-36-foot house was planned with four rooms on the first floor and four on the second, plus a laundry and bath. The 10-foot-wide verandas were on the west and south sides. Borden was a builder and served the county as freeholder and Shrewsbury as a member of the first borough council.

The Borden Homestead at 917 Broad Street is a three-bay, side-gabled Greek Revival house dating from the 1840s. Note the frieze windows in the upper half-story. This 1970s picture is deceptive about its size, a rear ell having greatly expanded its space. (Shrewsbury Historical Society Collection.)

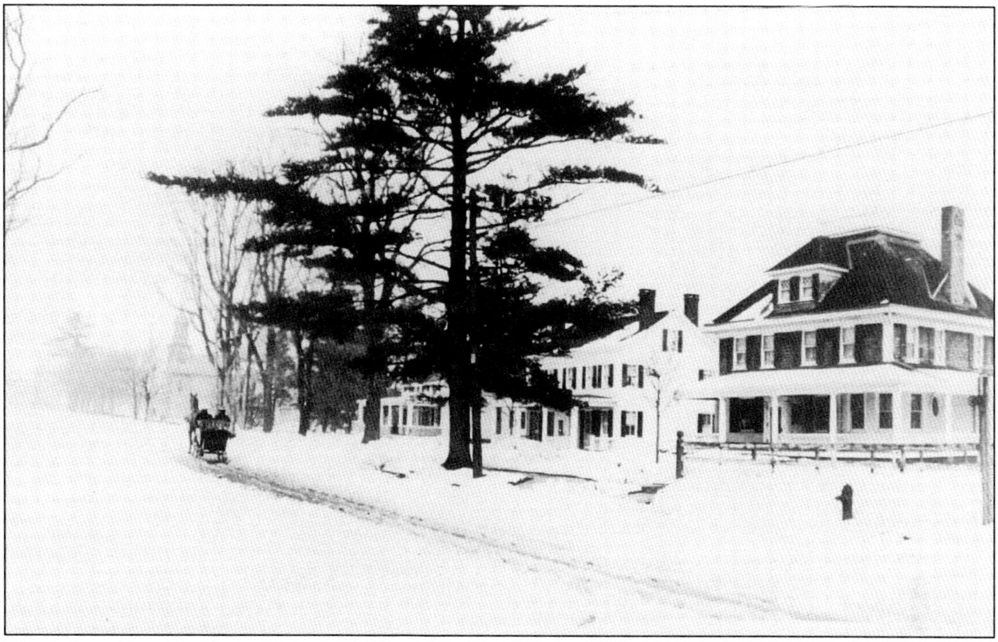

The Harry Borden House is viewed here in the context of the east side of Broad Street, looking north in the snow, with Christ Church in the background. The image comes from a *c.* 1910 postcard.

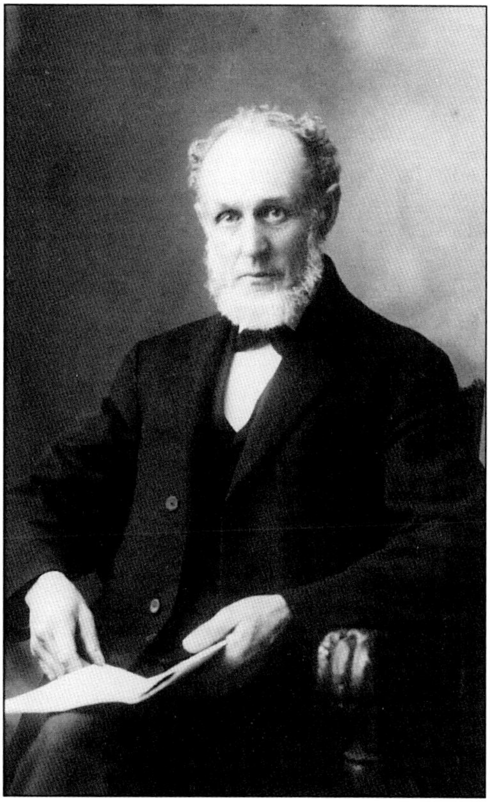

The professorial-looking W. Lambert Borden was a well-known Shrewsbury contractor and builder, and a member of the Presbyterian Church. The sixty-four-year-old Borden died January 24, 1908, following a half-mile walk from his home to Gabriel Nelson's house, where he took his meals.

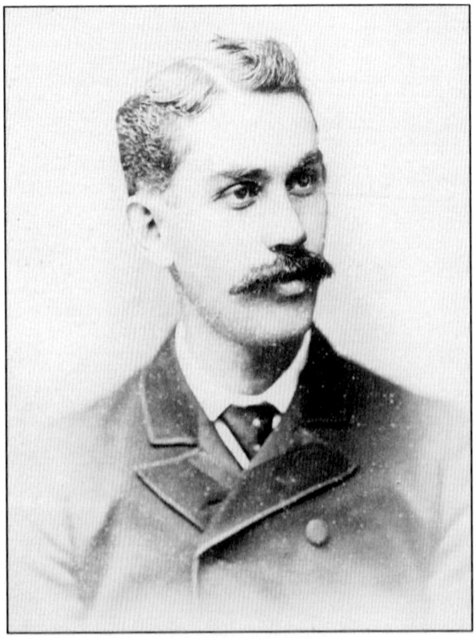

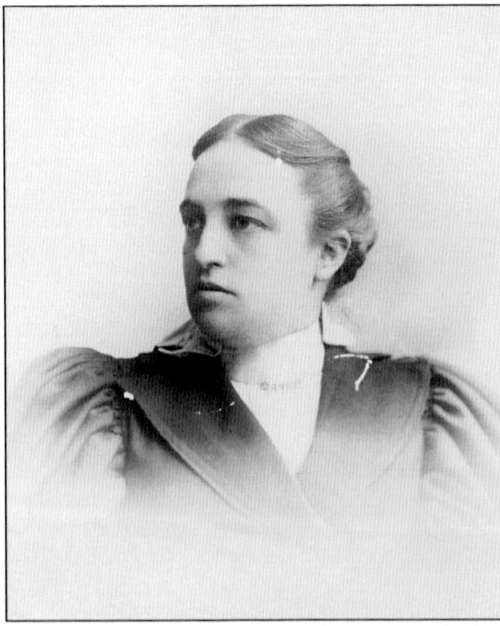

Abram Holmes Borden was born in 1866, the son of Francis and Hannah Lambert Holmes Borden. Widely known as "Holmie," he long-conducted a Shrewsbury grocery business (pp. 27–29). He was active in civic affairs, holding a number of positions, including charter member of the Shrewsbury Fire Company, member of the board of education, and Shrewsbury Township's overseer of the poor, a capacity he was serving in at the time of his death in 1923. His wife, the former Emily Julia Bunn, died in 1920. Her portrait is in the collection of the Shrewsbury Historical Society.

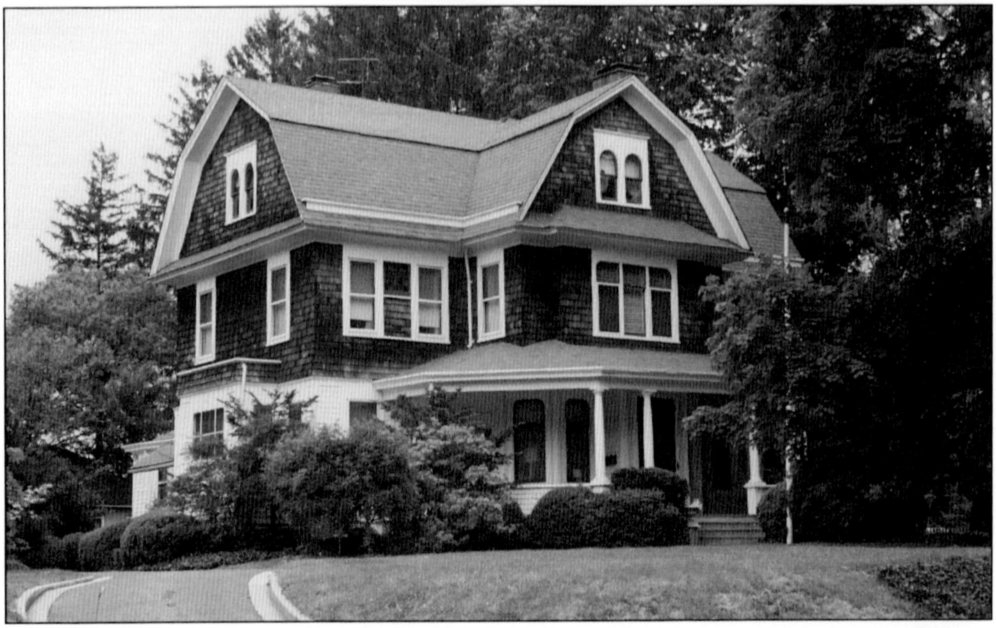

A. Holmes Borden bought about one-half acre from the Tallman estate, moved the small house and a large shed on the property, and hired his brothers, who traded as Borden Bros., to build this fine, Colonial Revival-Shingle house that still stands at 912 Broad Street.

Four

Sycamore Avenue

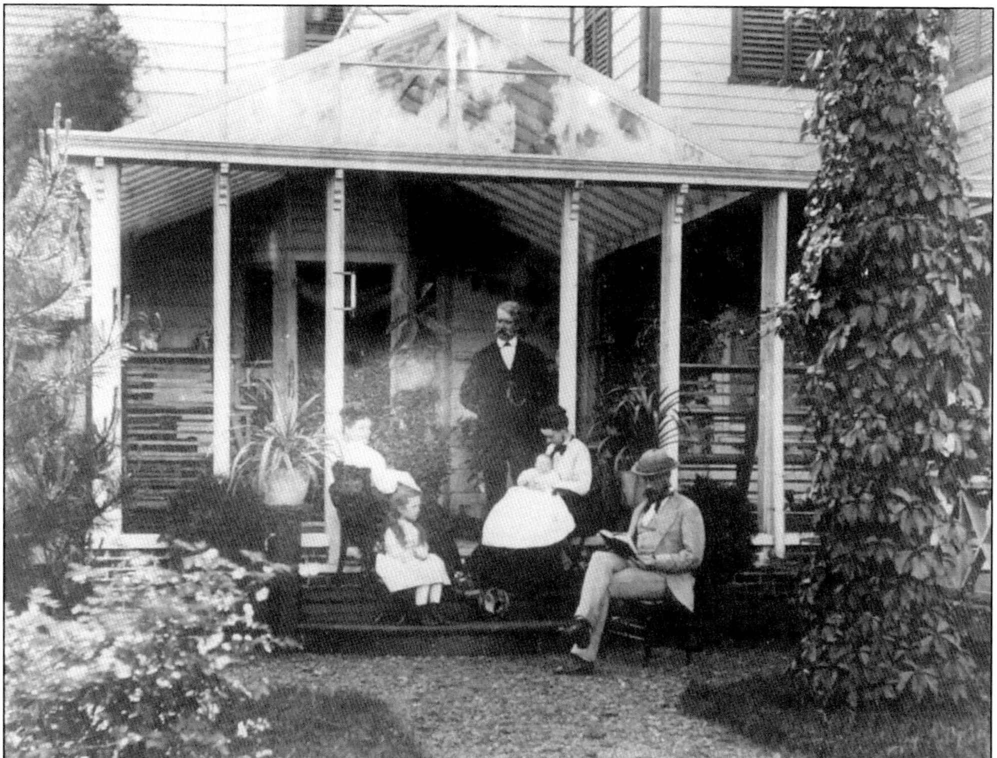

Dr. William Van Buren (p. 74) stands over a family group at the rear porch of his residence at 457 Sycamore Avenue (p. 74). Seated on the left is his daughter, Mrs. Meert, with her daughter, Louise Meert, beneath her. Another daughter, Mrs. Brugiere, is seated under the doctor's left arm holding baby Victor Meert. His son-in-law, Mr. Meert, seems detached at right, oblivious to the difficulties this group photograph would create over a century later: there are only six people visible, but identification guide on the photograph claims there are seven. (Shrewsbury Historical Society.)

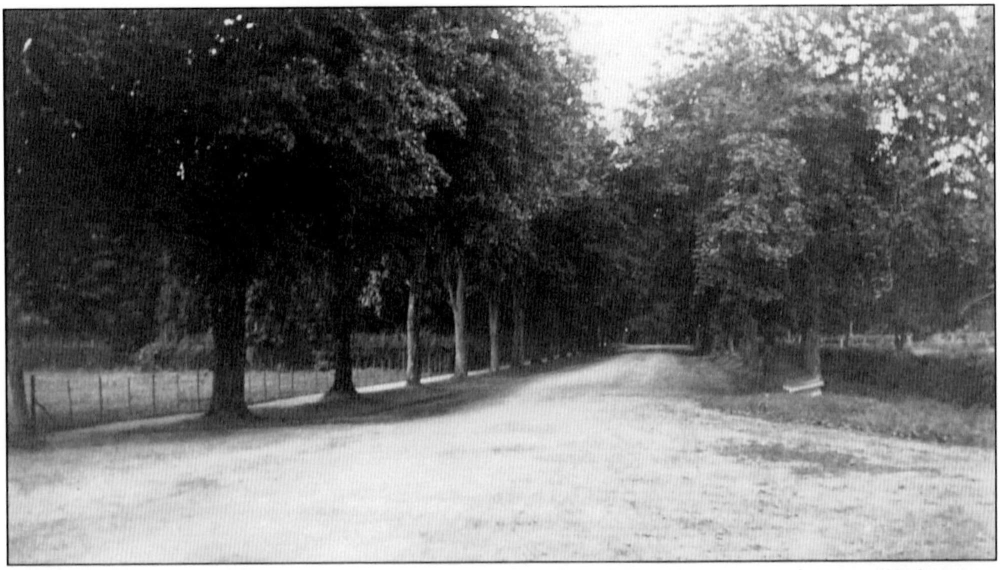

Sycamore Avenue looking west from the railroad in the 1890s was a pastoral scene. Today, one of the town's busiest intersections, on the Tinton Falls border at Shrewsbury Avenue, would be in the distance.

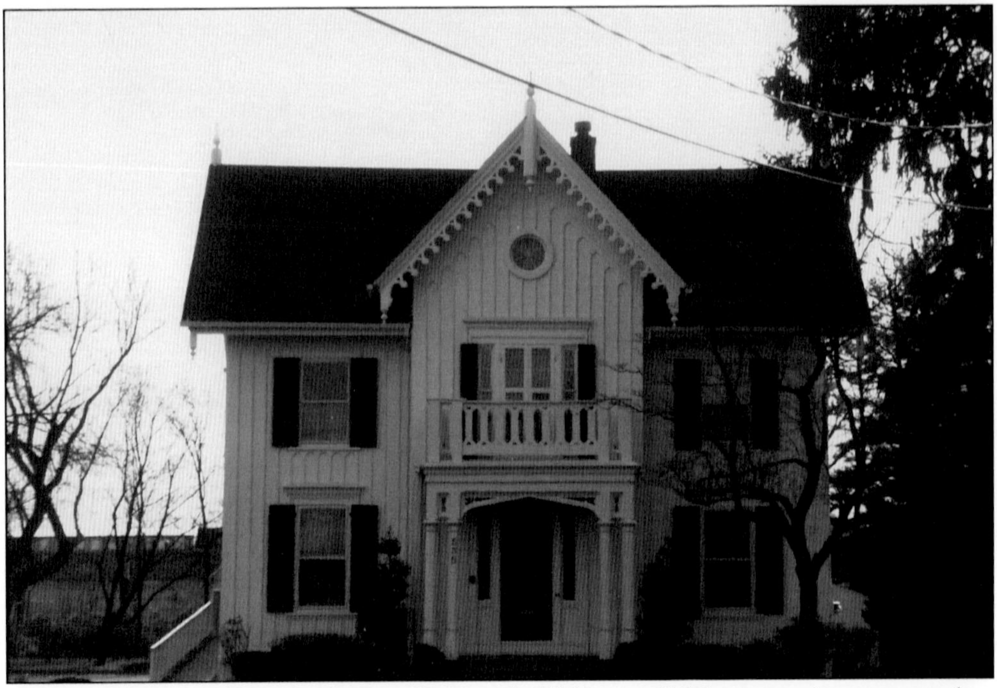

The Gothic Revival design for the Peter B. Campbell House at 535 Sycamore Avenue was taken from Samuel Sloan's 1852 pattern book *The Model Architect*. Campbell was a leading breeder of horses, and he treated them, although he was not known to be a veterinary doctor. The building was adapted for use as the Plastic Surgery Center, headed by Dr. Steven B. Norwitz, via an expansion designed by Red Bank architect Robert De Santis. Its sympathetic blending of new construction with the original structure makes it Shrewsbury's outstanding example of adaptive use.

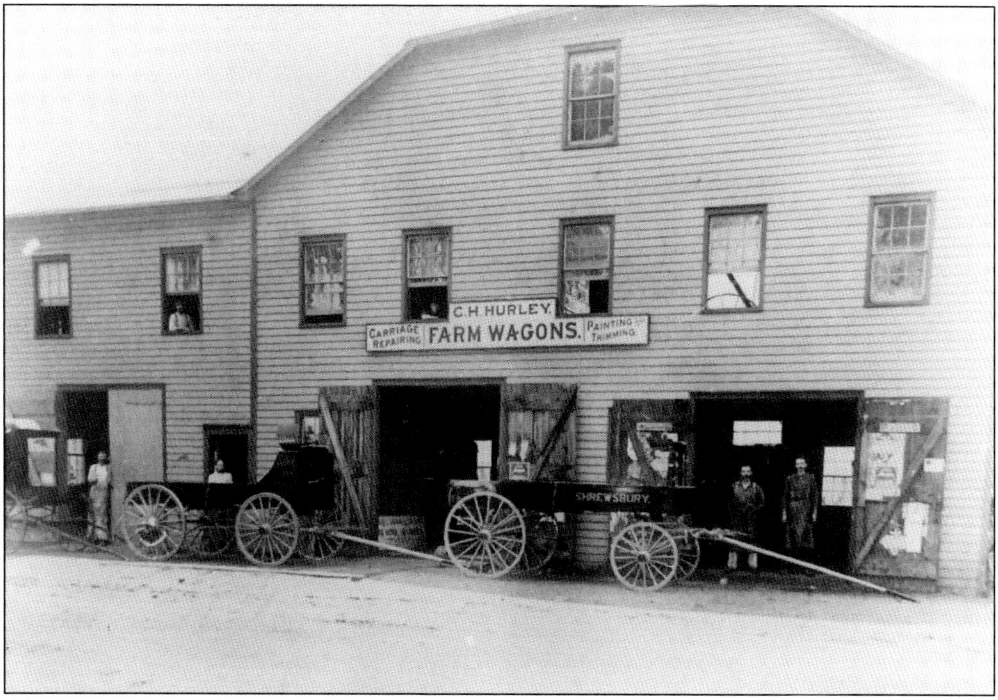

Charles H. Hurley began work in Richard B. Campbell's blacksmith and wheelwright shop around 1871 in a building that burned in 1875. A replacement was built by Edmund T. Williams, who owned extensive property in the area west of the New Jersey Southern Railroad. Hurley acquired it in 1889. He added farm machinery and implements in 1889, creating the first operation of its kind in Monmouth County, and sold the business in 1920. The structure grew over the years and is still recognizable as the office and store of the Lawes Company. This view from the collection of the Shrewsbury Historical Society appears to pre-date 1890.

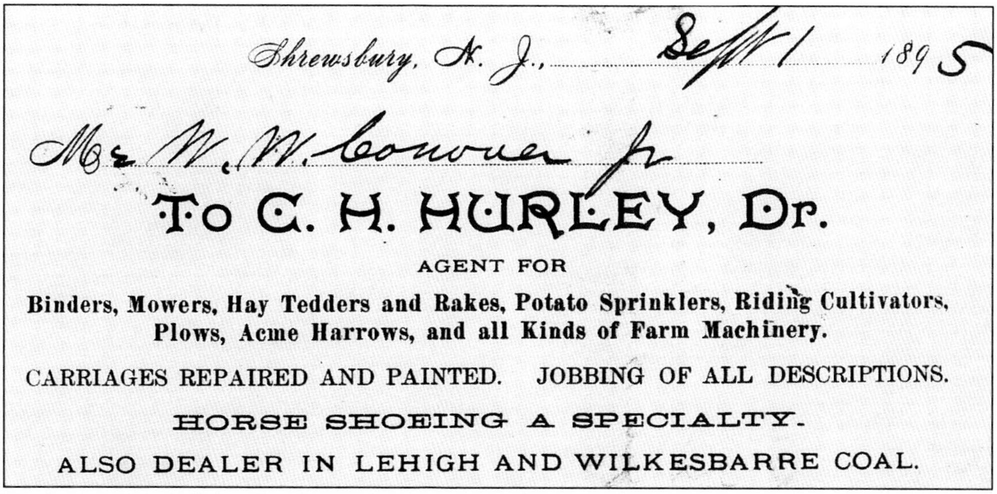

Shrewsbury, N. J., Sept 1 1895

Mr. W. W. Conover Jr

To C. H. HURLEY, Dr.

AGENT FOR

Binders, Mowers, Hay Tedders and Rakes, Potato Sprinklers, Riding Cultivators, Plows, Acme Harrows, and all Kinds of Farm Machinery.

CARRIAGES REPAIRED AND PAINTED. JOBBING OF ALL DESCRIPTIONS.

HORSE SHOEING A SPECIALTY.

ALSO DEALER IN LEHIGH AND WILKESBARRE COAL.

Hurley's 1890s bill head reflects the important farm machines of the day. The coal dealing presaged the longtime principal product of the 1926 successor, Lawes. (Shrewsbury Historical Society Collection.)

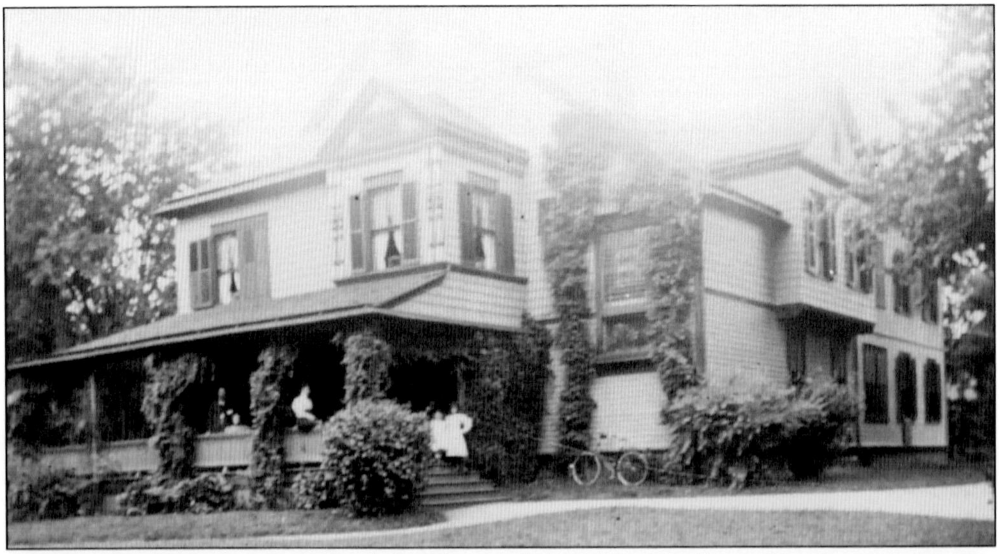

Waldron Post Brown, a partner of the New York banking firm Brown Brothers, bought the former Dr. Smith Cutter place on the north side of Sycamore Avenue, eventually moving its house to the rear of the property and building this two-and-one-half-story Queen Anne-style structure named "Brenda Lodge," at number 486. Although "Anno Domini 1877" appears in the pediment of the south facade's second-story gable, the house appears to be 1890s. It remains well-preserved, with a high degree of integrity, with even the porch remaining open. (Shrewsbury Historical Society Collection.)

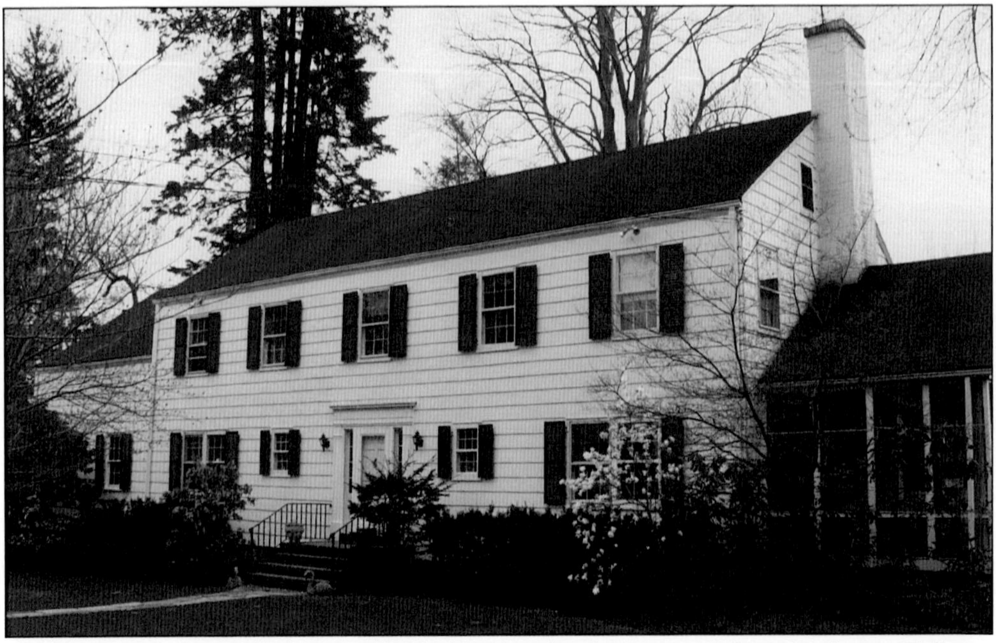

In 1937, Forrest S. Smith, a Jersey City lawyer, bought about an acre from the former Tallman estate (now Borough Hall property) and hired Robert Shannon, a Jersey City architect, to design this Colonial Revival house at 451 Sycamore Avenue. A generous set-back from the street and the use of an older architectural style provide a fine example of a newer house blending with older surroundings.

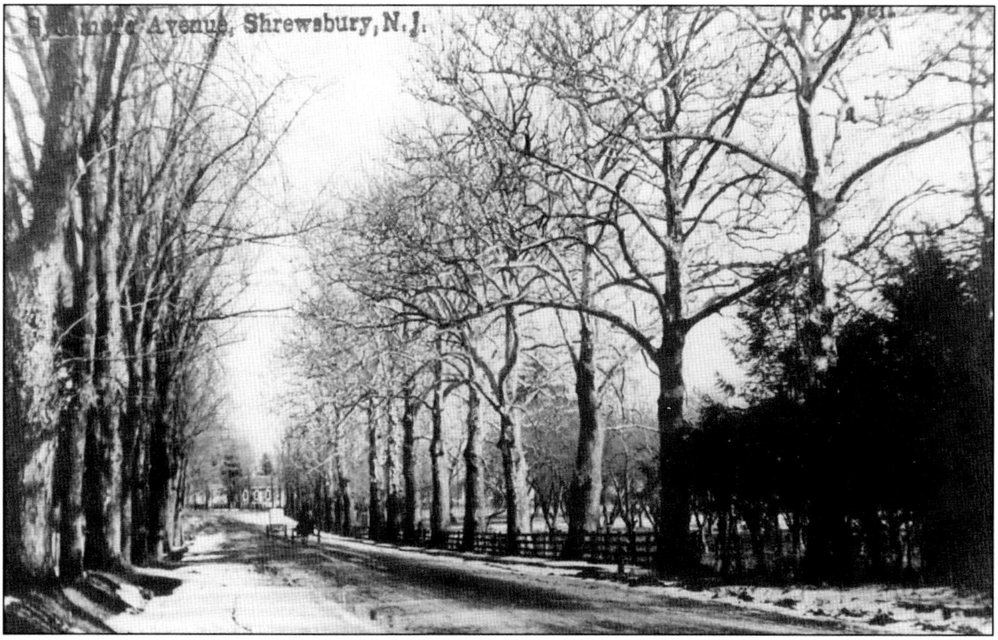

This *c*. 1905 Charles Foxwell photograph looking east shows Sycamore Avenue lined with its fine, old trees. (John Rhody Collection.)

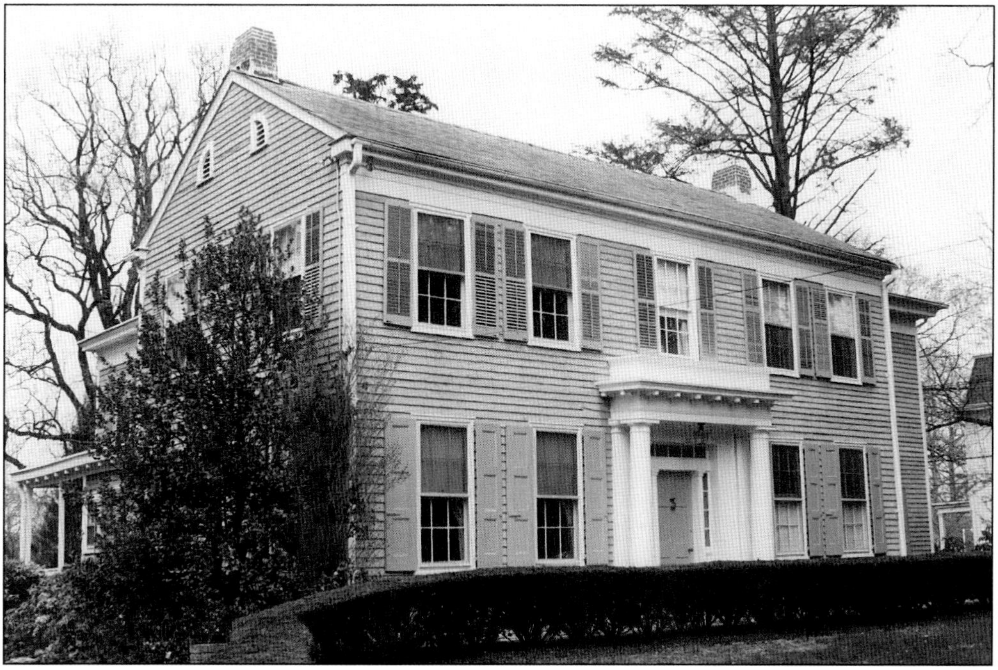

E. Delafield Smith assembled farm parcels on the north side of Sycamore Avenue in 1870–71, occupying number 458, known as the "Corlies place." He was corporate counsel for the City of New York, becoming entangled in the political turmoil of the 1870s, with his notoriety resulting in a renaming of this to "the Delafield Smith House." Smith died in 1878. The house has been expanded and remodeled on several occasions, including during the residency of Ashbel W. Borden, a noted builder who married Smith's daughter Charlotte.

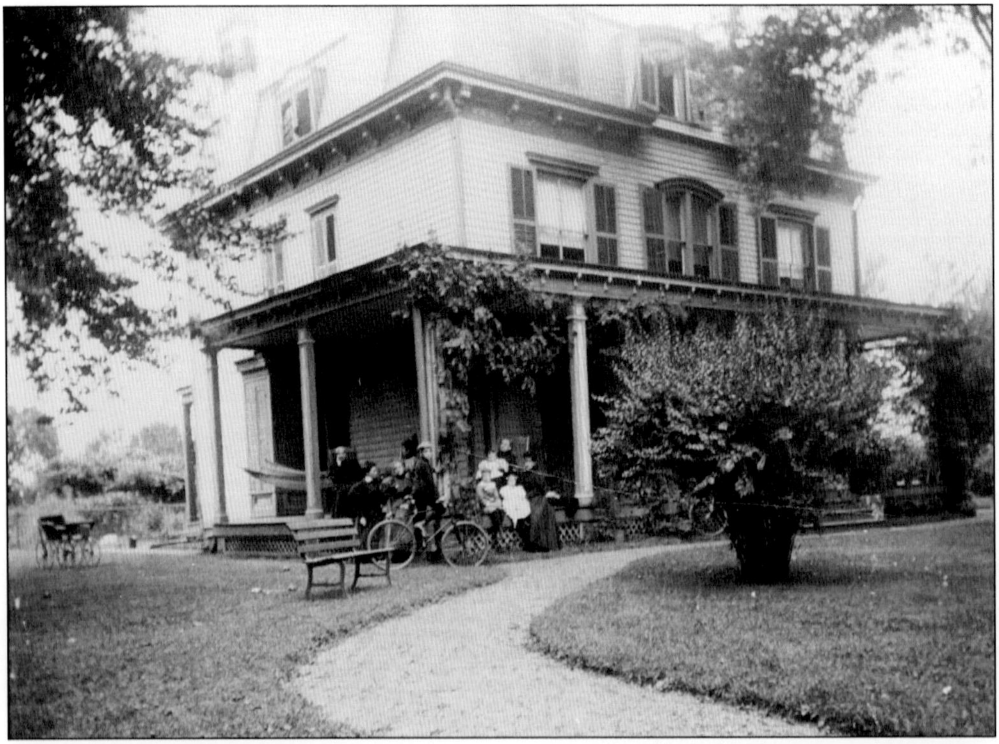

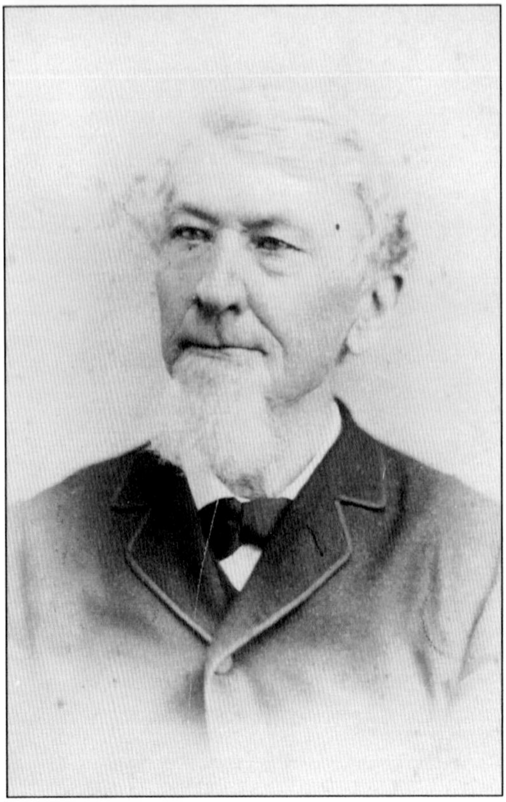

James Broadmeadow began purchasing his north side of Sycamore Avenue property in the 1860s, acquiring acreage in several transactions. He built this Second Empire-style house in the 1870s. Its appearance was similar to this *c.* 1890s photograph in the collection of the Shrewsbury Historical Society, with changed details.

James Broadmeadow was born in England, and he emigrated to the U.S. with his family at age ten, *c.* 1825. Work began in his grandfather's Richmond, Virginia, steel business in the early 1840s, which he left late in the decade to join the California gold rush. After staying two years, he returned east and opened a pickling and preserving factory in New York. It is said he is the first to have had tomatoes packed cold. In 1863 Broadmeadow built the Shrewsbury factory (p. 83) more commonly associated with E.C. Hazard, later moving to Red Bank where he also built a canning factory. Broadmeadow died at home, aged eighty, in 1895. (Shrewsbury Historical Society Collection.)

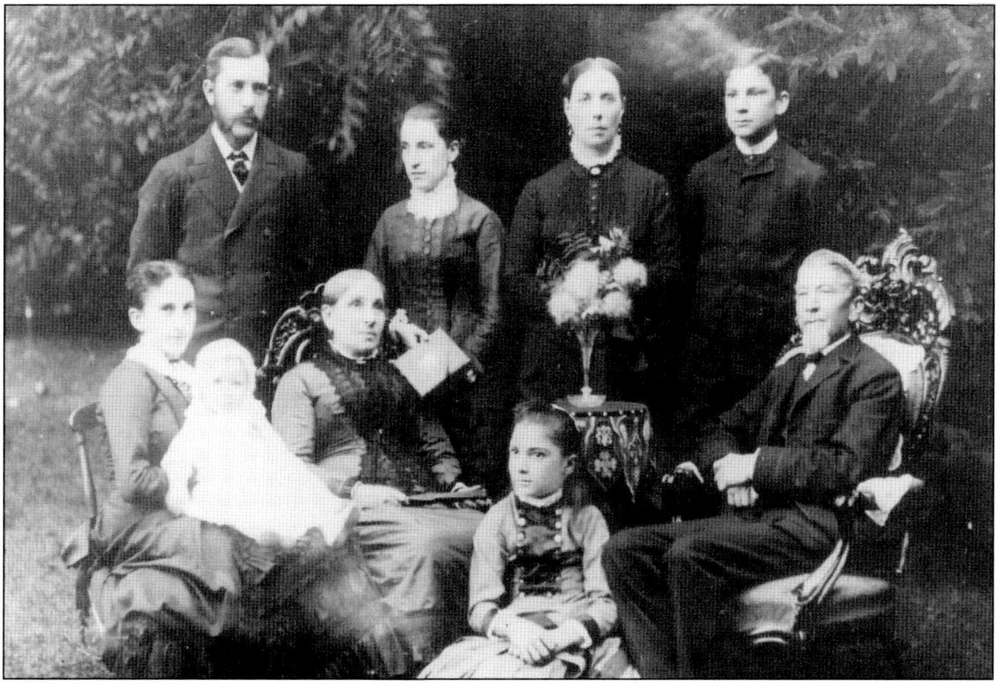

The Broadmeadow family strikes a regal pose. Patriarch James, at about age sixty-five, is seated on the right, with his wife, Lavinia, to the left of the flowers. Frances Broadmeadow Tallman is on the left, with daughter Lavinia in her lap. Lavinia was born in 1879, dating the photograph *c.* 1880. Standing are: Stephen Tallman, Ida Florence Broadmeadow, Ann Murtha, and Walter James Broadmeadow. Lillian Broadmeadow is seated at front. (Shrewsbury Historical Society Collection.)

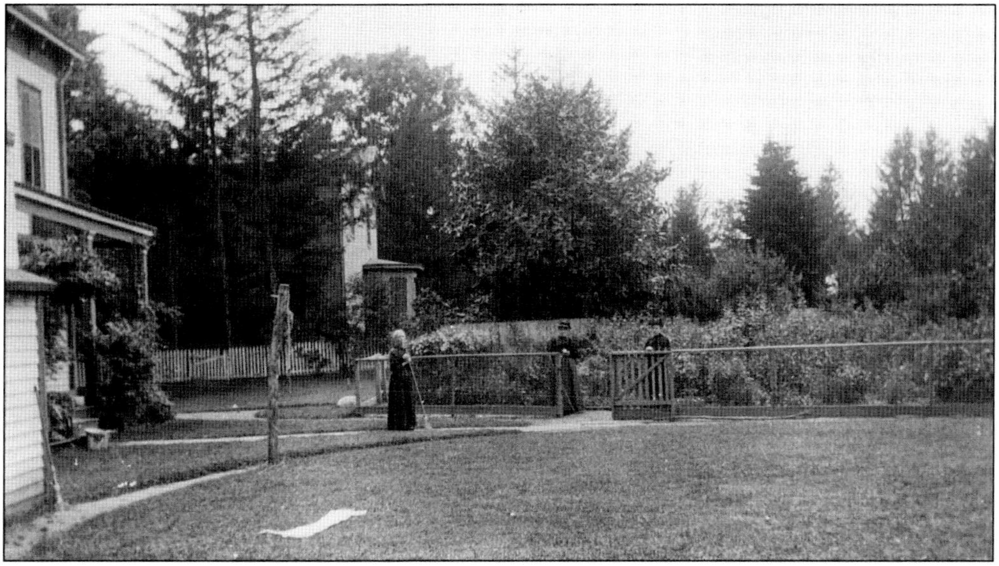

This is an unusual scene of the back of the Broadmeadow property with a domestic pausing from her work. Ann Murtha, born in Ireland, served the family for decades. Their closeness and affection may be inferred from her burial in the family plot at the Presbyterian church. (Shrewsbury Historical Society Collection.)

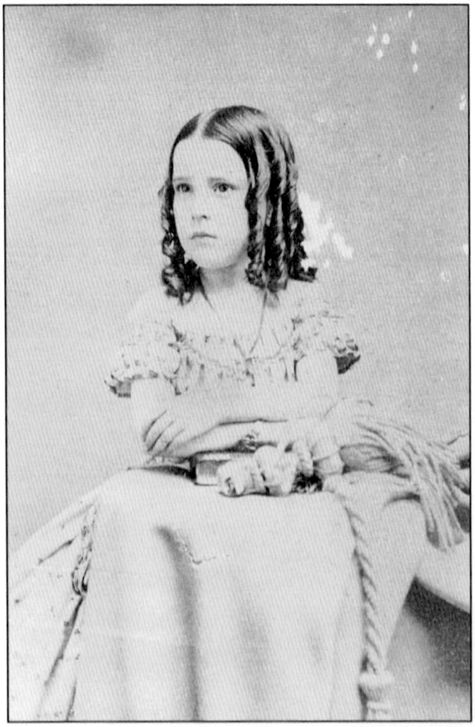

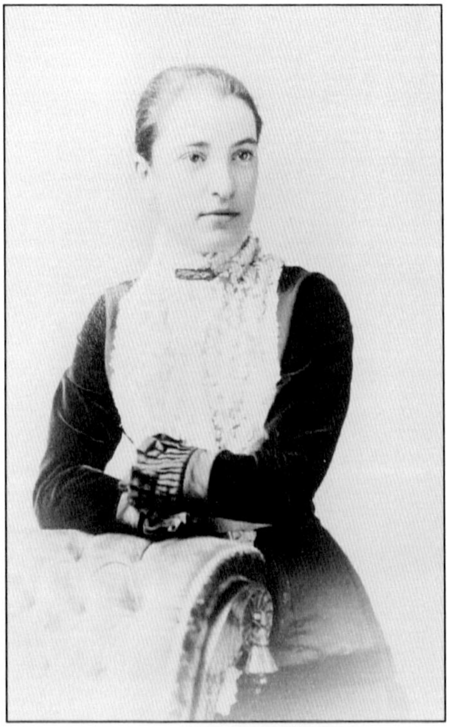

Ida Florence Broadmeadow, born 1857 to James and Lavinia, graduated from Freehold's Young Ladies Seminary in 1875 and enjoyed an eighteen-year teaching career—her position when pictured at left. Widowed in 1902, "perpetual mourning set in," according to a daughter, but she survived to age ninety-seven. (Shrewsbury Historical Society Collection.)

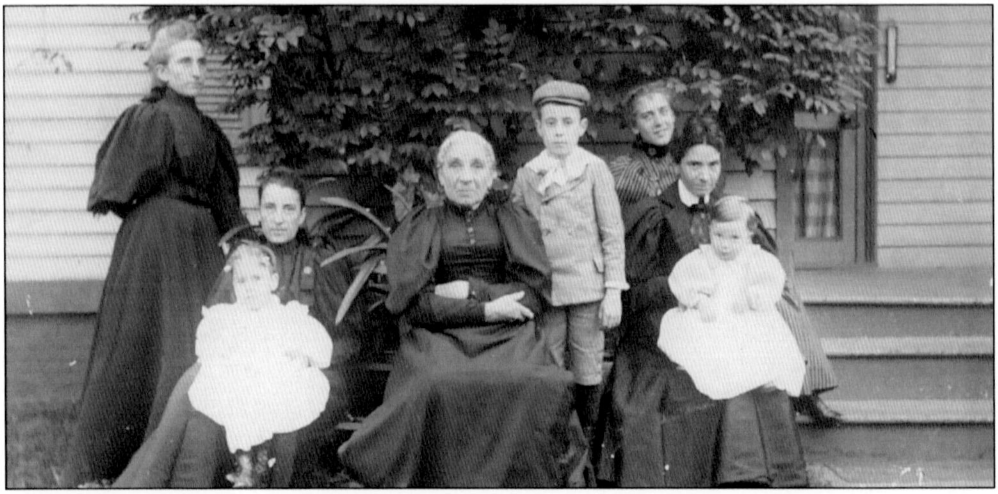

The family of James Broadmeadow (p. 70) after his death on September 1, 1895, strikes a somber mourning pose. His widow Lavinia is in the center. At her right are Martha B. Tallman and Ida B. Prince, with Ethel A. Prince in her lap, to her left. At right rear is Lavinia Tallman, Martha's daughter, whose expression may imply she is too young and pretty to be remembered without a smile. Below her is Lillian B. Bunn, with Charles Horatio Bunn in her lap. Longtime maid Ann Murtha is in the doorway, with at least the bottom of her dress visible. (Shrewsbury Historical Society Collection.)

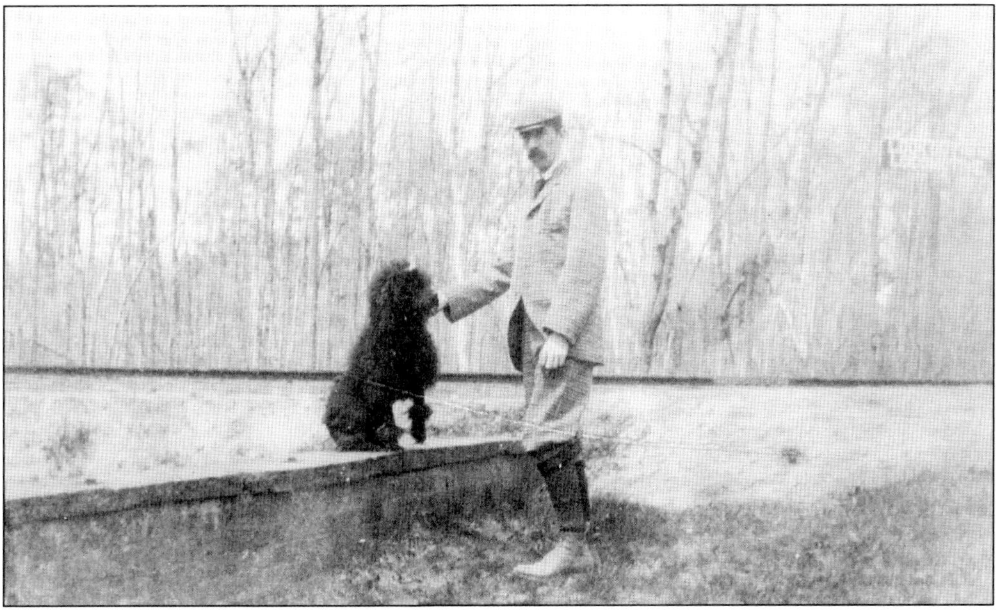

Ernest de Coppet, born *c.* 1874 at New Brunswick, New Jersey, is shown here *c.* 1900 at Thornbrooke. He spent his youth in Switzerland and was educated abroad, returning to America around 1900 to join the family brokerage firm, known in time as Jacquelin & de Coppet. Ernest lived in Garden City, New York, spent much time in California, and died in New York in 1937. (Shrewsbury Historical Society Collection.)

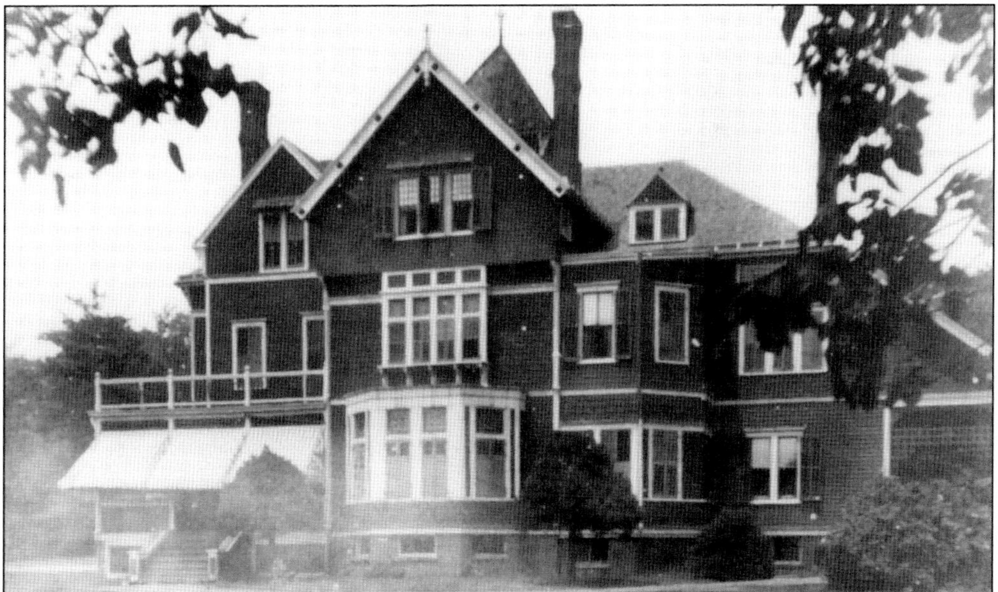

The two-and-one-half-story Queen Anne-style house at 469 Sycamore Avenue was named "Thornbrooke" by Louis C. de Coppet, who married the former Adele Thorn. This view of the south elevation (not visible from the street) is a *c.* 1900 picture in the collection of the Shrewsbury Historical Society. The house, now painted yellow, still stands looking not unlike the old view, with some change of detail.

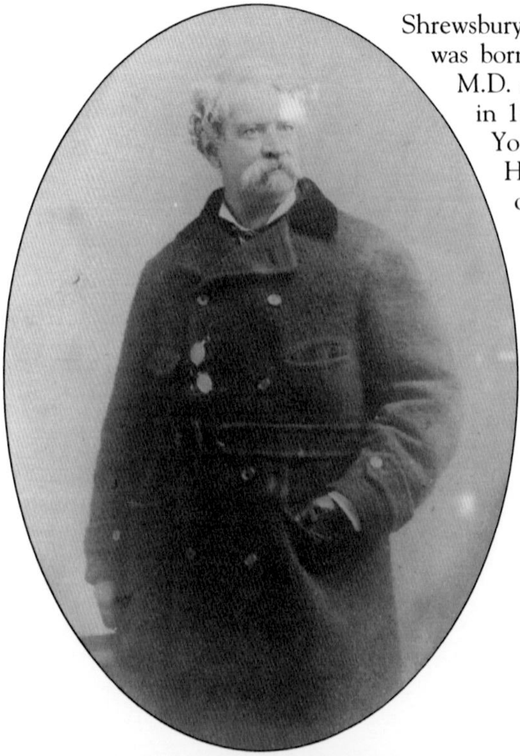

Shrewsbury summer resident William Holme Van Buren was born in 1819 in Philadelphia and received an M.D. degree from the University of Pennsylvania in 1840. He began practicing medicine in New York in 1845, becoming a surgeon at Bellevue Hospital and the professor of genito-urinary organs and venereal diseases at the University of the City of New York. He served as member of the executive committee of the United States Sanitary Committee during the Civil War. He traveled in Europe after the war, returning to New York as a consultant, lecturer, and writer of several medical texts. Van Buren died in New York in 1883. (Shrewsbury Historical Society Collection.)

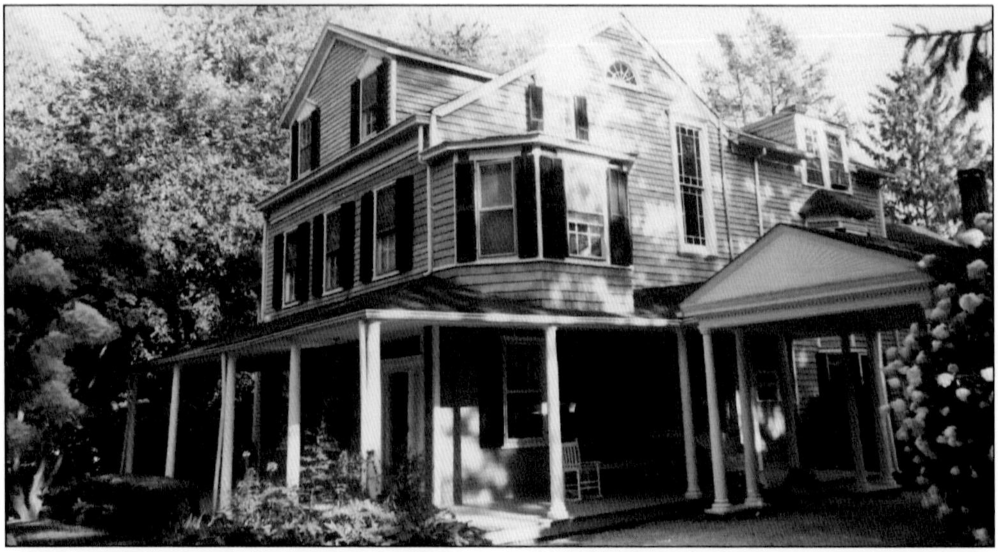

Robert Parker's original *c.* 1830s two-and-one-half-story side-gabled house at 457 Sycamore Avenue can seen by ignoring the porch, porte-cochere, large front dormer, bay window, and rear extension. Dr. William Holme Van Buren bought the place in 1867 and began expansions. The house may be considered a landmark in the establishment of the Catholic Church in Monmouth County, as Bishop Michael Corrigan often called on and stayed with Dr. Van Buren in his travels while building a church network in the1870s. The property was auctioned at a court-ordered sale in 1894, with Thomas and Mary Walling buying the house and Van Buren's daughter, Adelaide, buying an adjoining farm.

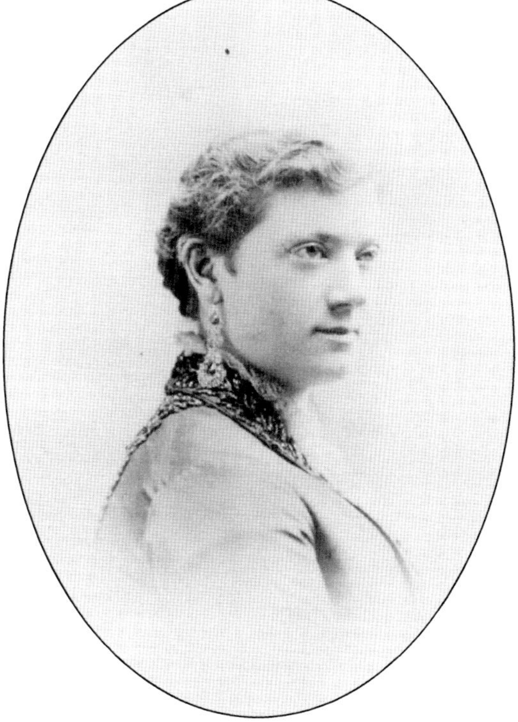

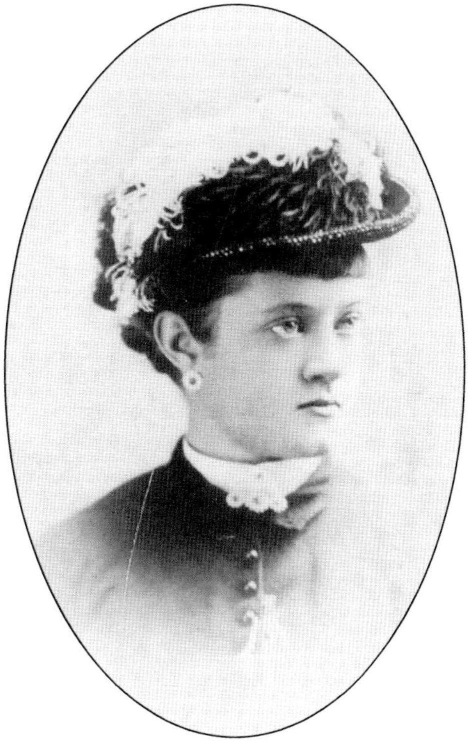

William Van Buren married Louisa Dunmore Mott in 1842. One of their two daughters, Adelaide Meert, is pictured at left, with her daughter Louise at right. Both pictures were taken in the 1880s, and are in the collection of the Shrewsbury Historical Society .

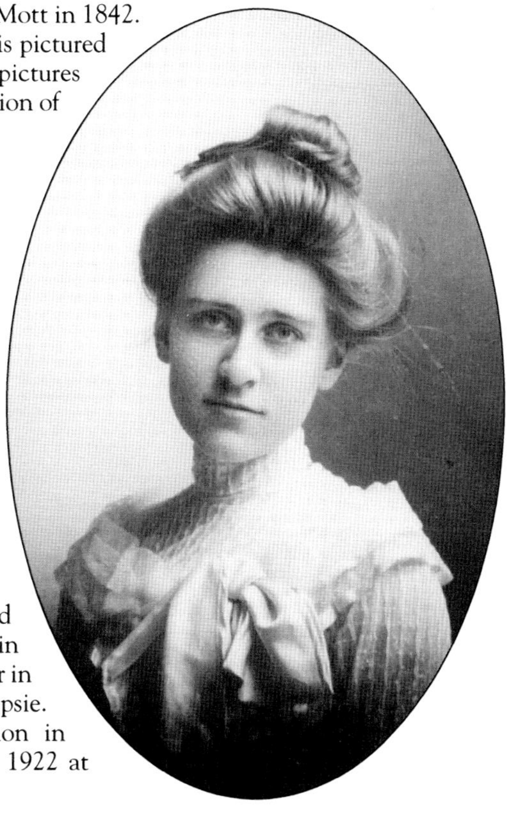

Lavinia Tallman, the daughter of Stephen and the former Martha Broadmeadow, was born in 1879 in Shrewsbury. She graduated from Vassar in 1904, when this picture was taken in Poughkeepsie. Lavinia's teaching career included instruction in English and religious education. She died in 1922 at Orange, New Jersey.

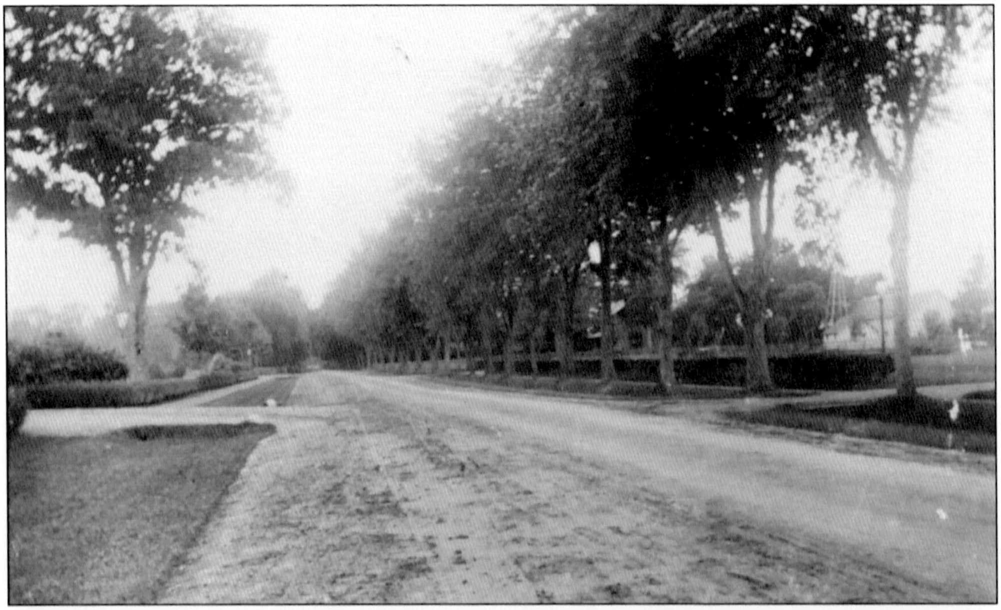

A view of Sycamore Avenue from the Broadmeadow House, about 350 yards east of the scene on the top of p. 66. The set-back of houses from the street line helps preserve the old character of the avenue. However, the present pavement alone makes this scene seem out of the distant past. (Shrewsbury Historical Society Collection.)

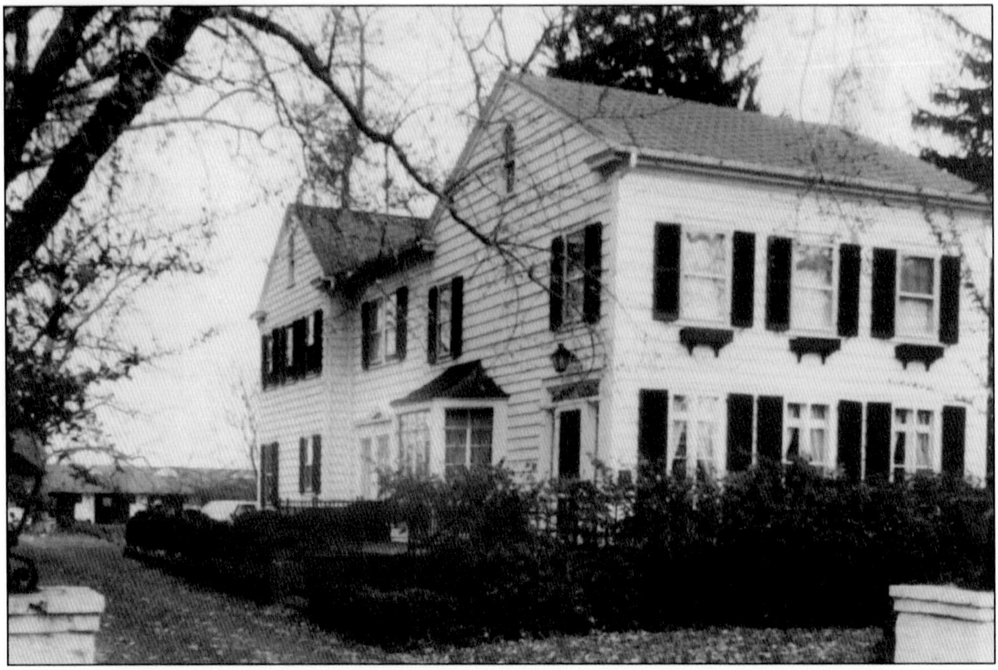

An old house is believed to sit at the core of the much-expanded 440 Sycamore Avenue structure, perhaps best known as the former home of longtime Shrewsbury mayor and New Jersey Senate President Alfred N. Beadleston. Stable and farm buildings in the rear reflect the importance of equestrian events in Shrewsbury's sporting past. This 1970s photograph is in the collection of the Shrewsbury Historical Society.

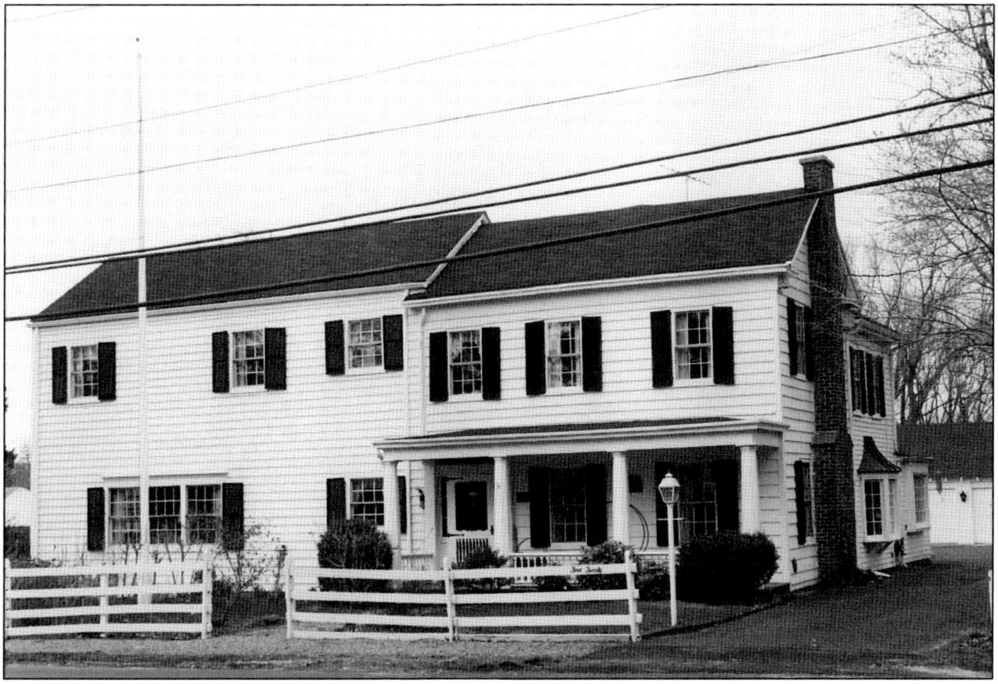

The mid-nineteenth-century house at 420 Sycamore Avenue was doubled in size in the recent past, the outlines of newer and older sections readily visible. Known as the Arthur Swift House for the late nineteenth/early twentieth century owner, in 1919 it was sold to Mrs. L.L. White and remodeled. Mrs. White was then owner of the present borough hall (p. 34).

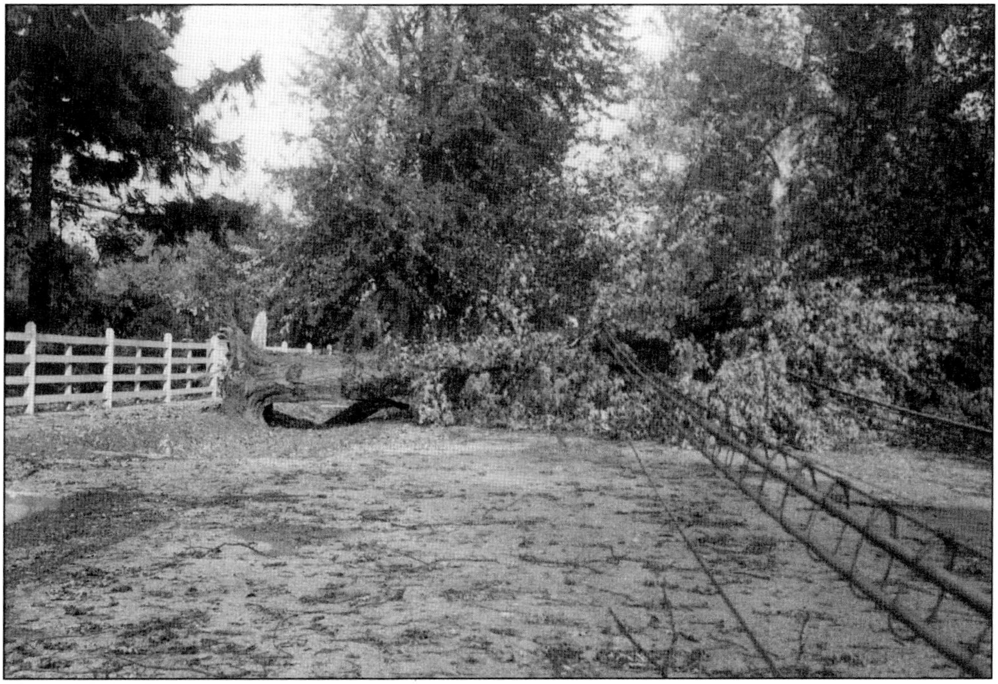

Storms as well as age have taken a toll among Sycamore Avenue's stately trees. This scene is after the 1938 hurricane, opposite the house on the bottom of p. 76.

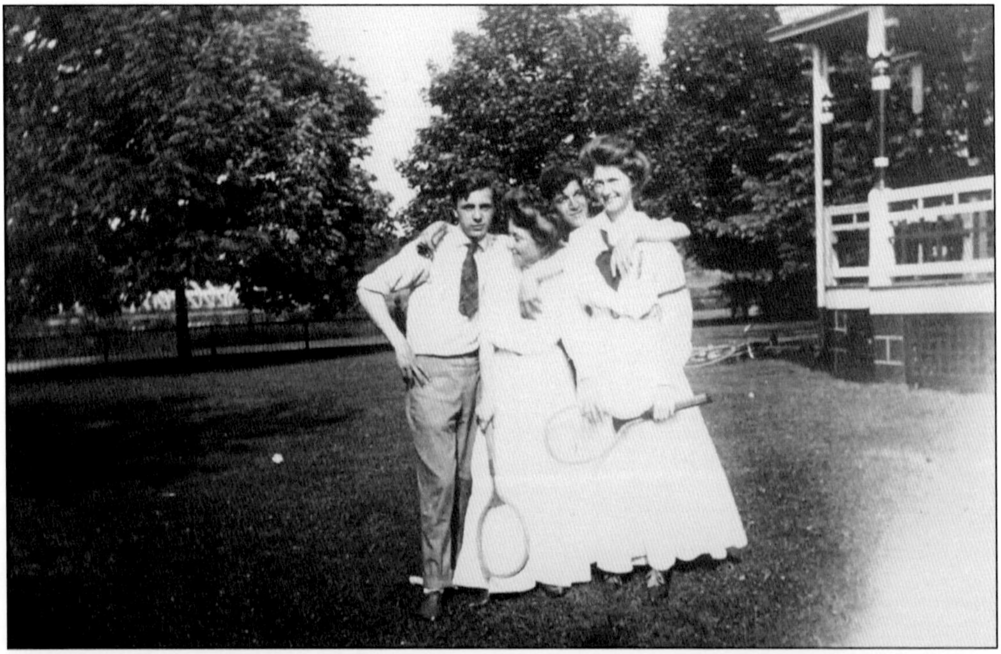

Would one risk spoiling that appealing pompadour with a vigorous game of tennis? Could one play a vigorous game of tennis in those skirts? This *c.* 1910 photograph is from the collection of the Shrewsbury Historical Society.

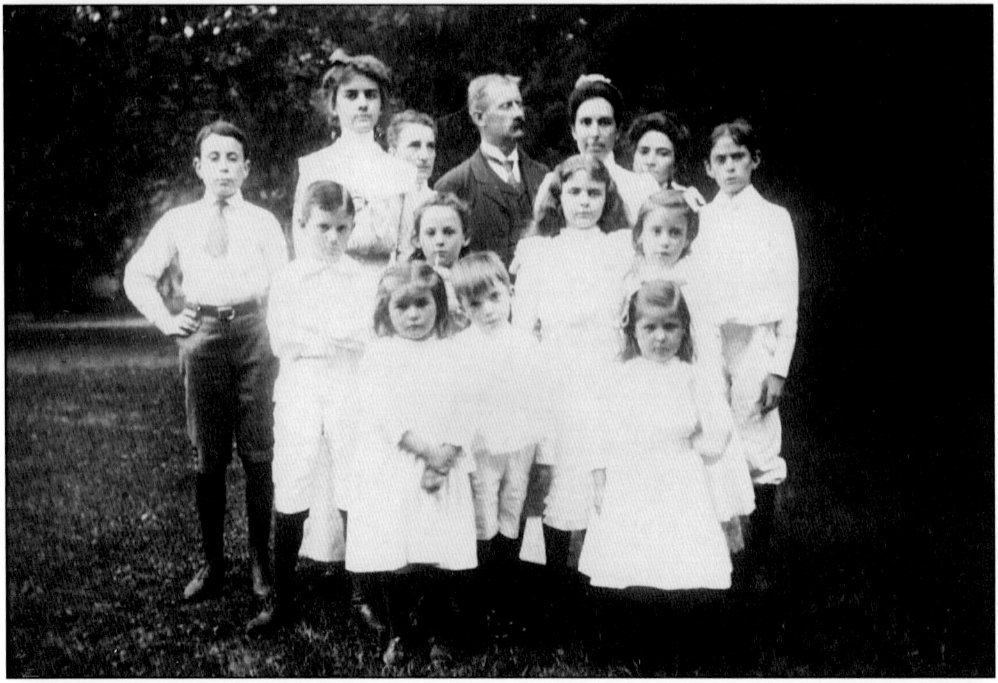

Sad faces are justified in this September 6, 1901 photograph of celebrants at the 87th birthday party for Ethel Prince. The label of the original at the Shrewsbury Historical Society indicates that G.S. Prince has just brought word of the shooting of President William McKinley, who died from his wounds on September 14, 1901.

Standing over the Reverend Thaddeus Wilson (p. 18) are Thomas Curtis, Randolph Borden (p. 80), James Steen, and Benjamin Wyckoff. Steen was a Princeton-educated lawyer, an elder in the Presbyterian Church, a student and writer of local history, and a Democratic political activist who led the campaign to bar race track betting in 1893.

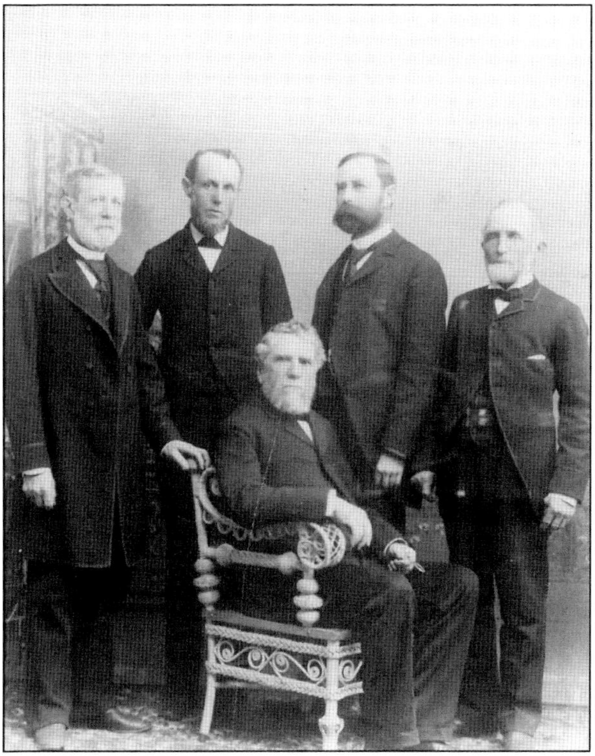

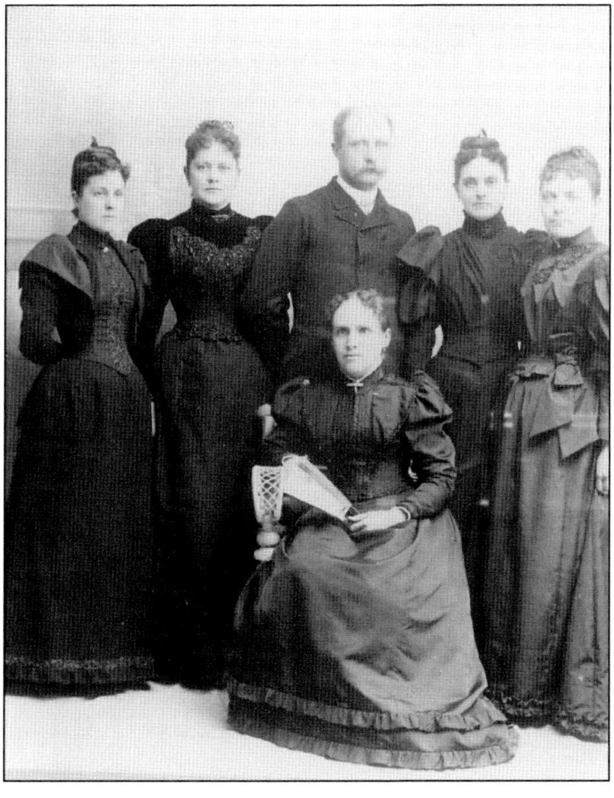

This late-1880s companion to the photograph above likely has a tie to a Presbyterian church matter, but the subjects were not identified. There appears to be a familial resemblance among the standing women.

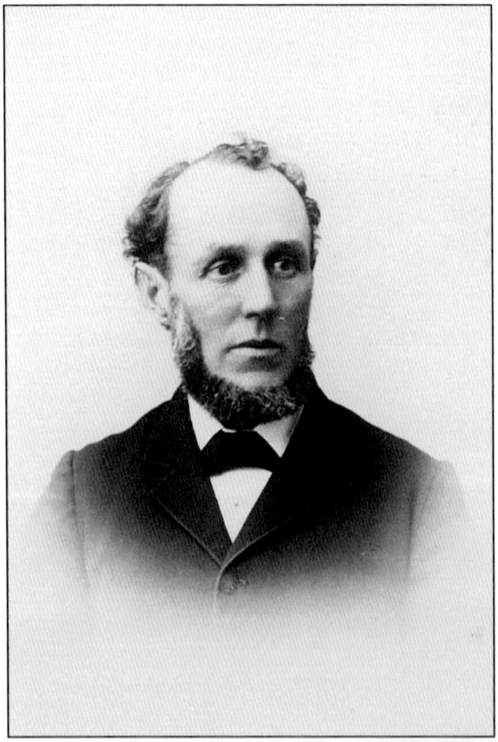

Randolph Borden was a builder for many years, in partnership with his brother Ashbel, erecting many large houses and other buildings, including St. Luke's Methodist Church in Long Branch and the no-longer-standing Laurel-in-the-Pines Hotel in Lakewood. He died in 1918 at age seventy-two, and was survived by three daughters, Nellie, Mary, and Elizabeth.

The earliest part of the house at 345 Sycamore Avenue likely dates from the fourth quarter of the eighteenth century. Long owned by the Holmes family, it was the Randolph Borden house after a marital tie, when this *c.* 1900 photograph was taken following Borden's 1890s expansion of the house.

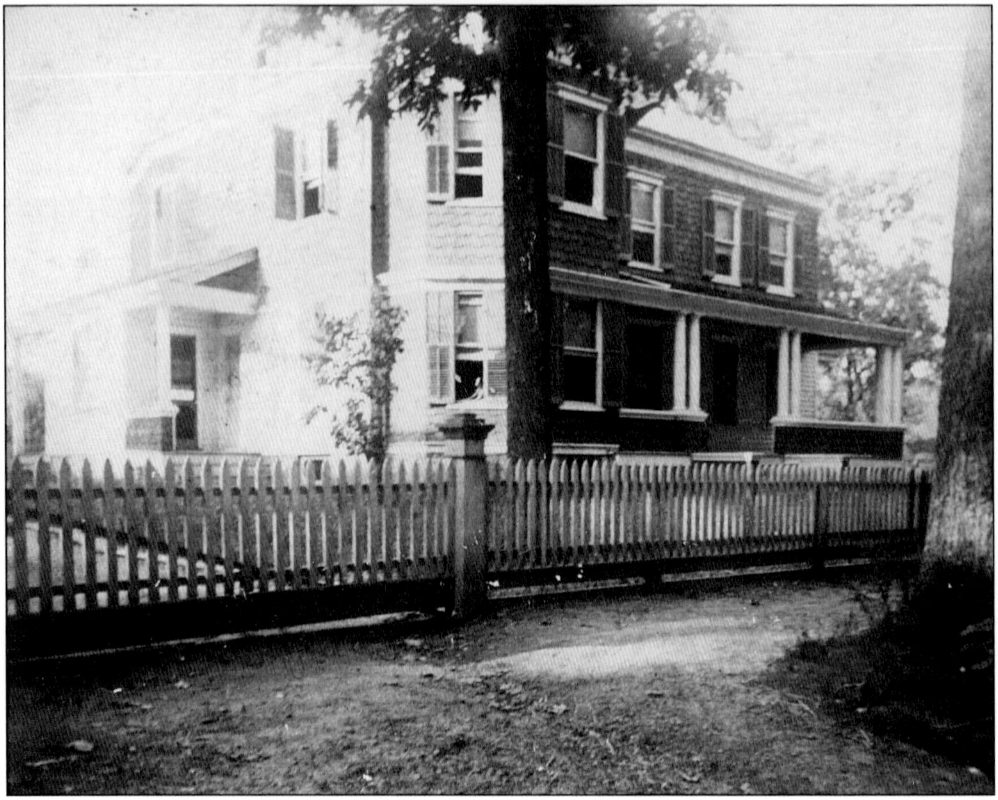

Charles Francis Borden, son of A. Holmes Borden (p. 64), born August 6, 1887, is pictured in his World War I uniform. Pvt. Borden served as a machine gunner with Co. A of the 310th Machine Gun Battalion. He was a ruling elder of the Shrewsbury Presbyterian Church and a member of the Monmouth Chapter, Sons of the American Revolution, and several other organizations. He owned a real estate and insurance business at his home, where he died December 19, 1920.

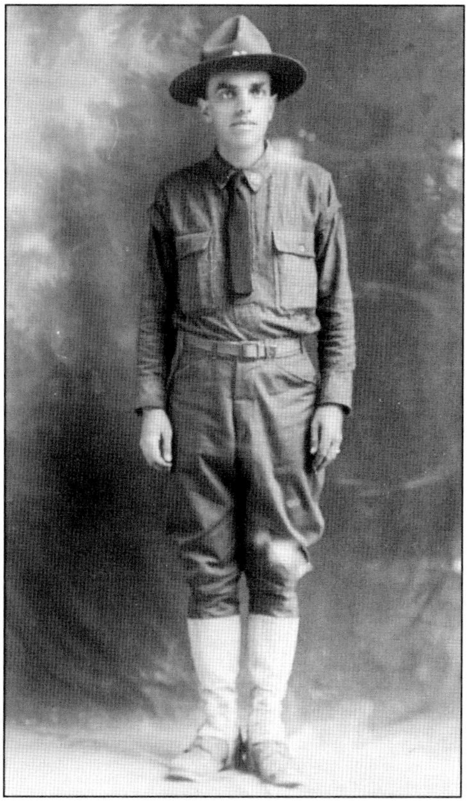

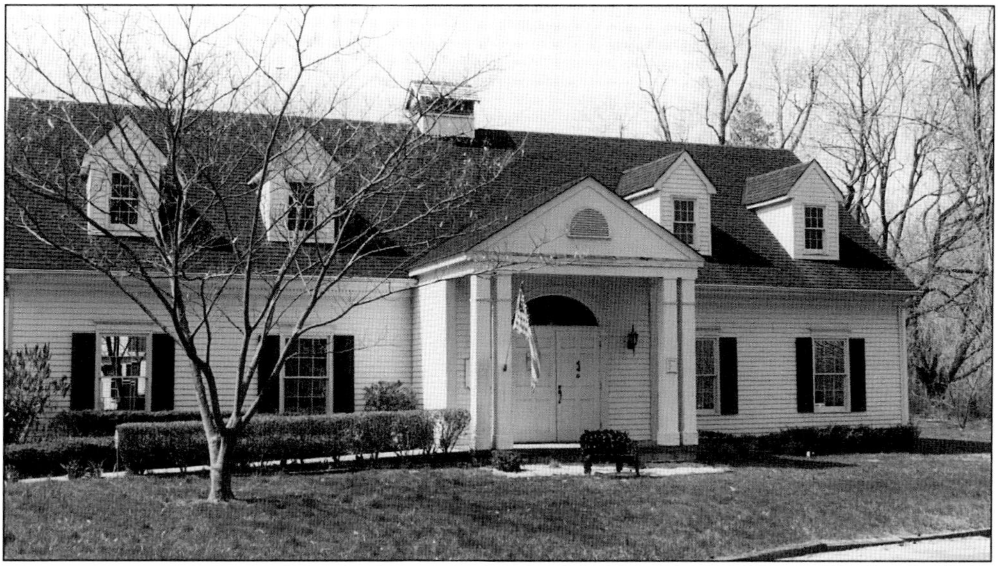

The Shrewsbury Borough School's Jerseyana Club and SARAH (see p. 31) are antecedents of the Shrewsbury Historical Society. Dr. Ervin Harlacher, co-chair with Louise Jost of SARAH, suggested to her that a society be formed. The disbanding Jerseyana Club donated their artifacts. The museum and research center was built on the site of the Wardell carriage house, destroyed by fire in 1976. Architect Samuel Abate designed the building to be harmonious with Shrewsbury's colonial roots after a contemporary design was rejected. It opened in 1982.

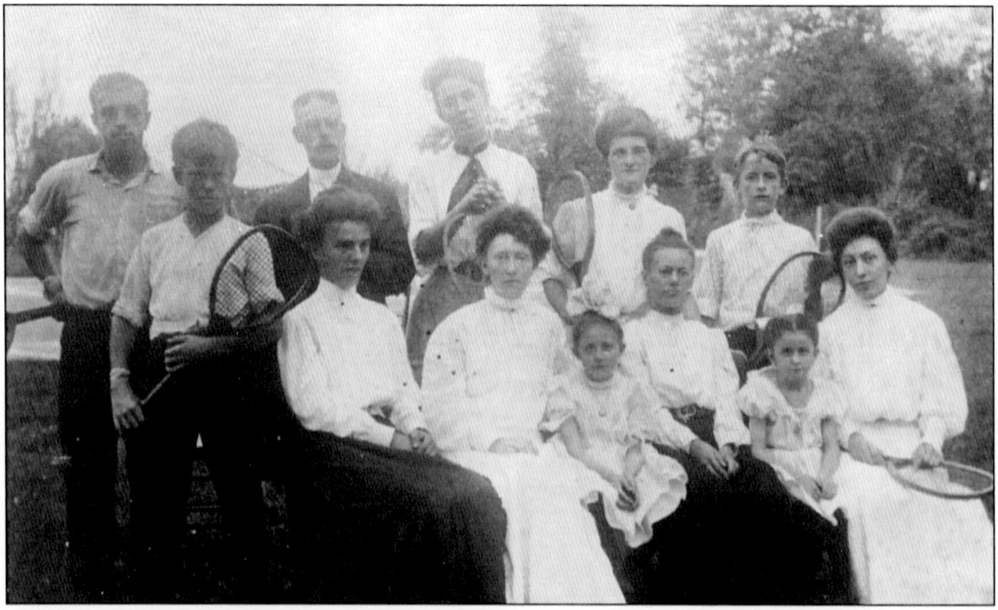

A tennis court was laid out at the Randolph Borden house in 1902. This photograph was probably taken there a few years later.

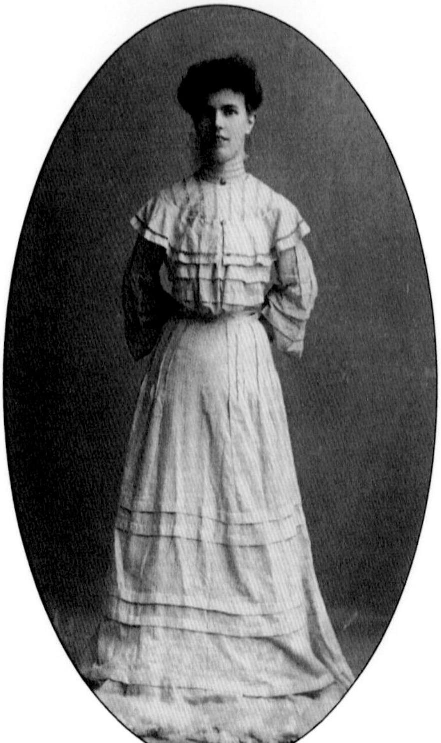

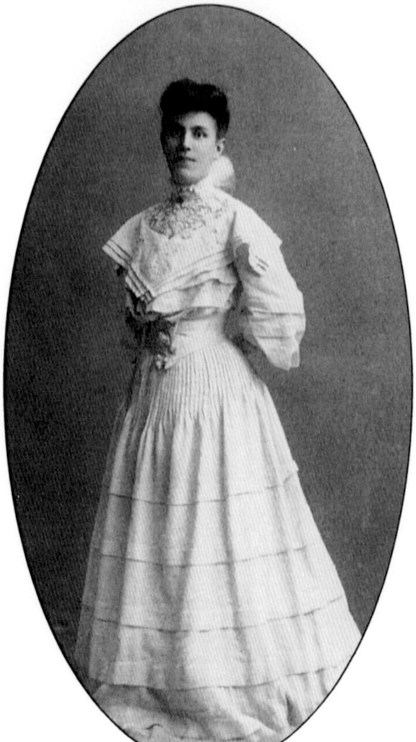

Mary and Elizabeth (known as Bess) Borden were two of Randolph and Caroline Borden's three daughters. Bess, the only one of the three to marry, married G. Harold Nevius. These pictures are from the late 1890s. The two women died in October and February, 1969, respectively.

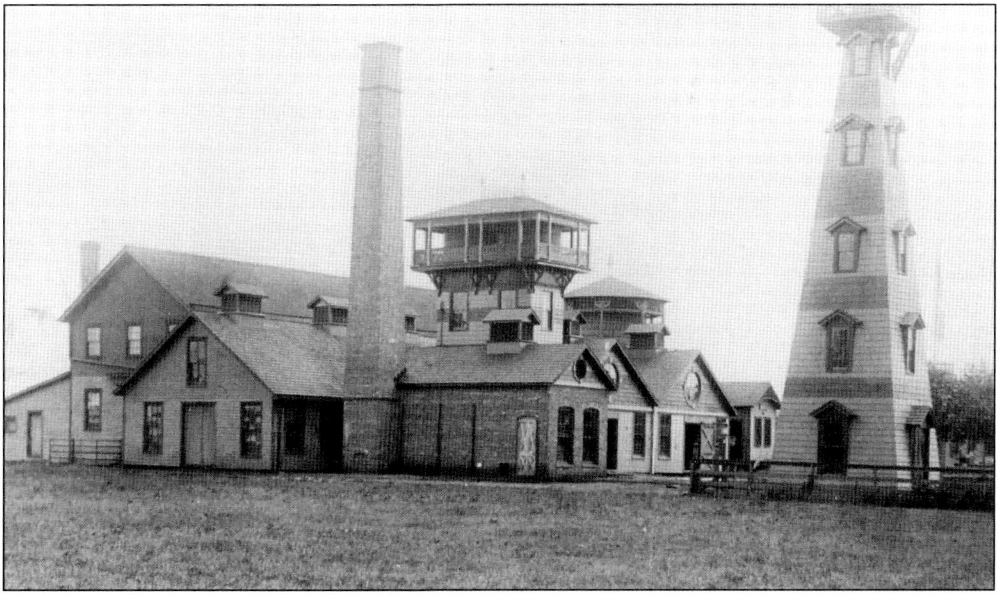

James Broadmeadow began canning tomatoes in Shrewsbury in 1863, and sold his factory to Gordon Sickles in 1866, moving to Red Bank where he continued in the business. Edward Clarke Hazard bought the Shrewsbury plant and about 34 acres in 1883. The plant, destroyed by fire in 1888 and rebuilt, was described in 1891 as being 76-by-200 feet, two stories in height, to which an addition was planned. Hazard used tomato kettles lined with pure silver to avoid the ill-effects acids had on other metals. Shrewsbury Ketchup became their best-known product. The date of this nineteenth-century photograph by Stauffer of Asbury Park is unknown.

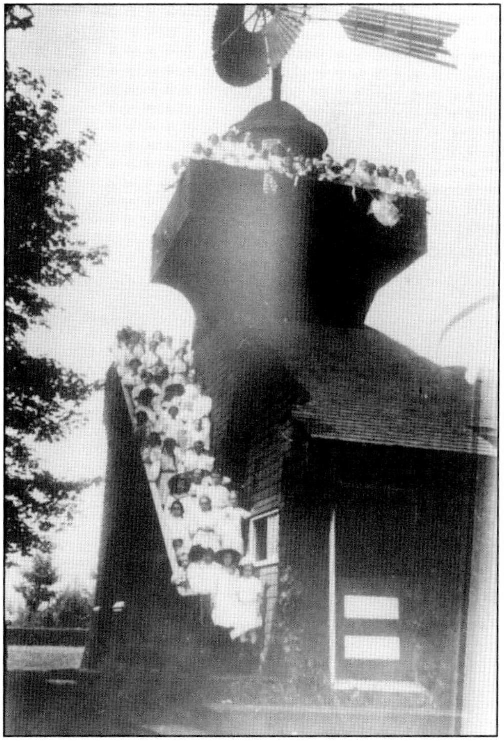

Hazard also manufactured a number of other condiments and canned a variety of vegetables in Shrewsbury. Some were grown on Hazard farms, which included a 112-acre tract bought in 1891, but most were bought from local farmers. A typical price advertised in 1907 and 1909 was $10 per ton of tomatoes. Hazard made news in 1890 by successfully growing mushrooms. Other condiments produced included mayonnaise and their Burnt Onion Sauce, which imparted cooked onion flavor to foods. This unidentified, undated group photograph on the plant's water tower is in the collection of the Shrewsbury Historical Society.

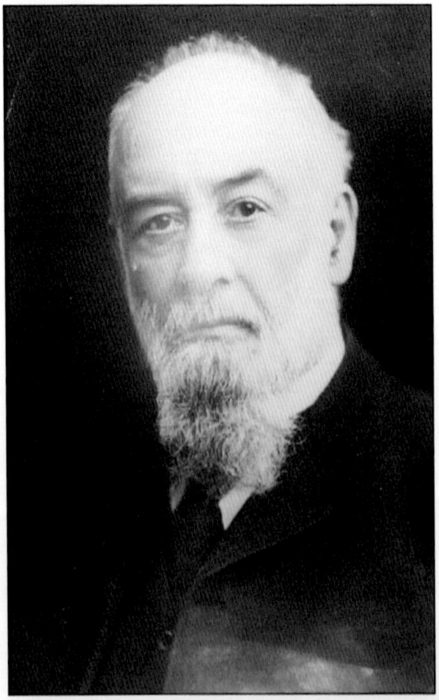

Edward Clarke Hazard was born 1831 in Rhode Island and began his business career in 1849 in New York selling soap, then grocery items. He opened a grocery business, E.C. Hazard & Company, in the early 1860s, eventually expanding into canning. Hazard married three times. Cribbage was his serious recreational pursuit, with Hazard having simplified and copyrighted its playing rules. Hazard died in 1905. He is buried in Christ Church's Shrewsbury cemetery, his Daniel Chester French stone one of the monumental highlights of the yard. (Shrewsbury Historical Society Collection.)

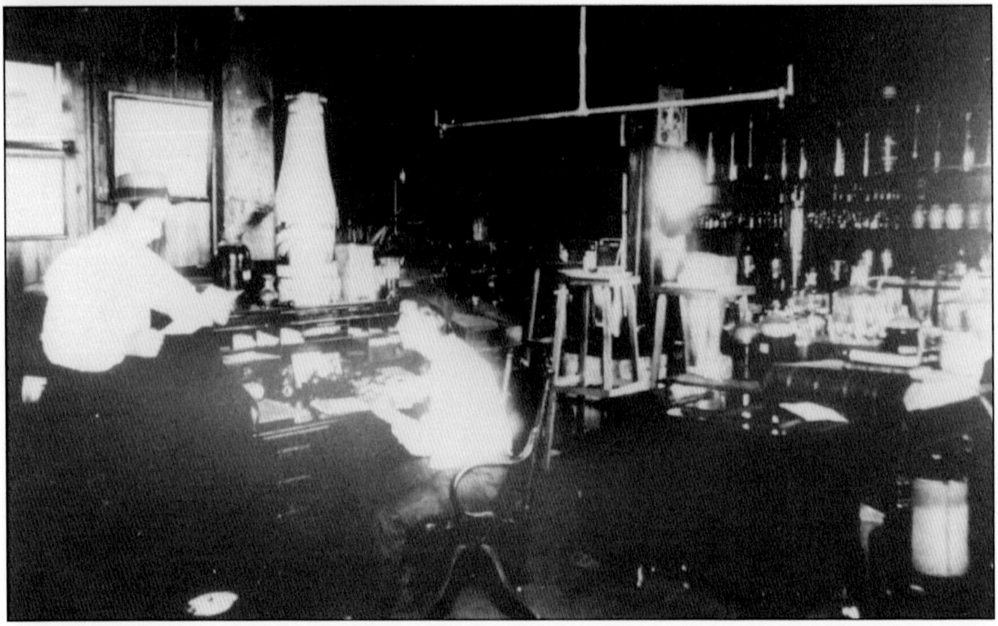

This undated photograph is likely the Hazard office and their well-equipped laboratory. The facility developed many of its own processes and used some custom-built machinery. Serious fires visited the Shrewsbury plant twice, and financial failure once. The place was rebuilt after an 1888 fire. The firm declared bankruptcy in 1907, after the founder's death in 1905, but reorganized the following year. A fire destroyed the plant in 1914 when it was owned by Harry Lord Powers. Wrangling with the family that sold him the business resulted in at least one suit involving insurance proceeds. This dissension may have contributed to the decline of Powers' operation. (Shrewsbury Historical Society Collection.)

The former Florence Frothingham married Edward Clarke Hazard in the late 1870s. They had seven children. She survived him by eighteen years, dying in New York on March 16, 1923, and is buried with him at Christ Church.

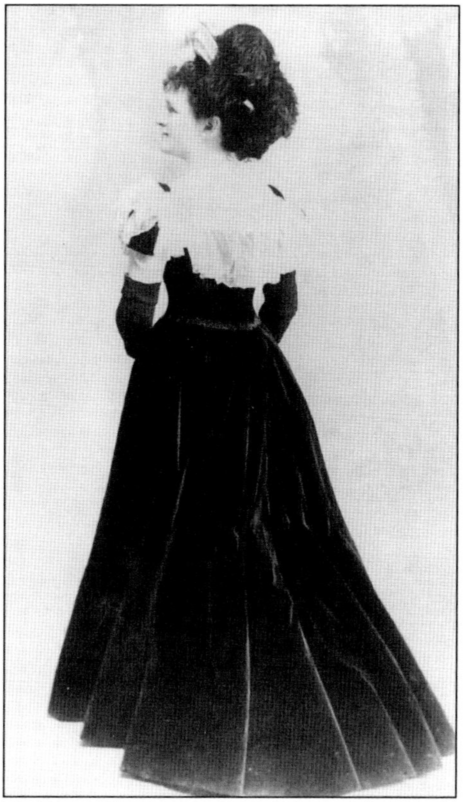

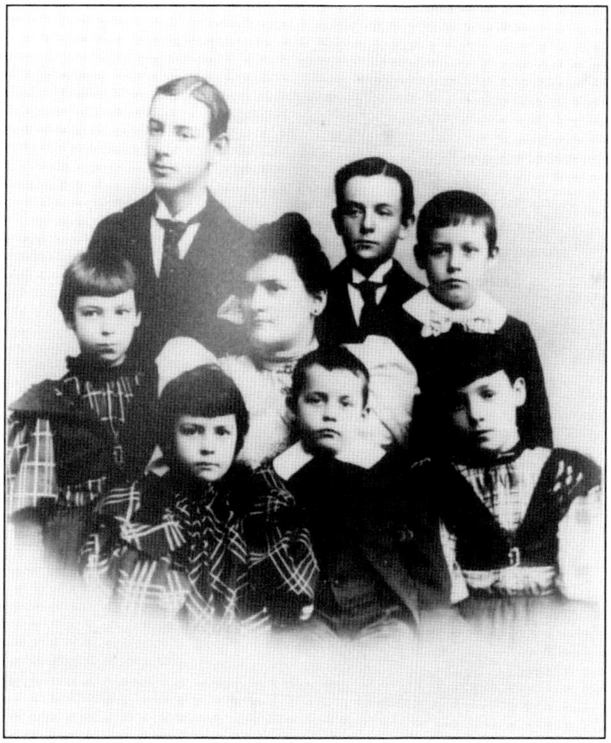

Florence Frothingham Hazard (center) posed with her seven children in a picture from the mid to late 1890s. Elmer, her eldest son, became a doctor and founded the Hazard Hospital in Long Branch, an institution known for extensive charity work. (Shrewsbury Historical Society Collection.)

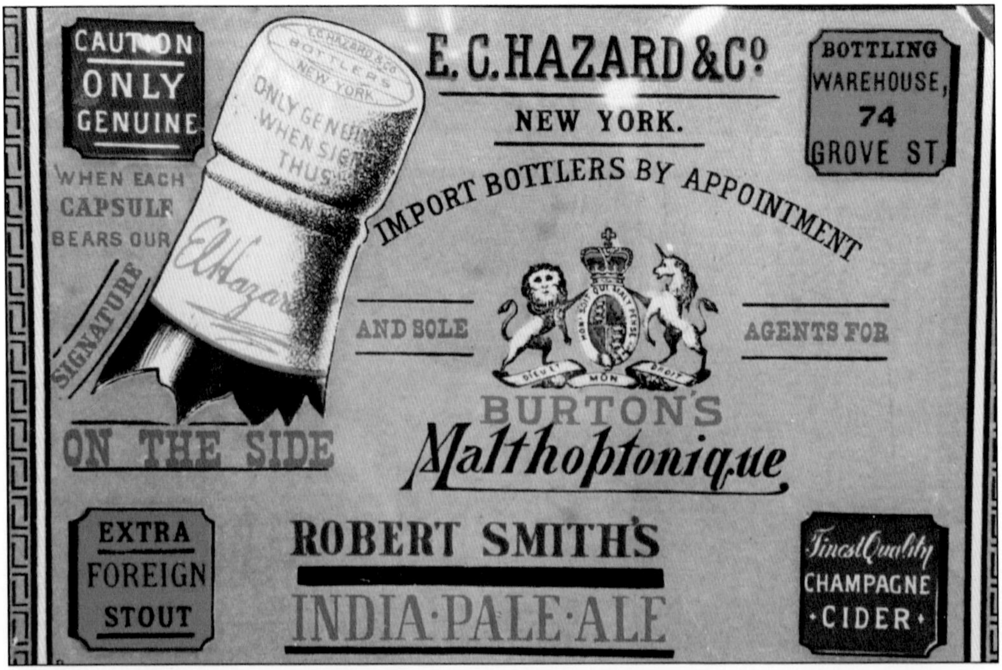

Hazard's was best known locally for their ketchup, condiment, and canning operations. However, the firm received its start as grocers and its New York dealership sold a wide variety of fancy goods. The 1888 *Illustrated New York* described their wares: ". . . choice canned fruits, meats and vegetables . . . grocer's sundries and specialties . . . the finest and best spices . . . choicest cereals . . . the choicest brands of wines, liquors and ales, also the popular and favorite brands of cigars." This ale label dates later, after the firm acquired the Grove Street location. (Shrewsbury Historical Society's Hazard Label Collection.)

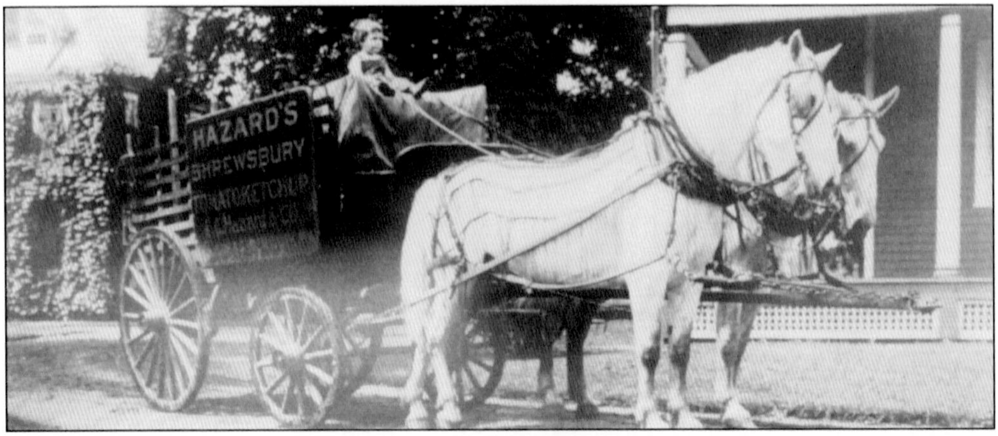

A 1908 Hazard ad states "If your grocer cannot furnish we will deliver at your door," although probably not with this turn-of-the-century wagon. They had distributors from coast to coast and in Puerto Rico. The youngster is not identified, but children were a regular presence. A February 25, 1891 *Register* account states "Along one side of the factory, partitioned off with boxes, etc., is a children's play 'store.' The place was stocked with a variety of Hazard products. A handwritten sign announced the firm name: Hazard, Green and Tallman." The latter two were local families with children contemporary with young Hazards. (Shrewsbury Historical Society Collection.)

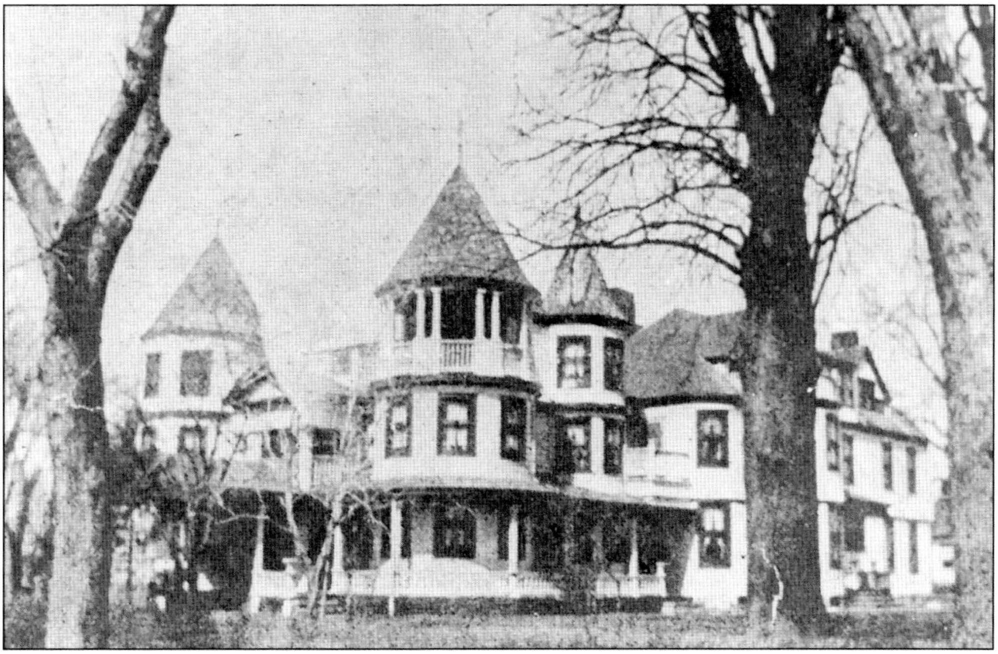

This is not a hotel, nor a boarding school, but the Hazard family residence on the north side of Sycamore Avenue. The Gordon Sickles home is present somewhere, but E.C. Hazard enveloped the older house with several additions. Information about the house is scanty. It had a large ballroom and was the site of notable socials. Two of the round towers were added in 1901.

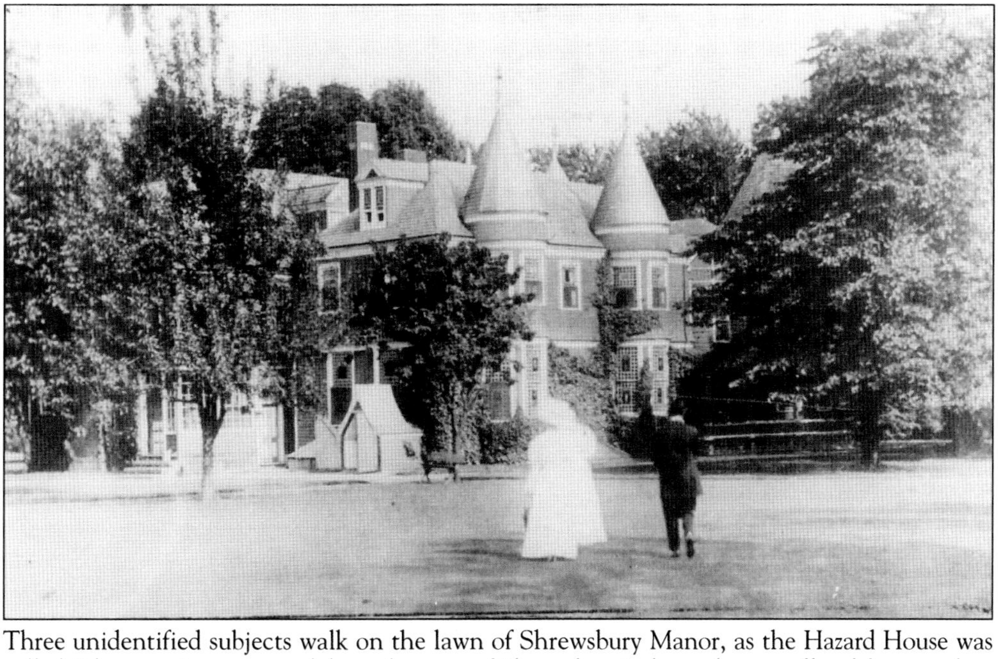

Three unidentified subjects walk on the lawn of Shrewsbury Manor, as the Hazard House was called. The mansion, once celebrated as one of Shrewsbury's show places, suffered from neglect and was in a deteriorated condition when it was demolished in 1937. (Shrewsbury Historical Society Collection.)

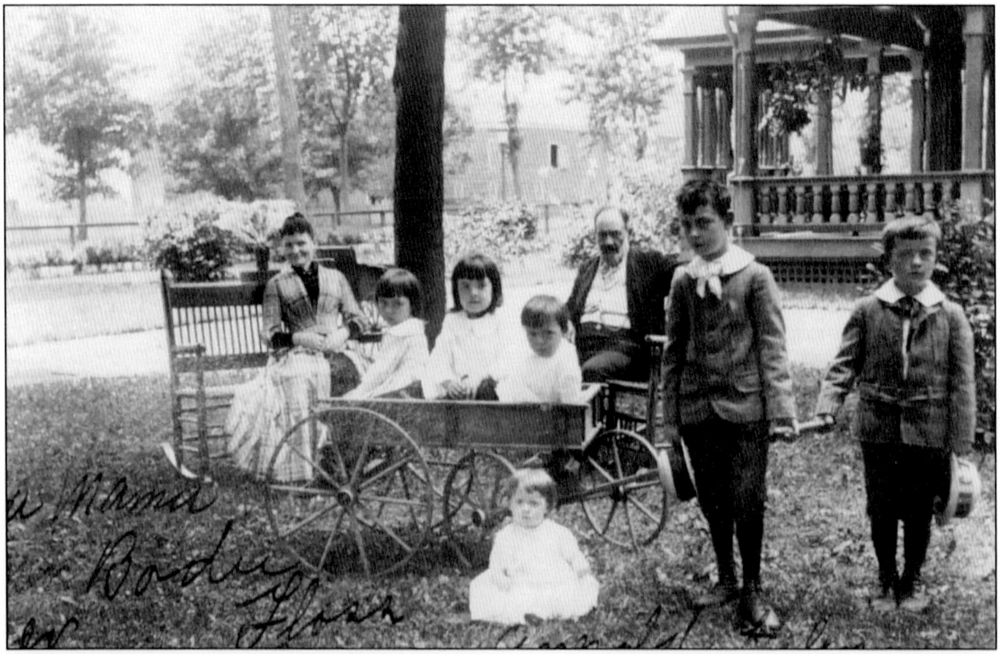

From the February 25, 1891 *Register*: "Mr. Hazard is peculiarly happy in his home life. He is passionately fond of his children and can afford to gratify their every whim." The two elder Hazard sons, Elmer and Bowdoin, are at right in this 1880s image. The younger children are Florence, Bessie, Arnold, and Helen. (Shrewsbury Historical Society Collection.)

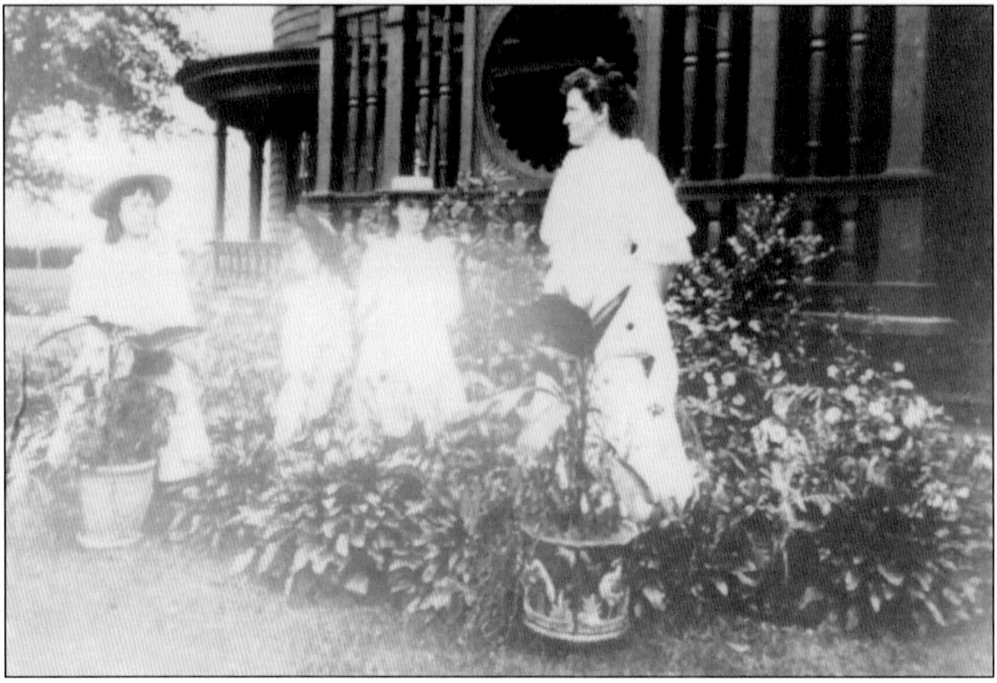

Florence Hazard (at right) posed with her three daughters, Florence (at far left, known as Flossie), Helen (second from left), and Elizabeth (known as Bessie). This picture from the early 1890s was taken at Shrewsbury Manor. (Shrewsbury Historical Society Collection.)

Florence Ellsworth Hazard married Prince Franz von Auersperg of Austria in 1899 at Shrewsbury, a linkage of money and title. He had lived an adventurous life and lost a fortune, with his escapades having allegedly caused many a duel. Prior to his success at love, he had run an elevator at a "swell" New York hotel and trained as a physician at Long Island Medical College. (Shrewsbury Historical Society Collection.)

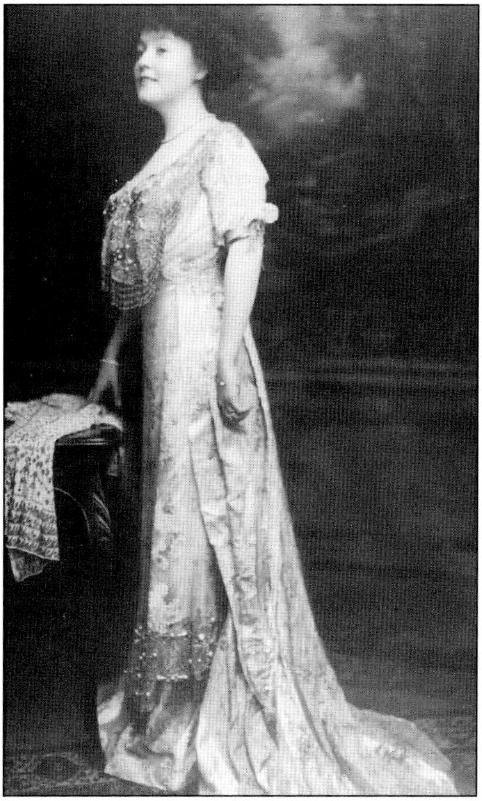

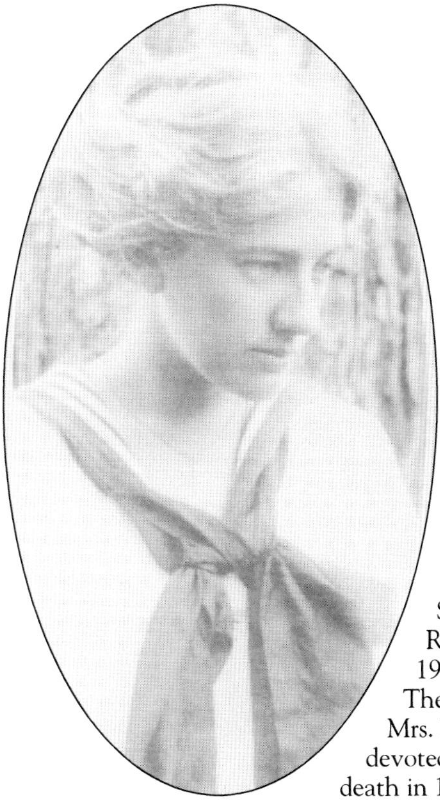

Georgie Remington Burton, a native of East Greenwich, Rhode Island, was born in 1883 and married Bowdoin Frothingham Hazard in 1906. She opened Burton Hall, a preparatory school in Red Bank, *c.* 1916. Georgie and Bowdoin divorced in 1917, but she retained close familial ties to the Hazards. They lived at 440 Sycamore Avenue, then owned by Mrs. Edward C. Hazard. The highly regarded school had a devoted following and endured until shortly before Georgie's death in 1965.

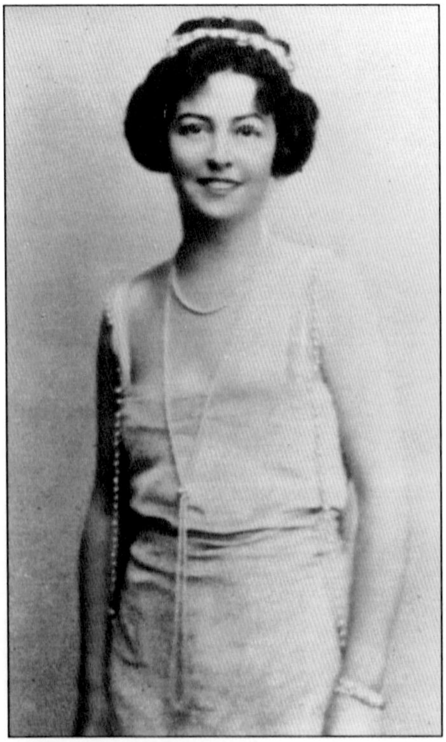

The marriage of the twenty-one-year-old Helen F. Hazard to the sixty-year-old brewer Alfred N. Beadleston made front page news in 1909. Their son, of the same name as his father, is the former Shrewsbury mayor (p. 127) and longtime leader of the New Jersey Senate. Helen Hazard later married Julian McCarthy Little, surviving him by three years, dying in 1937. (Shrewsbury Historical Society Collection.)

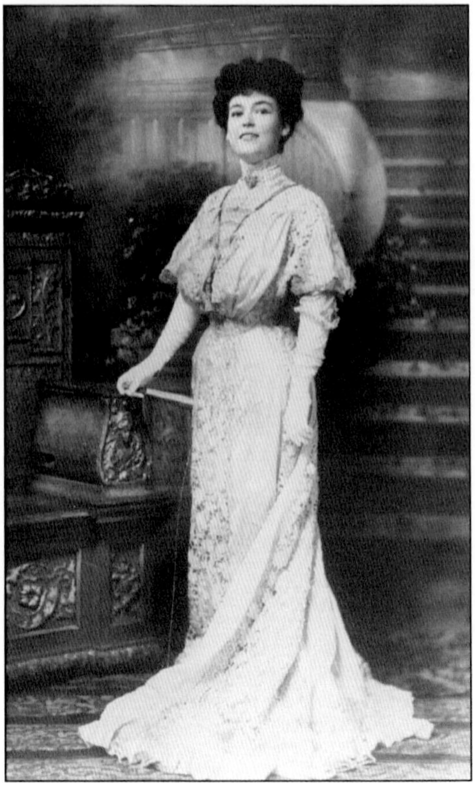

Elizabeth Hazard's marriage to Harry Lord Powers (p. 91) provided the union that would add a partner for succession in the family business, a transition that would not prove harmonious. (Shrewsbury Historical Society Collection.)

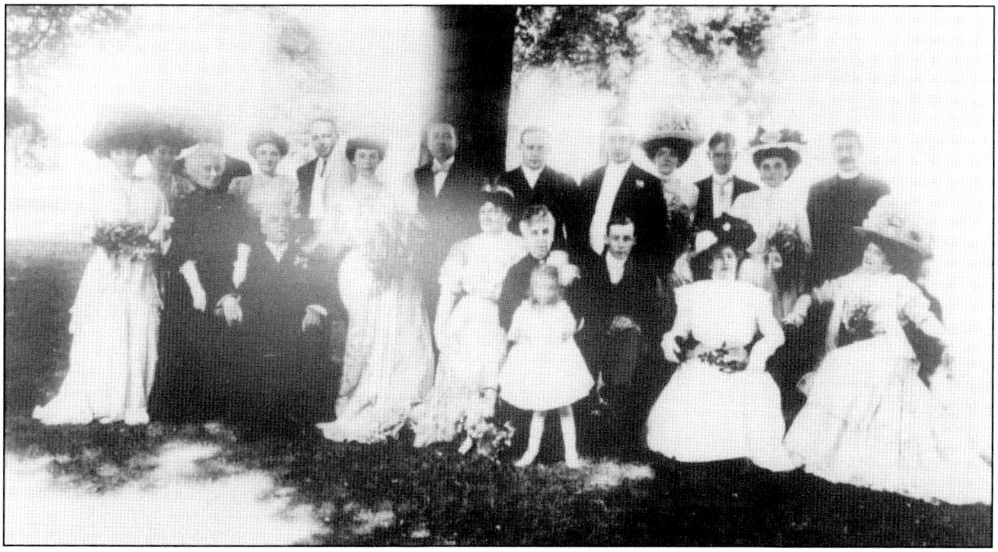

Elizabeth Robinson Hazard married Harry Lord Powers on September 27, 1908. Although the original photograph in the collection of the Shrewsbury Historical Society is without identification, inferences can be made. The bride is presumably left of center with the large bouquet of lilies of the valley. Her husband is presumably in front of the tree, having earned the privilege of taking off his jacket. The widowed Mrs. Hazard is behind the small child while Powers' parents are left of the bride. Can you hazard a guess as to the bride's two sisters, subjects with apparent familial resemblance? The clergyman at right is the Reverend Tilton, pastor of a New York church.

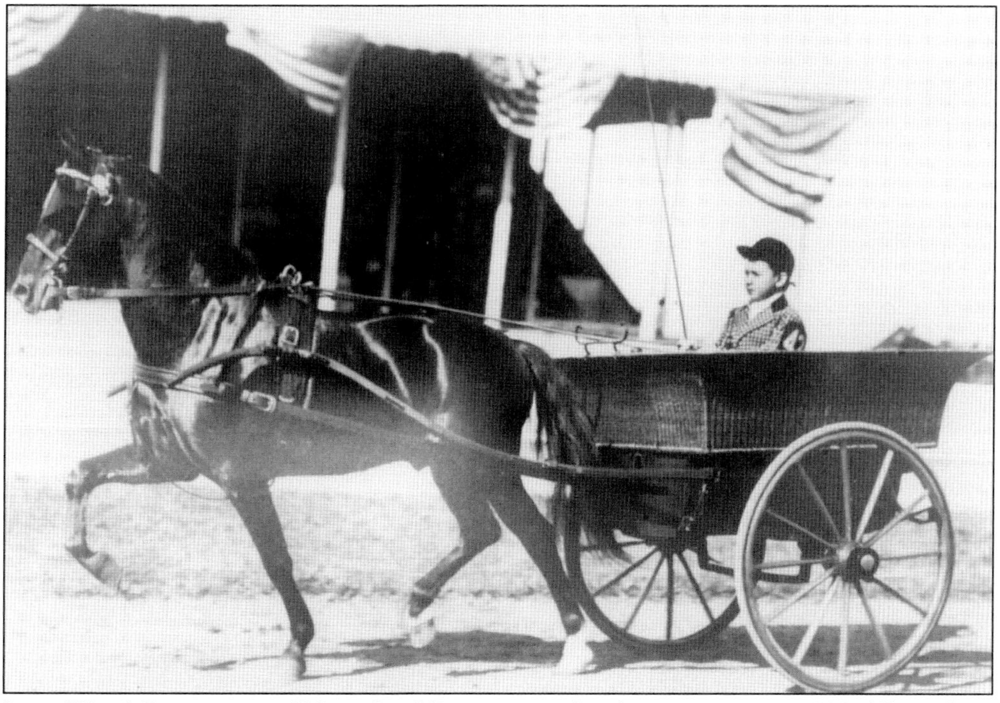

Jessie Wood Powers, son of Harry Lord Powers, posed in his pony cart, *c.* 1920. (Shrewsbury Historical Society Collection.)

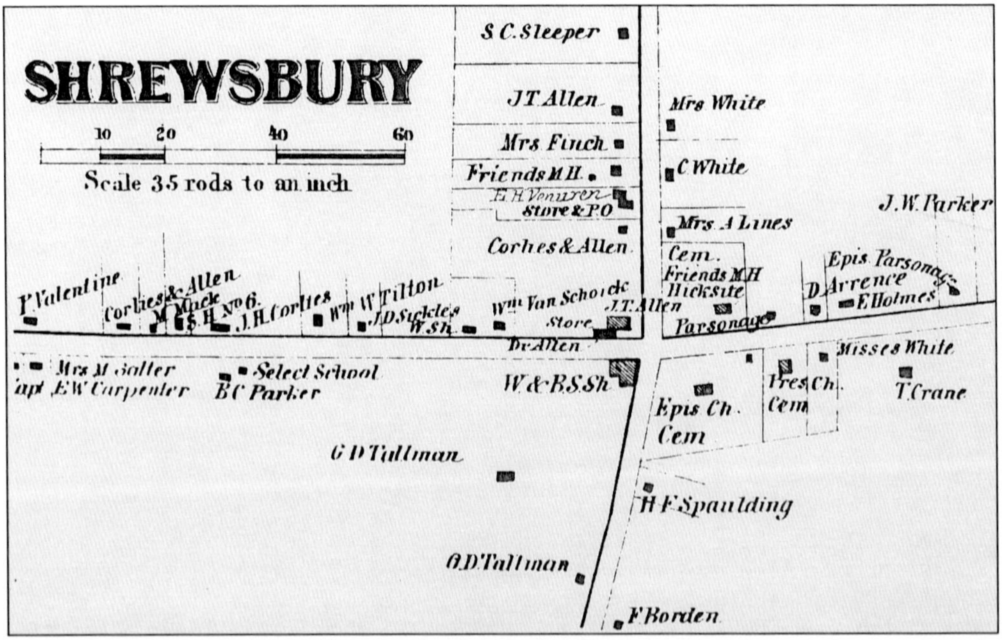

The large scale inset of the village on the Beers 1860 sheet map of Monmouth County is the oldest widely circulating map of Shrewsbury. Many of the landmarks shown here still exist, but there are also differences with the present landscape. At the Four Corners, the wheelwright and blacksmith shop was in place then and the division between Friends groups is shown. Corlies and Allen, later at the Allen House, had Broad Street and Sycamore Avenue locations. Broad Street runs up and down, while Sycamore Avenue runs across the page. Several of the depicted buildings can be found throughout this volume.

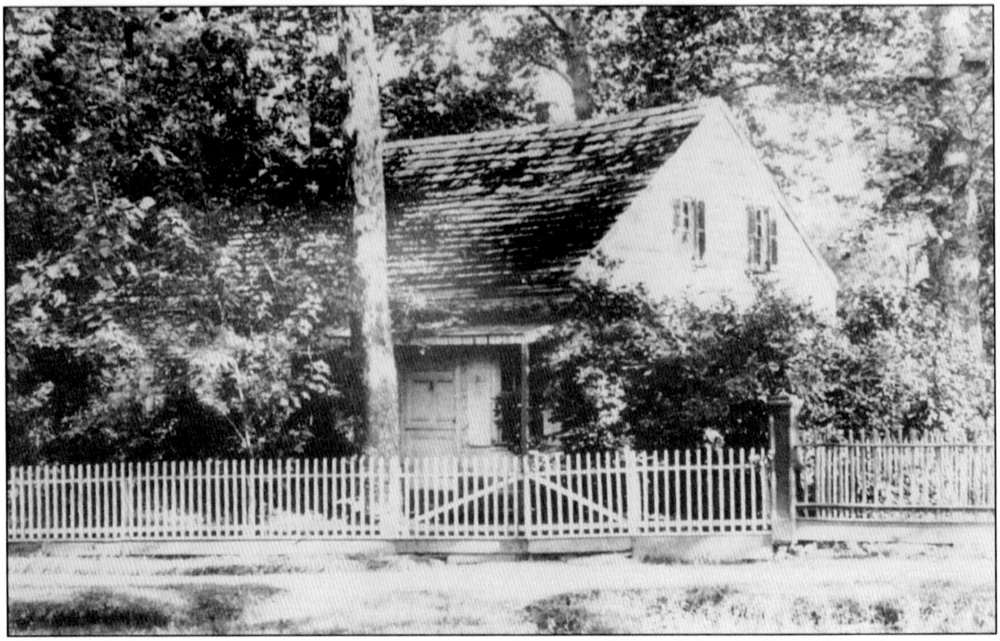

The Hoidel House, apparently on Sycamore Avenue, was demolished after a Van Vliet house was built behind it. (Shrewsbury Historical Society Collection.)

The large scale Shrewsbury village map, part of plate 29 of the 1889 *Wolverton Atlas of Monmouth County*, is arguably the town's most attractive map ever. At the top is Shrewsbury Avenue, then running only south to Sycamore. The large Colonel Edmund T. Williams' estate is gone without a trace, with a bank and other commercial buildings there now. Williams was a major figure in his time. The railroad provided reliable transportation for freight and passengers, but did not bring the usual major growth. Van Buren had two houses; the one on p. 74 is on the south side (or the left) of Sycamore Avenue. Tallman's outbuildings are shown, one likely the carriage house that burned in 1976. This image was made from a color reproduction available at the Shrewsbury Historical Society.

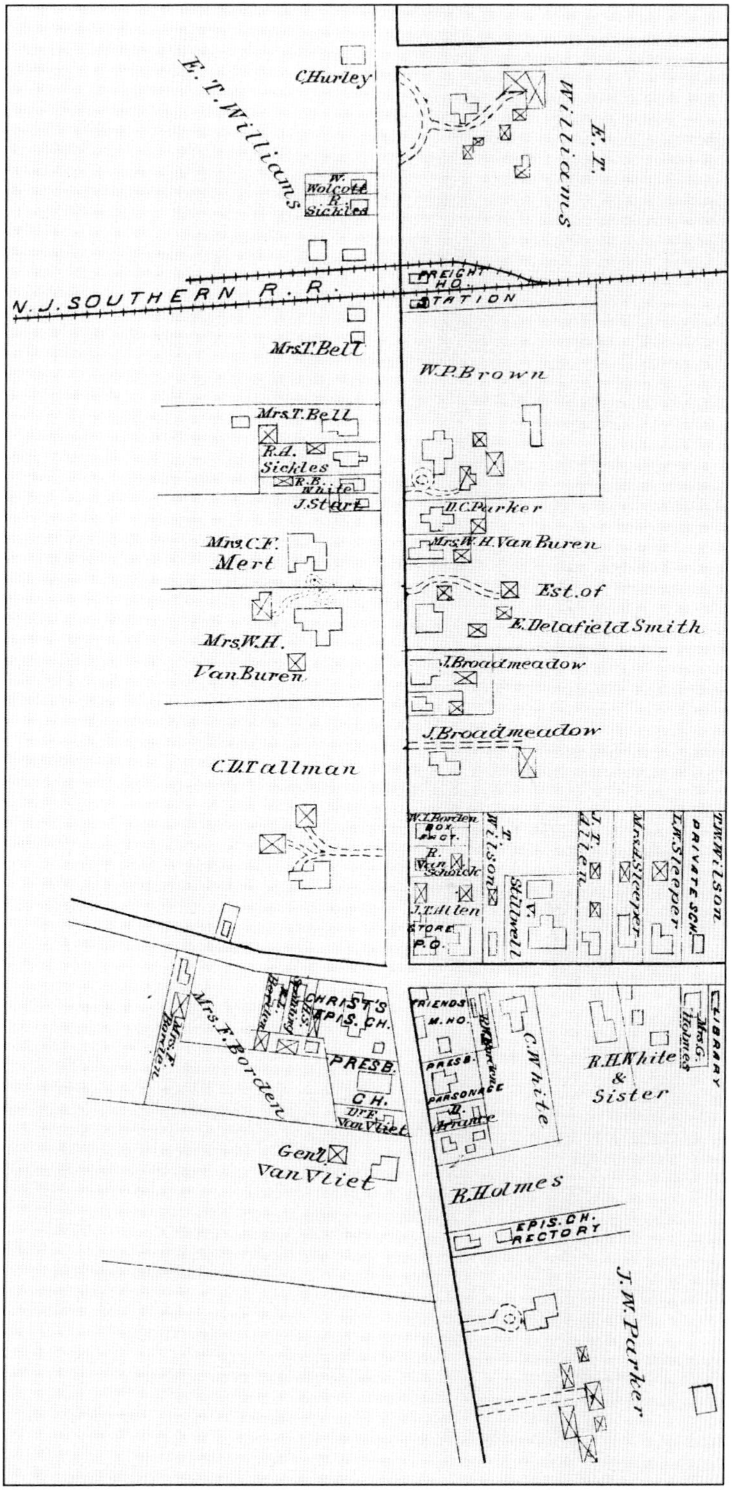

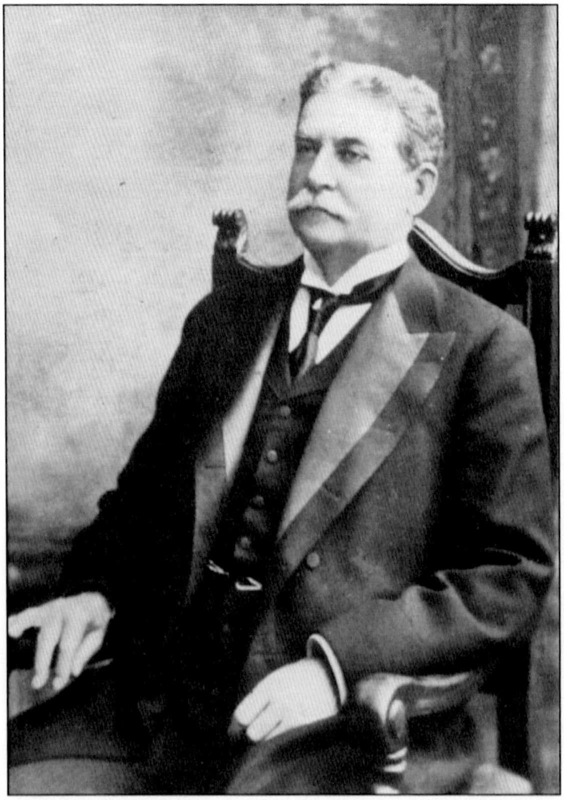

Lucien O. Appleby, a businessman born in 1842 in Smithfield, Rhode Island, was a widely known figure in late-nineteenth century turf circles. He began with trotters in New England in the 1860s, apparently to assume an outdoor activity for health purposes. Appleby achieved his great prominence later through flat racers. He died in New York in 1910.

Lucien Appleby bought around 118 acres of the former William Lippincott farm, later known as the Benjamin Stevens place, *c.* 1889, and built one of the finest horse stock farms in the east. This early Colonial Revival house was likely built shortly after his purchase. The farm was sold to William Fanshawe in 1905 and was owned by Christian Broderson when the house was destroyed by fire early on Thanksgiving morning, 1926.

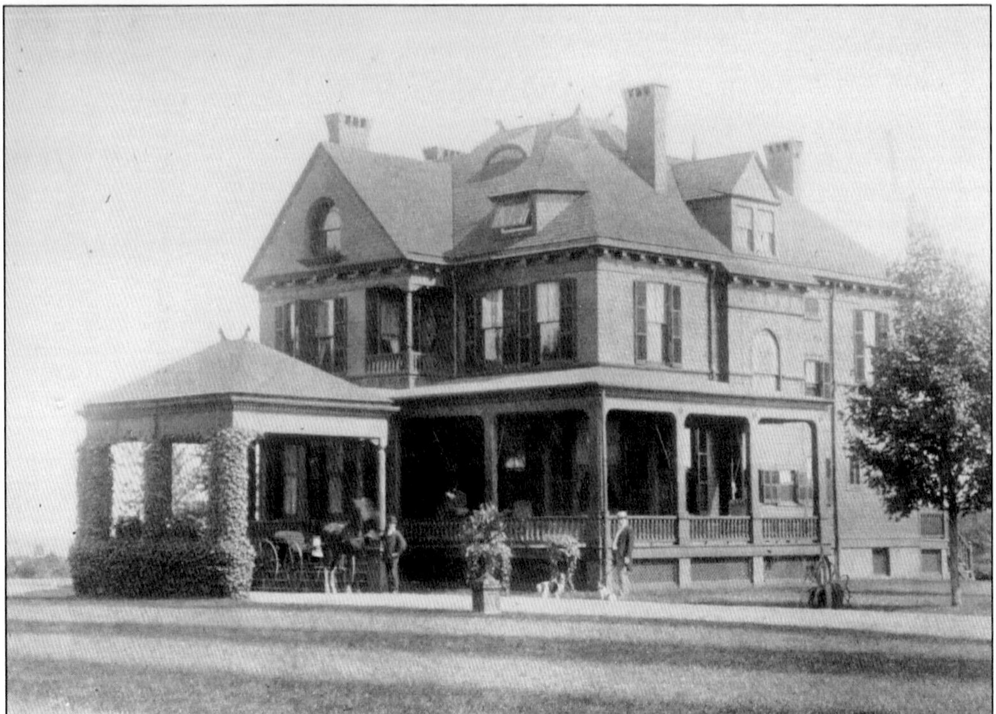

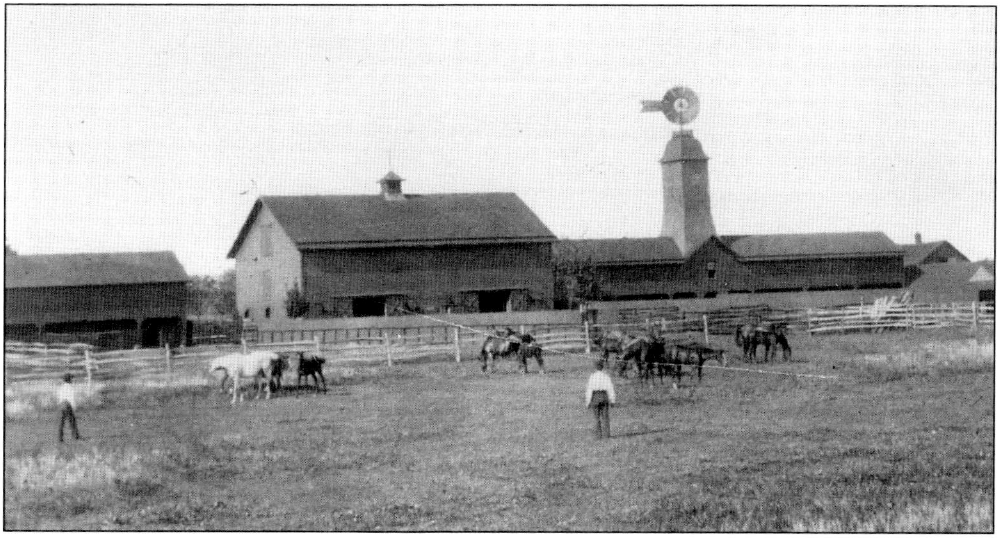

Appleby's farm, known as the Silver Brook Stud, was built with the most modern facilities of the 1890s. The stable has been described alternatively as having box stalls for sixty-five to one hundred horses. An extensive drainage system throughout the property emptied into a brook. The fences were locust posts and chestnut rails. Housing sits on the site now, developed around Silverbrook Road.

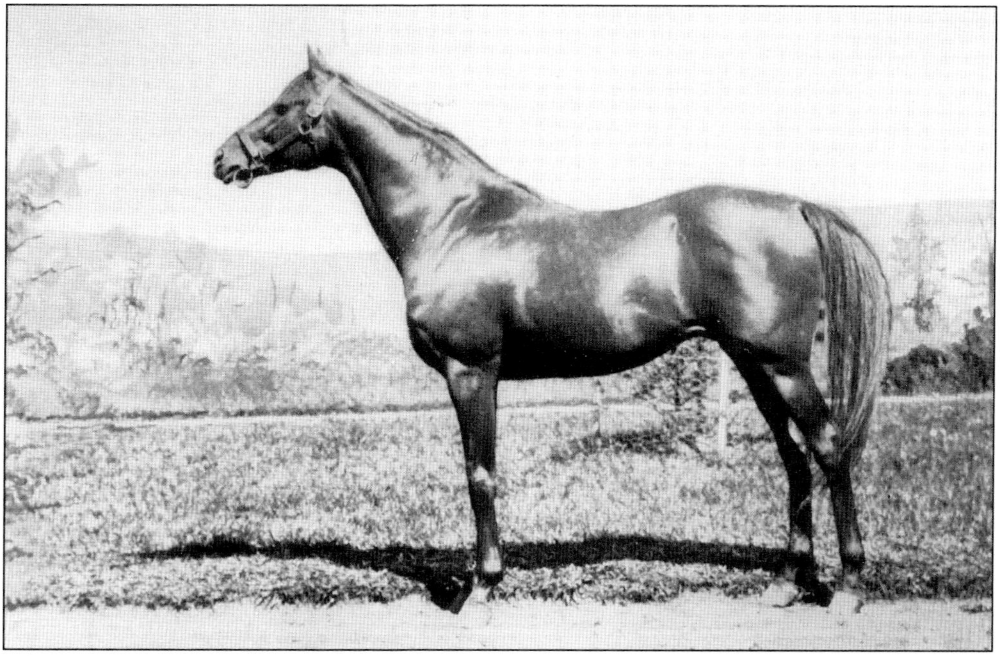

Silver Brook raised, raced, and bred many prize stallions, including Tristan (shown here). Foaled (born, to us non-horsemen) in 1885, Tristan had a distinguished record on the track, winning the first Metropolitan Handicap and other noted races. He was the sire of two horses with unlikely, historically notable names, Governor Griggs and Monroe Doctrine. The photographs on this and the preceding page are from *The American Turf*. Its promotional text quoted Appleby's intentions for Tristan as a "constant desire that the mares he serves shall be of a grade calculated to insure successful results with the product."

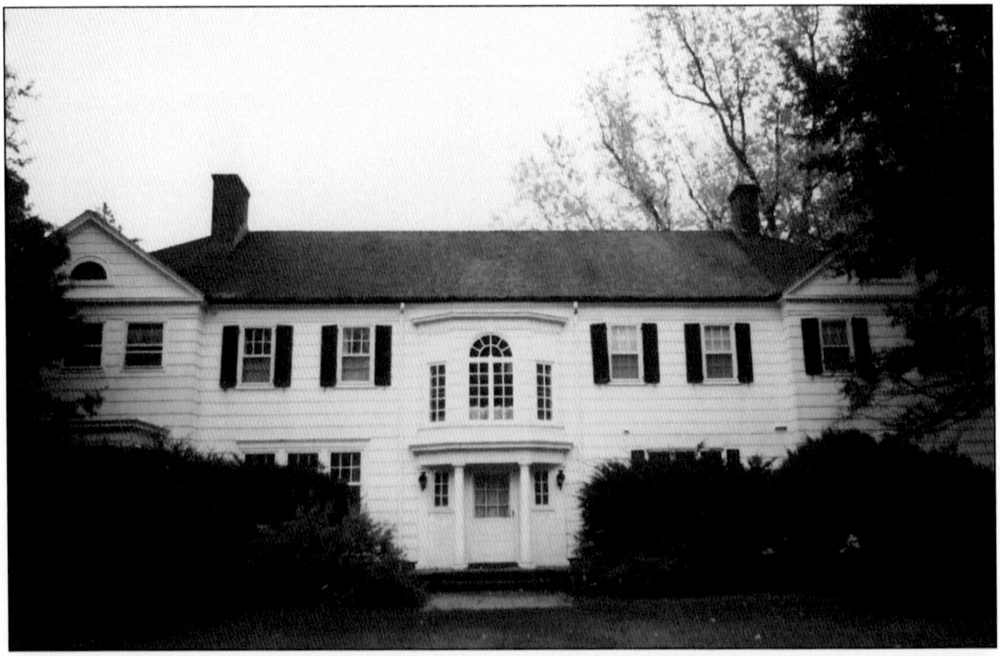

Dr. Paul Livingston of East Orange bought the 400-foot frontage running from Sycamore Avenue to Elm Place of Christian Broderson's Crystal Brook Park in 1927. He built this large Colonial Revival house, architect unknown, shortly thereafter. Located at 300 Sycamore Avenue, reconfiguration of the lot has re-located the entrance to Elm Place. A large center hall is the interior focus of this fine, austerely decorated Georgian plan house.

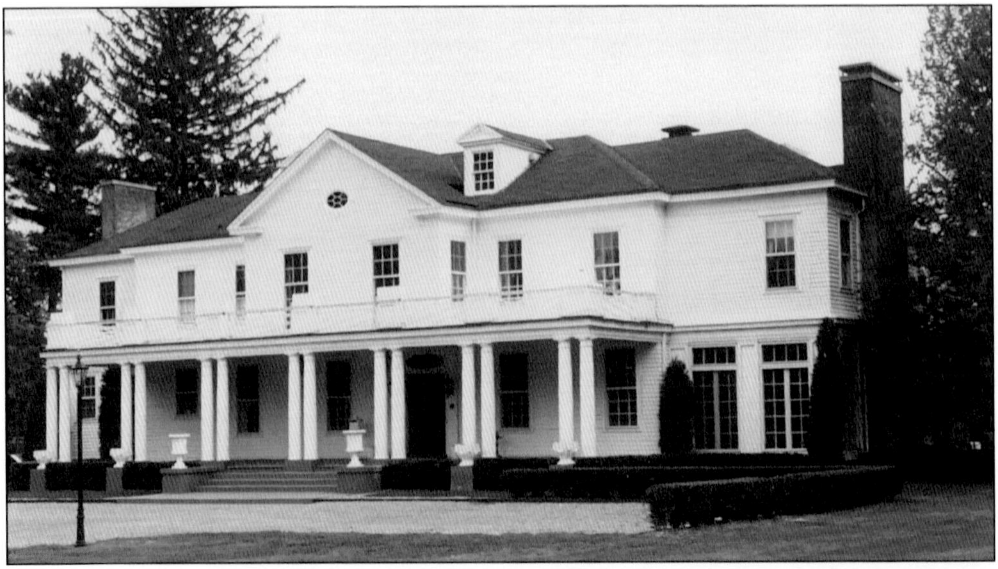

Part of the six-bay, main block, hipped-roof Colonial Revival at 130 Sycamore Avenue is the house John Hemingway Duncan designed for Louis V. Bell, built in 1910. A large wing was added to the rear, giving the house the present form of a "T." The wing was designed by Long Branch architect Leon Cubberley and built in 1917 for noted horsewoman Clara Peck. The house is still known as Chal Mar Farm, although its once-extensive acreage was separated from the house for the late-1980s Paddington Farm housing development.

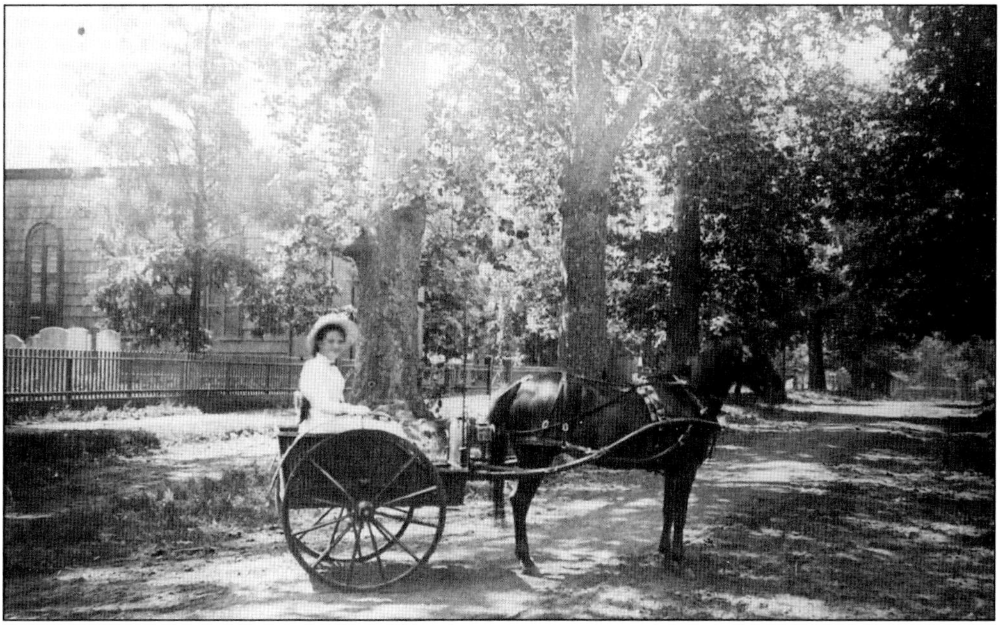

An unidentified girl poses with her horse on Sycamore Avenue looking west in the summer of 1884, with the old tollhouse visible in the distance. (Monmouth County Historical Association Collection.)

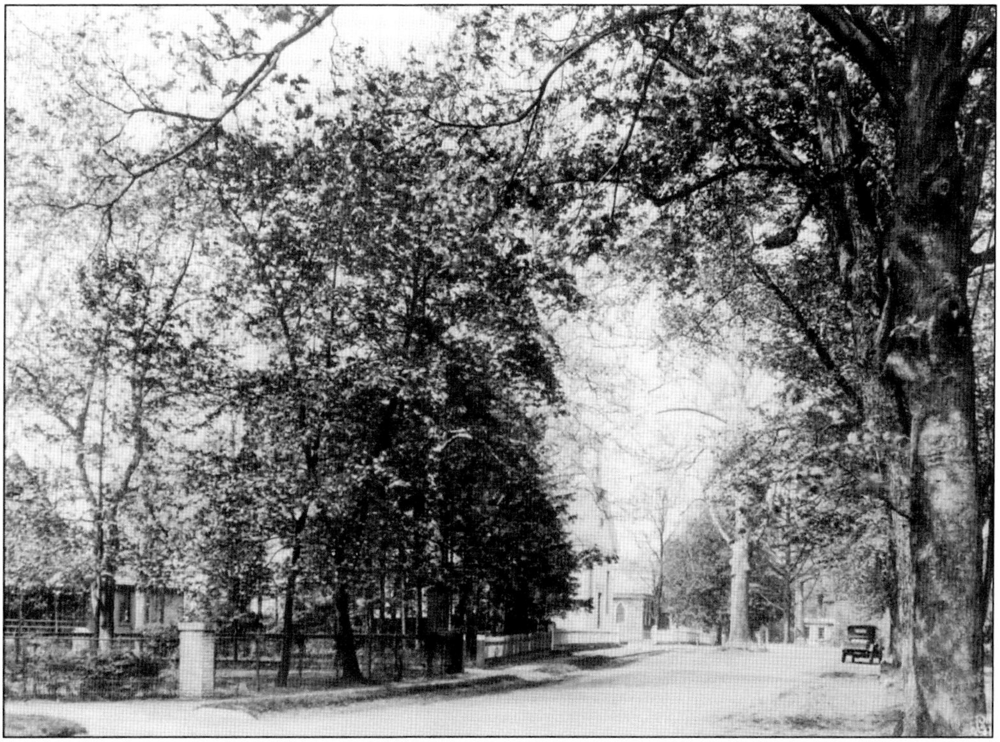

This view, the same as at the top of the page but about forty years later, reflects subtle change in a similar landscape. Travel by this time was by automobile, the new post office is near the corner, and time was taking its toll among the sycamores.

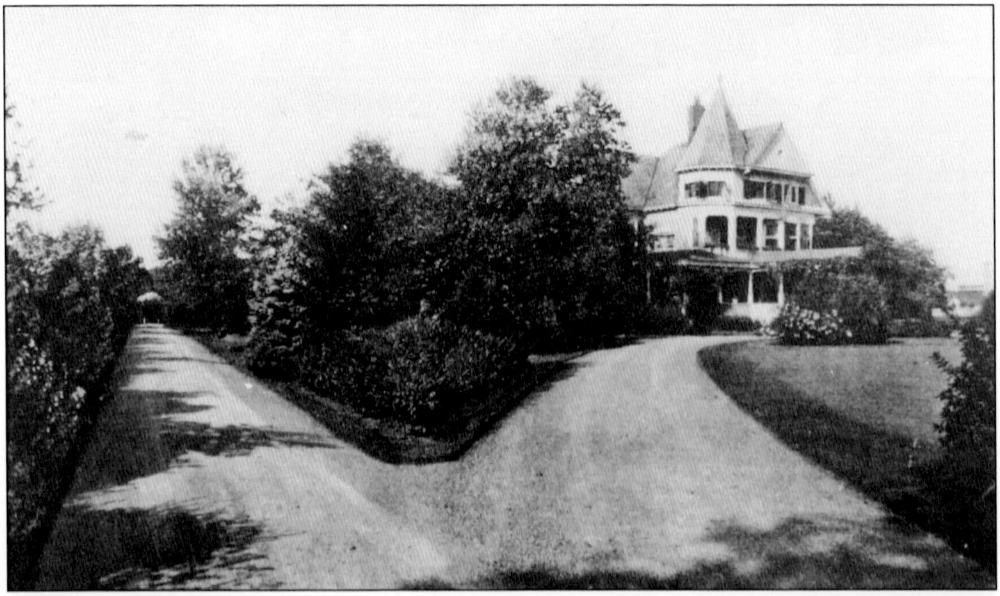

Mrs. Richard Roche of St. Louis bought about 30 acres of former Benjamin Parker property on the north side of Sycamore Avenue in 1891. The next year she built this large Queen Anne-style house, architect unknown, with the *Register* having projected on March 9, 1892, that "It will probably be the handsomest house in Shrewsbury when completed." This image is from a c. 1910 postcard. Mrs. Roche sold the home to John J. Mahoney of New York in 1899. (John Rhody Collection.)

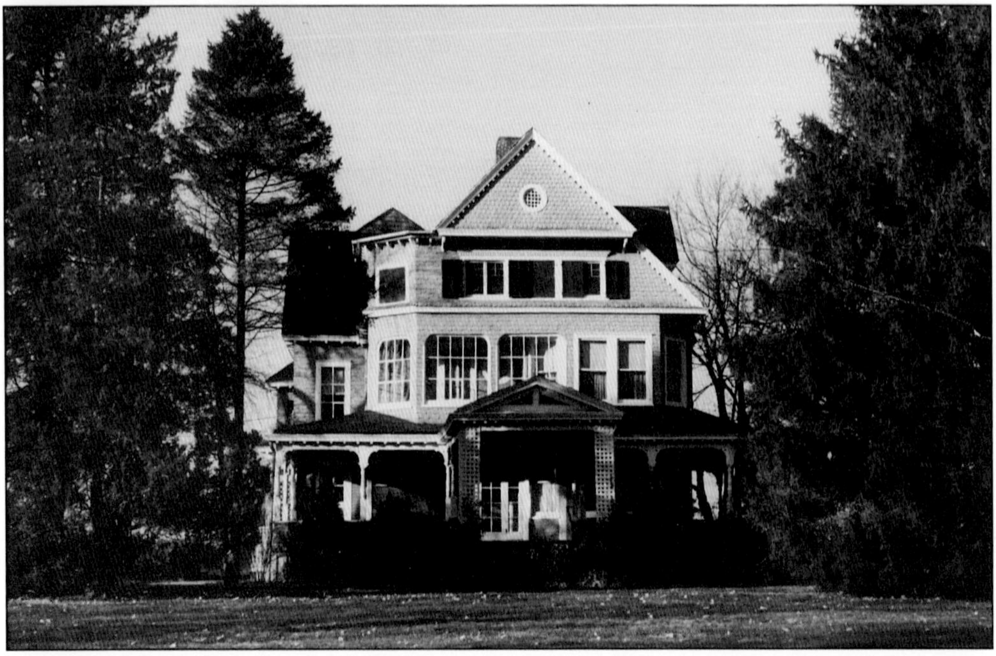

Few changes have been made to 291 Sycamore Avenue, other than the removal of the front tower. The intact property is one of the borough's larger pristine sites. The house is surrounded by mature trees, many much more mature than in this c. 1940s picture, obscuring the view from the street.

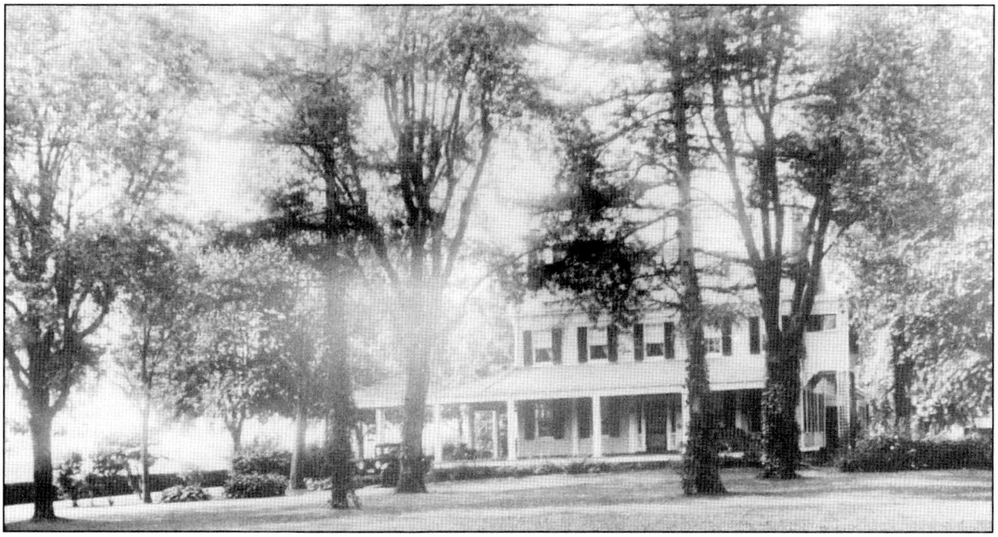

The origin of 197 Sycamore Avenue is a small eighteenth-century house, likely a single grade floor keeping room with an upstairs sleeping loft, which is not visible here as it was enveloped by a mid-nineteenth-century expansion. The property was part of the William Parker farm and had several noteworthy owners, including produce merchant and state assembly member Grover Lufburrow in the late 1800s and Bruce Campbell in the twentieth century. Note the second-story bathroom addition at right, supported by posts.

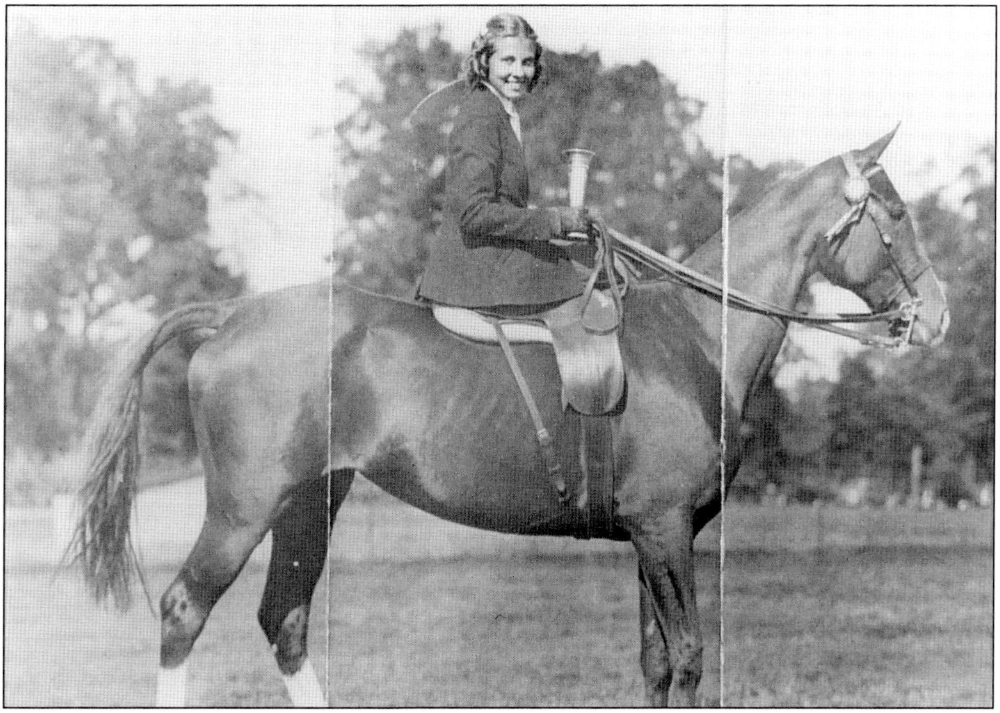

The beautiful Anna Louise Campbell (now Rudner) beams in the late 1930s with one of her equestrian trophies. She grew up at 197 Sycamore Avenue, stabling her horse in a farm building. Anna Louise is the sister of Robert (p. 22), a graduate of Skidmore, a member of the DAR, and a trustee of the Monmouth County Historical Association.

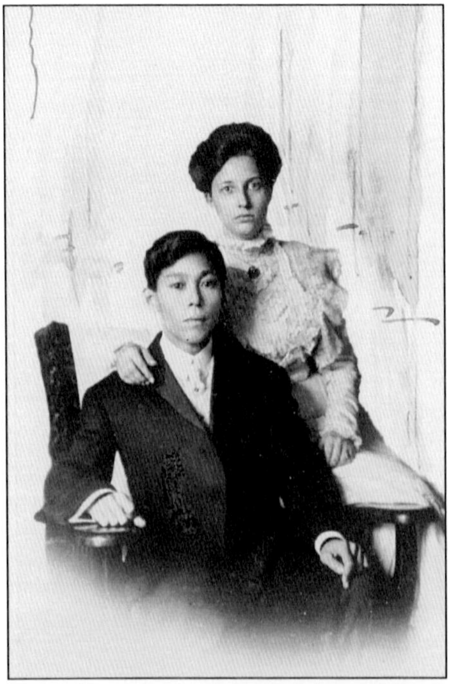

Kashiro Kodama, born in Japan in 1877, showed early independence by resettling in London, associating with an art dealer. After emigration to the United States and earlier residency in Illinois and upstate New York, the Kodamas bought eastern Sycamore Avenue farm property, its appeal enhanced by its proximity to the railroad. Kashiro commuted to his own Oriental art object business in New York. He is shown here in a pre-Shrewsbury portrait with his wife, Mabel Sydney, who was known by her middle name. Kashiro died in 1941.

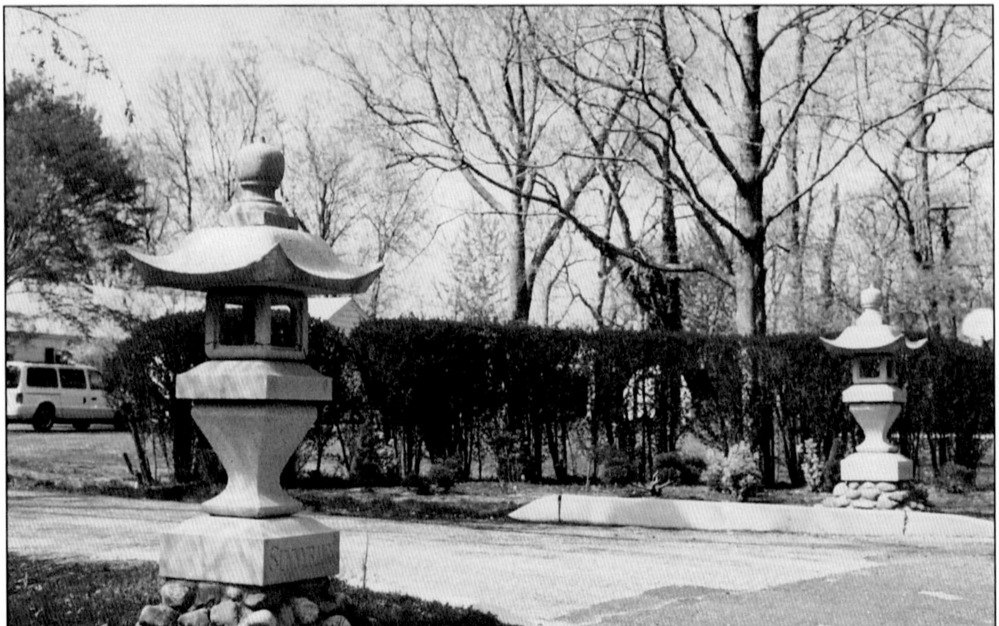

In 1921, Kashiro Kodama bought, in the name of his wife Mabel Sydney Kodama, about 25 acres of the Ethel Kenneth estate, located on the south side of Sycamore Avenue, just west of the Little Silver railroad station. They occupied its large, old house, also acquiring several outbuildings, including a superintendent's house, farm equipment, and farm stock. Kashiro erected one of Shrewsbury's most visible landmarks in 1928, these two ornamental posts known as Japanese lanterns, made of material he bought in Japan. The estate name "Sunnybank" appears in each base.

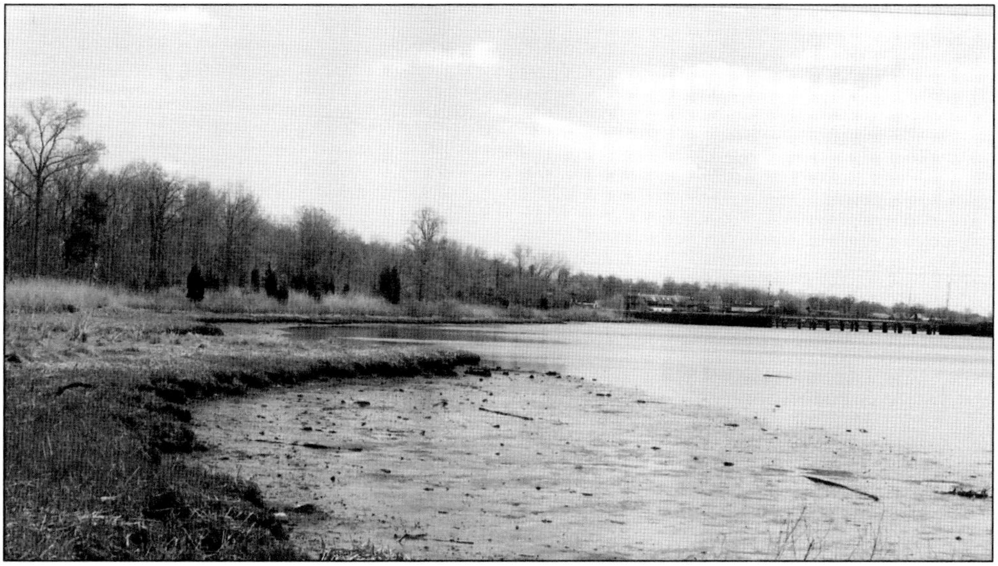

Sunnybank embraced a plot that ran from Sycamore Avenue south to Parkers Creek, a stream that forms Shrewsbury's southeastern border, and the "bank" in the estate name. This view is east toward Oceanport Avenue crossing between Little Silver and Oceanport. Kodama plotted the property for development in 1928, with a survey by J. Wesley Seaman. He had two artificial lakes built, erecting a new house beside one and selling the old place to Lawrence Iverson. The private Sunnybank community, without a public road, retains its intended ambiance of out-of-the-way peacefulness.

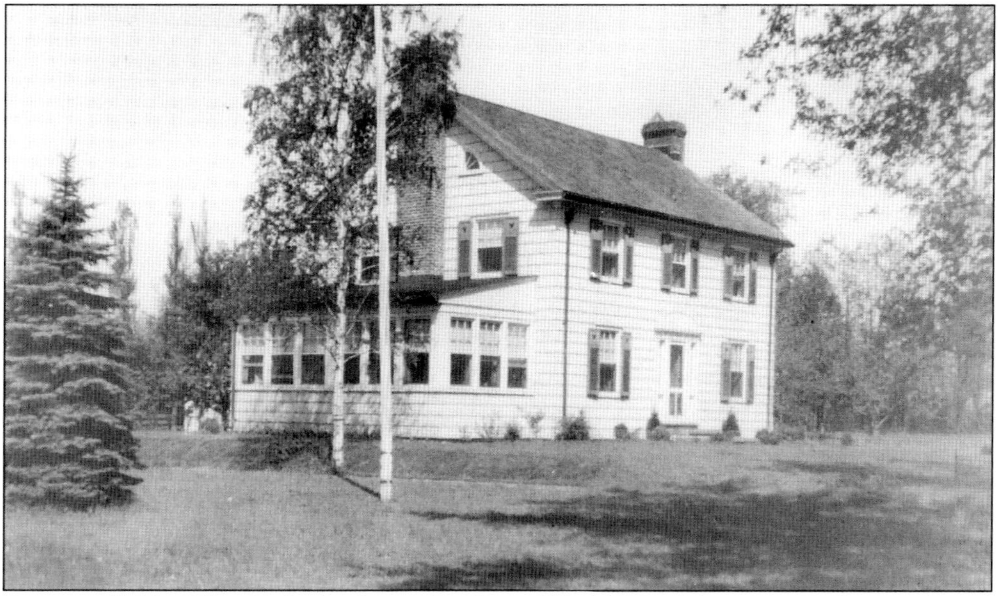

Benjamin F. Van Vliet built the first and only pre-World War II house on Kodama's planned development. It is a simple center-hall, Colonial Revival design by Frank Quackenbush, constructed in 1928 by Quackenbush and Nevius. Timing would not prove good, with a depression slowing housing considerably. The house, on the west side of Sunnybank Drive, is well preserved, with only a small entrance porch and the addition of a greenhouse on the south side changing this *c.* 1929 appearance. Post-war construction filled out Sunnybank.

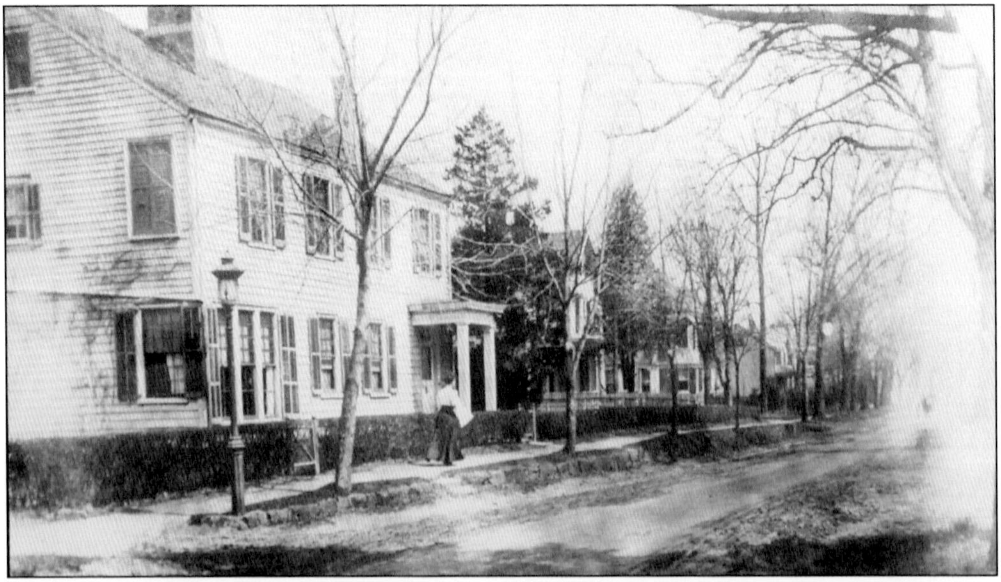

The Benjamin White House at 355 Sycamore Avenue, east of the Quaker Meeting House and opposite the Presbyterian church, was built in 1789. It was used as the Presbyterian Manse for a time and was known as Fordacre following its 1926 purchase by George Ford Morris, the noted animal artist, who was then returning to America following three years in Paris. Morris had a long and varied career, beginning in Chicago as an illustrator for *The Horseman* at age sixteen. Business activity included partnership in raising horses at the Green Meadow Farm, Freehold. This is an early-twentieth-century view.

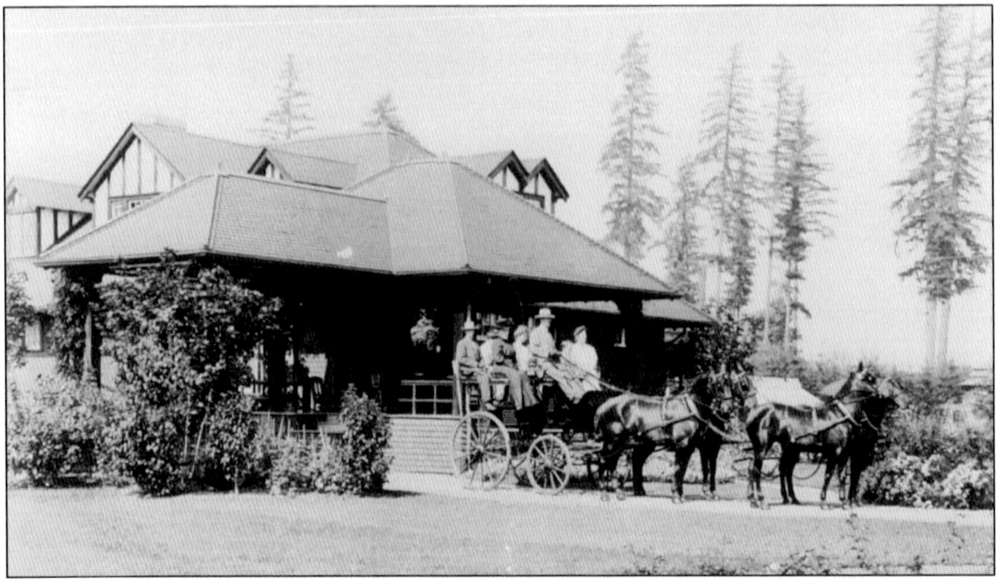

George Ford Morris traveled extensively and had a winter home and studio in Aiken, South Carolina, from 1929 to 1942. He is shown here at the reins in an undated photograph somewhere in the south. Morris was best known for his horse illustrations, with his magnum opus in print, *The Horse Book of the Century*, published in 1952, containing over 700 illustrations. He also painted dogs and other animals, including a line of art posters for livestock, horse, and dog shows. (Shrewsbury Historical Society Collection.)

Five

People, Places, and Events

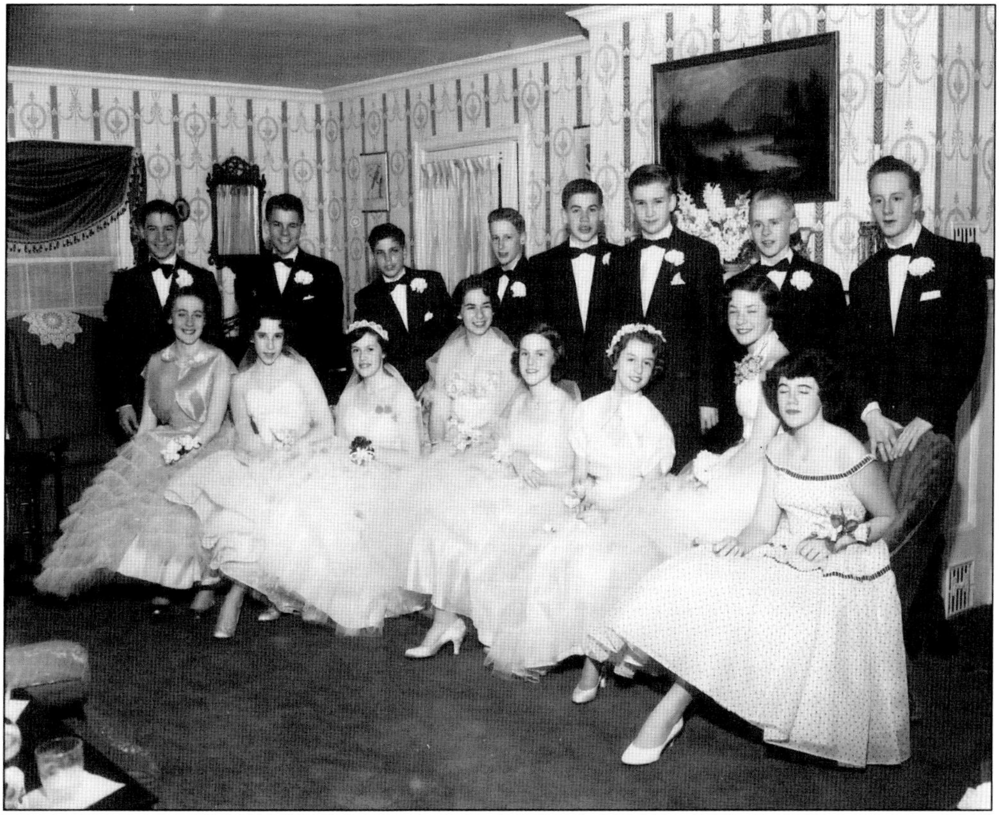

It is the night of a 1950s class dance, with these Shrewsbury students loving every moment, even their photography session. Patricia Dorn, third from the left, is naturally at ease in front of the camera as she is a member of the famed photography family. (Dorn's Collection.)

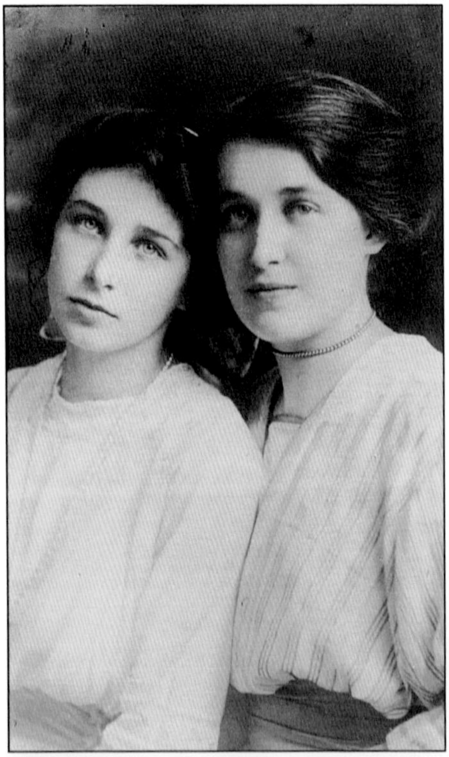

Yearning expressions and sisterly affection give a timeless appeal to two young women early in this century.

Holding a pose can be a difficult task for a portrait subject. The unknown subjects in this c. 1890s image are obviously in the same room, but, perhaps, four different worlds. After months of handling this photograph, the mug at left began to look familiar to the author. Look at the top of p. 79—that's the Reverend Wilson! (Shrewsbury Historical Society Collection.)

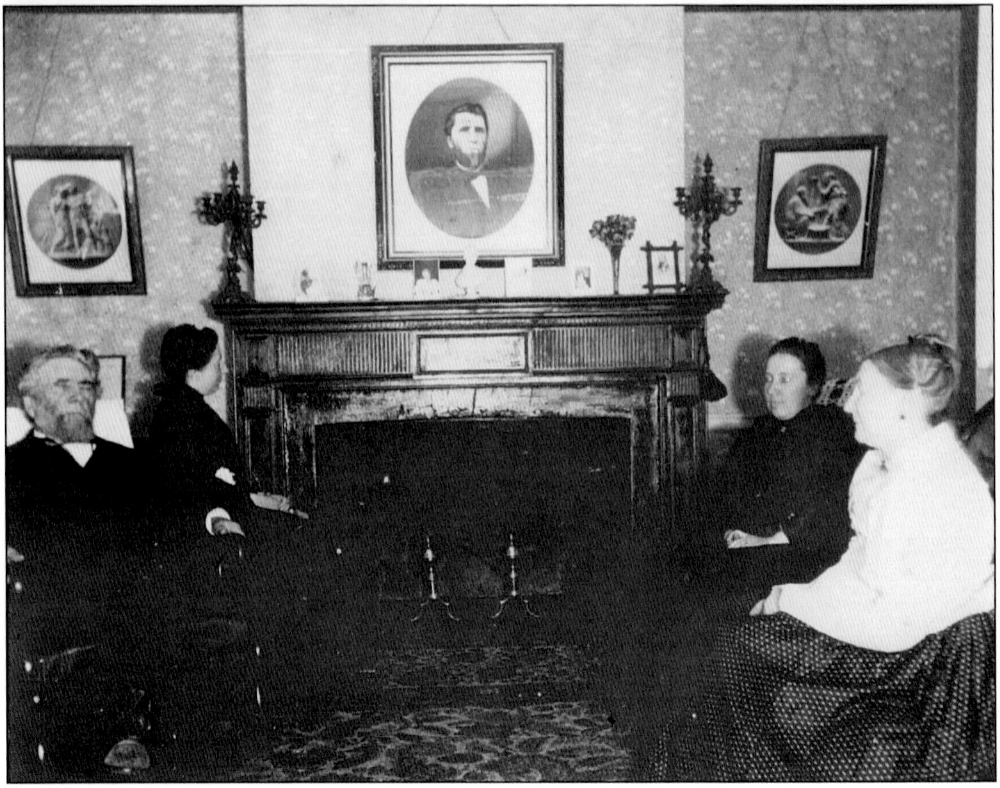

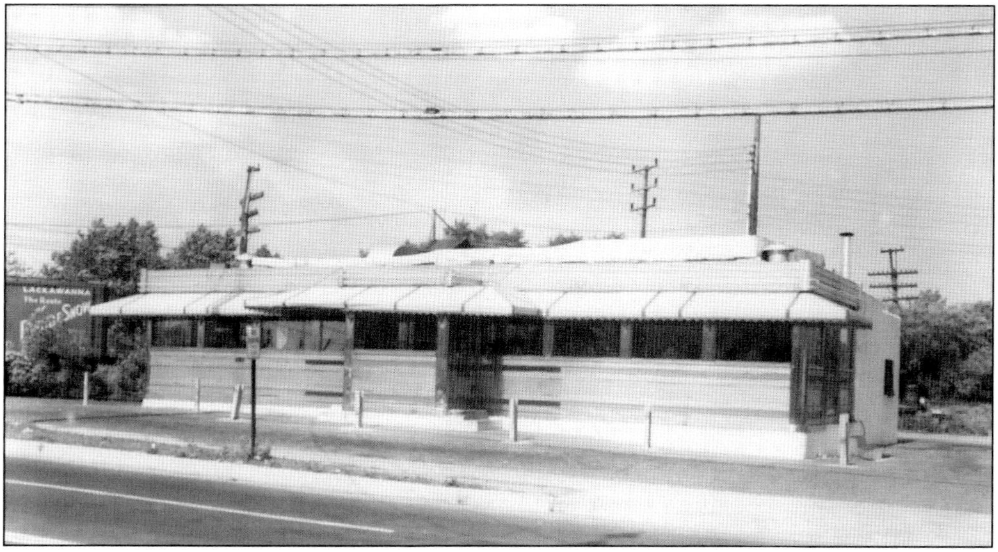

The diner once occupying the east side of Broad Street at the foot of Newman Springs Road was removed to permit construction of the left-turn road jug-handle. The 1950s picture post-dates the 1954 opening of the Garden State Parkway. The railroad forms Shrewsbury's eastern boundary at this point. The boxcar reflects passing railroad history, with the Lackawanna later merged with the Erie and then made part of Conrail in 1976. (Dorn's Collection.)

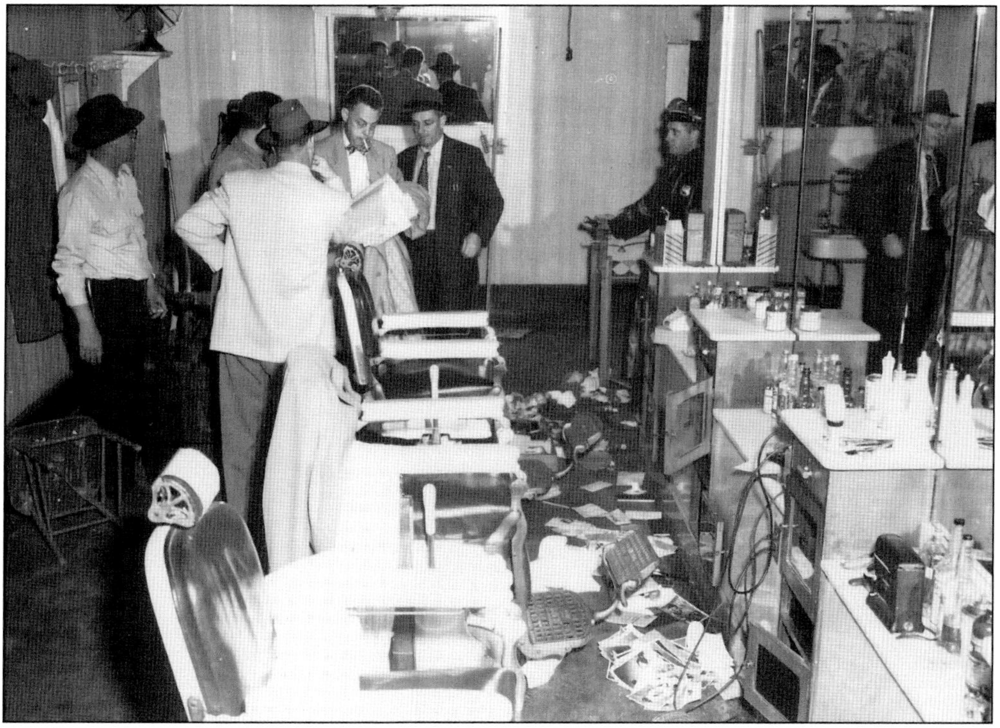

Frank's Barber Shop on Obre Place in the early 1950s is out-of-order. Is something missing? One cannot spot the Wildroot, inevitable in a shop of the period. The event appears to have been a gambling raid, an event with few definite details, but it did provide an opportunity to preserve pictorially a 1950s barber shop. (Dorn's Collection.)

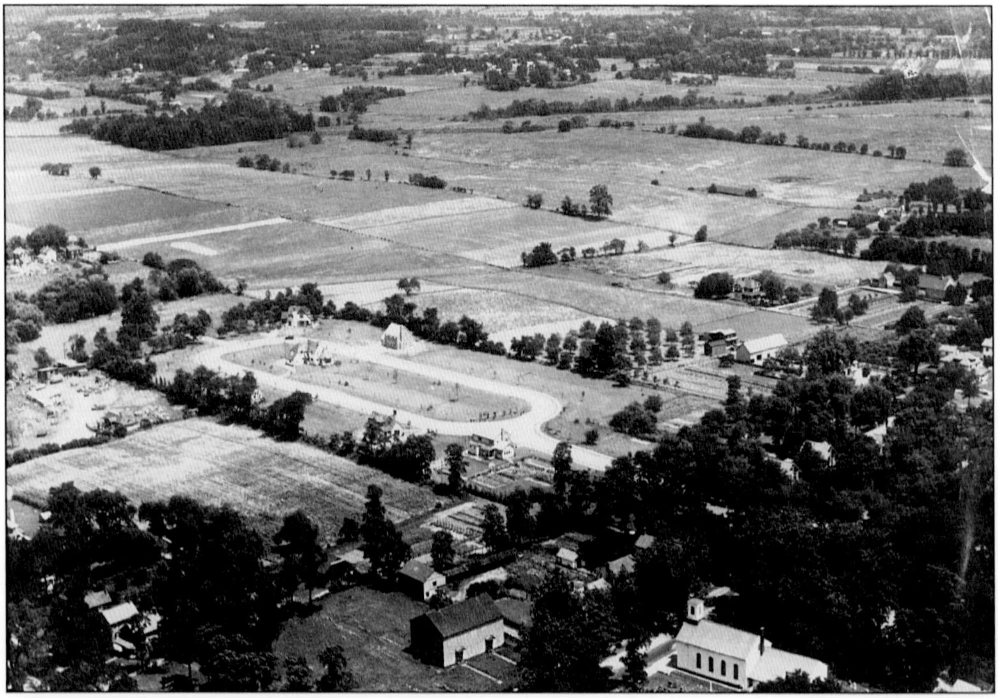

This *c.* 1928 aerial view looking northeast from the Four Corners portrays Buttonwood Park as the first major development north of Sycamore Avenue in a landscape that would soon be dotted with houses. The Presbyterian church and the Quaker Meeting House at bottom help provide the perspective. Farm structures belonging to the north side of Sycamore properties that would also be sub-divided are visible at right.

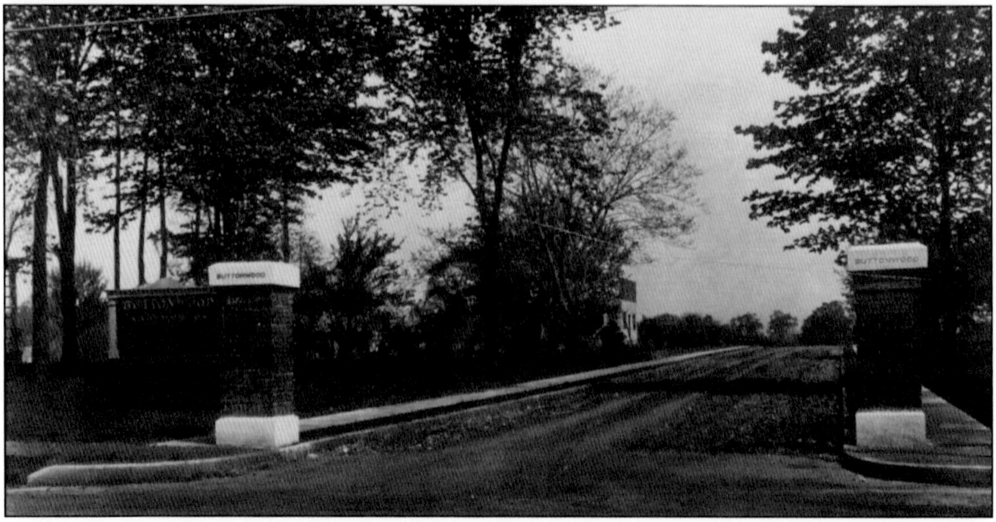

G. Harold Nevius, developer of Buttonwood Park, the town's first fine housing sub-division, planned the entrance to resemble a private estate. He built these brick gate posts to mark the entrance to a community that had the right of architectural approval, along with other restrictive covenants, written into its deeds. Electrical service was installed underground through lines that encircled the property at the rear of the house lots. Buttonwood is another name for sycamore. The posts still stand.

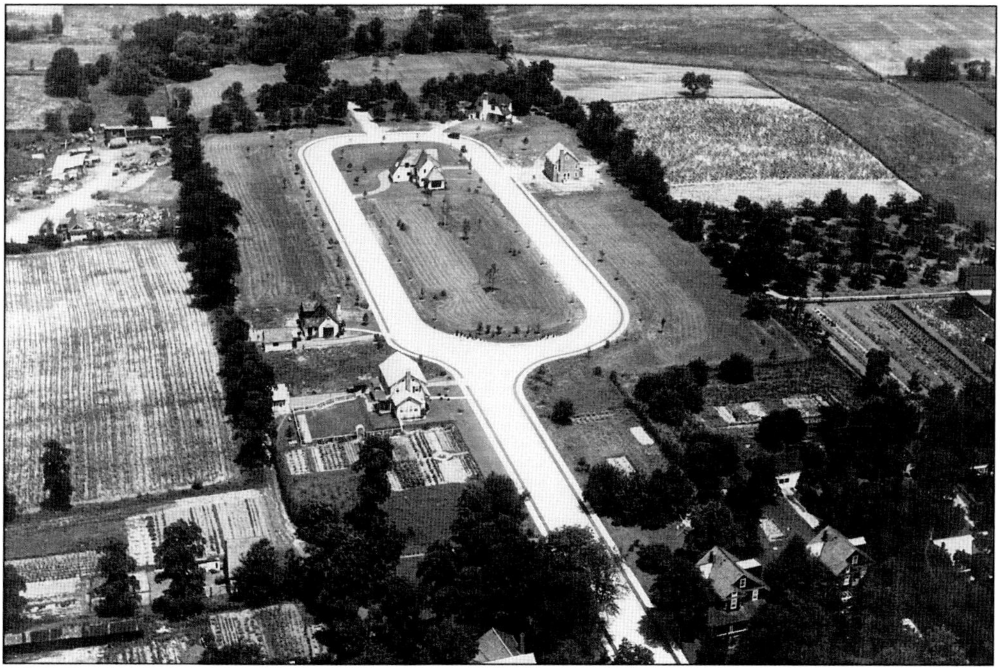

Early builders at Buttonwood can be identified from the map below. This c. 1928 aerial photograph is looking north from the Sycamore Avenue entrance. One of the developers, Frank Quackenbush, built his house at the oval to the right. The B.C. Downing place is in the interior of the oval, opposite Thomas Wylie's house. C. Baquet's place is at the entrance to the oval, while R. Van Camp's is north of it.

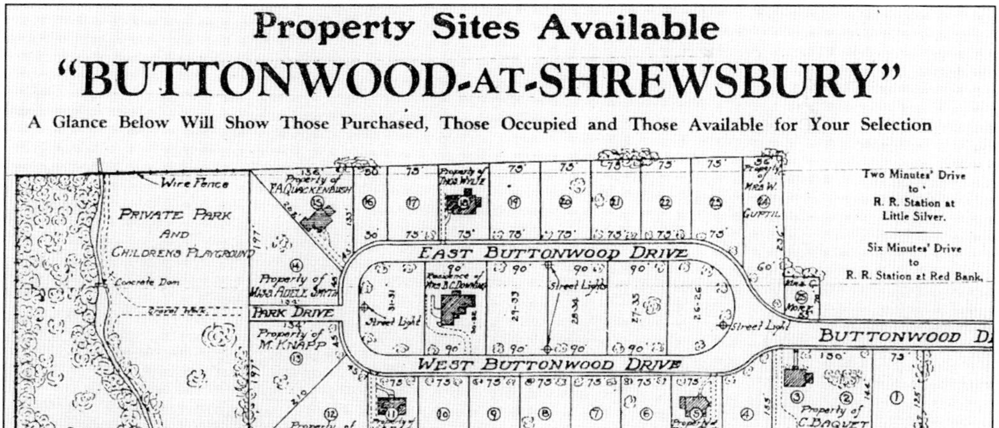

Arthur C. Swift surveyed and laid out Buttonwood Park. This is the developer's plan showing available lots in the spring of 1929, outlining each of the houses in the picture at top. Vincent J. Eck, an architect with an extensive practice for the Catholic Church, designed his own house, built at the northwest corner of the oval that year. The park land shown north of the house lots is now undeveloped open space owned by the borough.

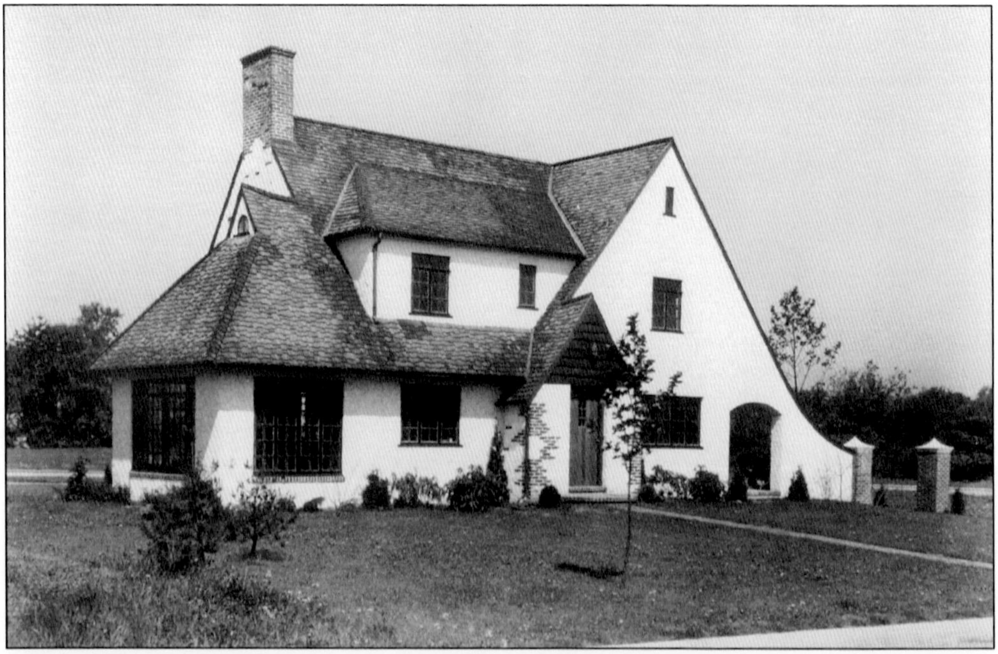

G. Harold Nevius built this house in 1927 in the middle of the oval to serve as a model. Shown here *c.* 1928, the home appeared in promotional pieces on Buttonwood. The Tudor Revival house was designed by Frank Quackenbush and is consistent with the predominant Buttonwood style, although without the half-timbering used elsewhere there. The well-preserved house still stands. Nevius lived at the Sycamore Avenue entrance to Buttonwood and rented this house.

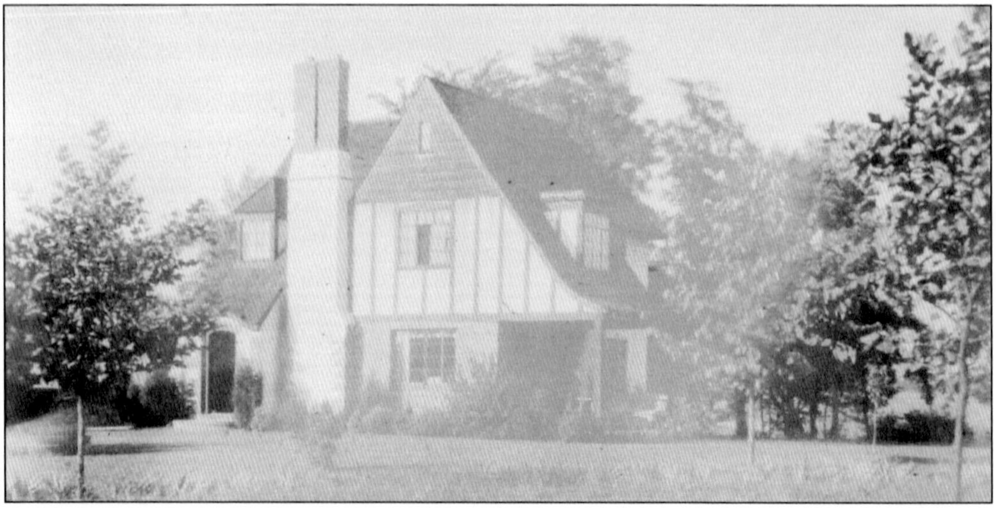

Frank Quackenbush, a naval veteran of World War I and the son of an Atlantic Highlands builder, was employed by a New York brokerage firm and was a resident in Red Bank when he built a nearby house intended for family occupancy, which he sold for the proverbial offer that could not be refused. He bought a lot in the northeastern corner of the Buttonwood oval, designed this Tudor Revival house for himself at number 27 Buttonwood Drive, and so impressed G. Harold Nevius that Quackenbush was persuaded to make a career change and was admitted to the former's firm. The house in this *c.* 1928 photograph is well-preserved today, with a kitchen added and the garage on the left expanded.

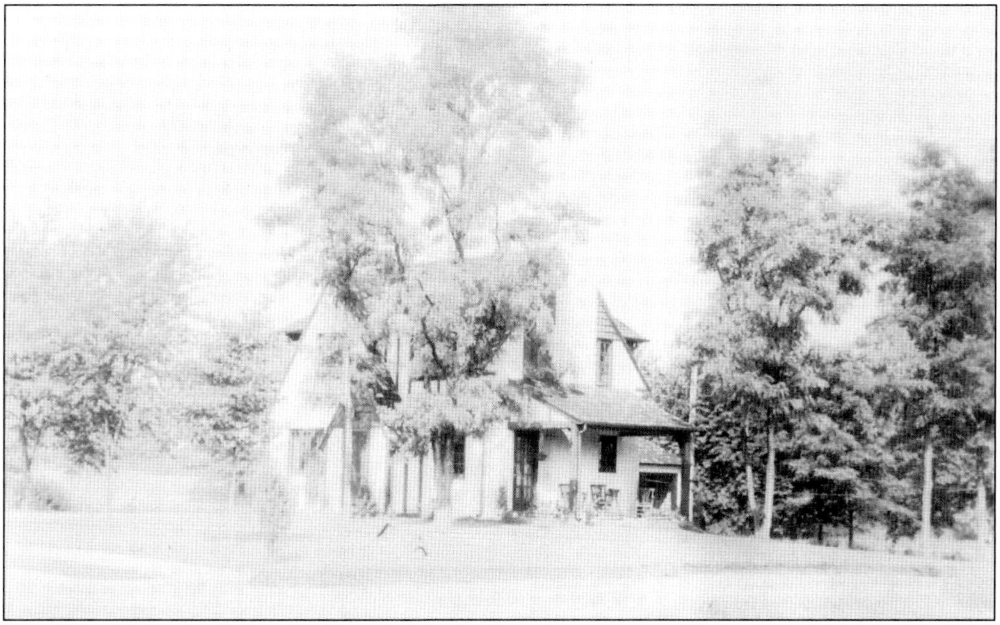

Morgan C. Knapp, an official with the Monmouth Boy Scout organization, had this Tudor Revival built in the northwestern corner of the oval, "the park end," in 1929 to a design by Frank Quackenbush. A steep shingled roof, casement windows, and half-timbered stuccoed walls characterize this artful residence. It has changed little since this *c.* 1930 view, with the porch at right now enclosed.

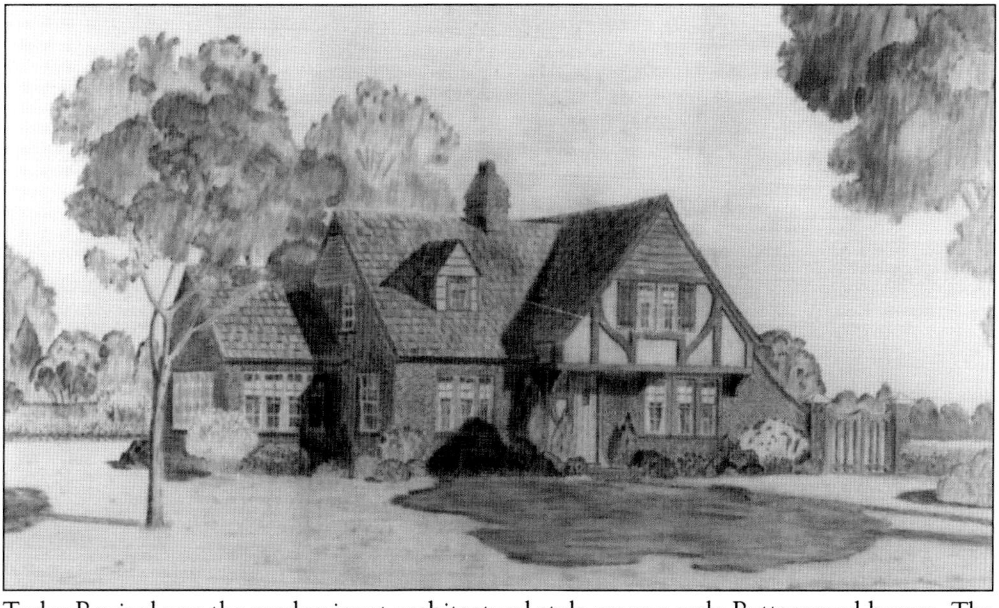

Tudor Revival was the predominant architectural style among early Buttonwood houses. The development had an architectural review restrictive covenant in their deeds, a condition remedied by co-developer Frank Quackenbush having designed most of the houses. This rendering from his hand embraces many motifs found at Buttonwood, but the actual house appears not to have been built there. The firm built elsewhere in the area, making one suspect this house may stand at another location.

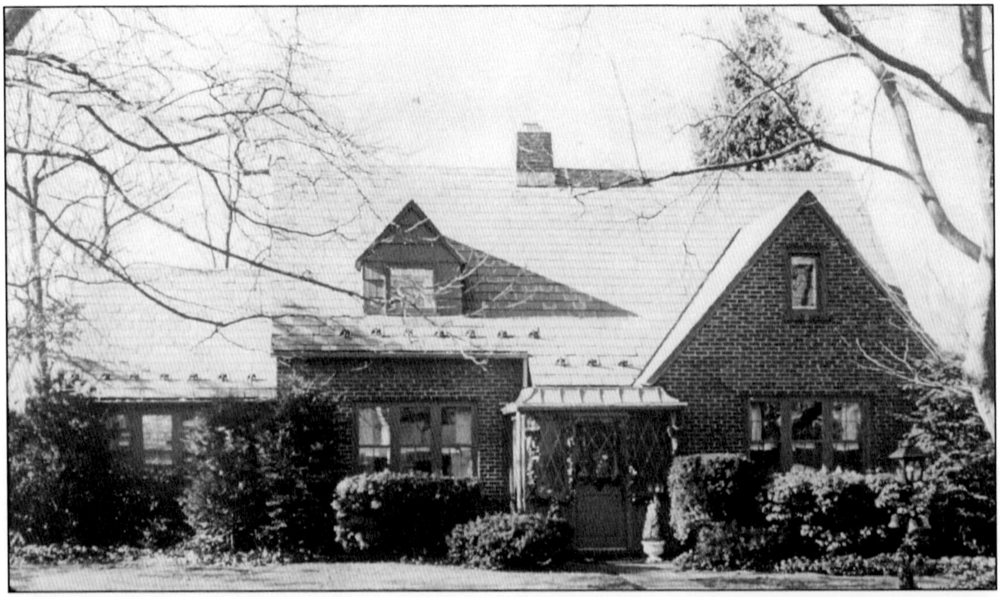

The Colonial Revival house shown in this c. 1980 picture at 15 Buttonwood Drive is likely the last of pre-war construction in the development. It was built c. 1935 and designed by Frank Quackenbush. The house's early history is obscure, but the developer Harold Nevius had the title twenty years later when it was sold to George and Dorothy Blair. The small entrance porch is a later addition.

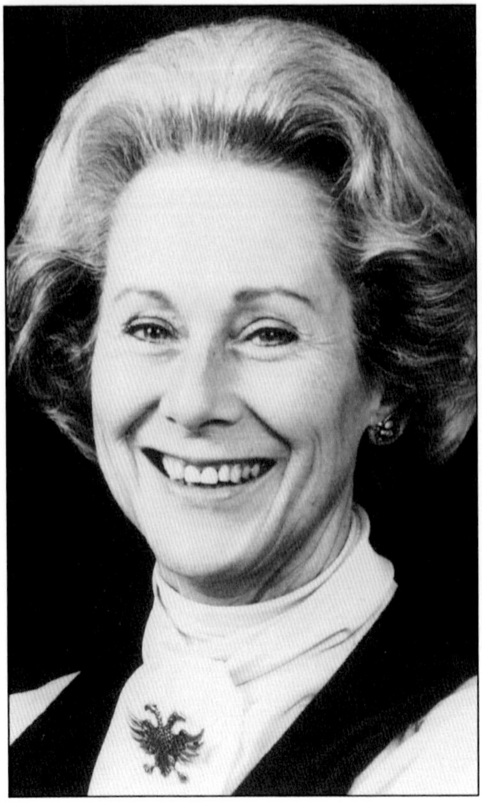

The warmth and esteem in which Dorothy Blair Manson was held by the people of Shrewsbury, and the warmth she returned to those she met, are qualities meriting mention before her lengthy accomplishments. The first woman to hold the office of mayor in Shrewsbury, she quietly filled an early goal to serve twelve years, following six on the borough council. She was proud of over fifty years service to the Girl Scouts and was a member of the Monmouth Council since its 1962 origin. Dorothy was the 1938 homecoming queen at Wayne State University in her native Michigan. She received several person of the year awards, was the first vestry woman of Christ Church (1971), and was their first sub-deacon (1988). In an earlier career, Dorothy was a successful dancer. In addition to all this, she was a trustee of the Shrewsbury Historical Society. Her untimely passing a few days after the society endorsed this book project left one sad note, this volume, in part as a memorial to her successful life, rather than as an expected shared pleasure with her over her beloved town's achievements.

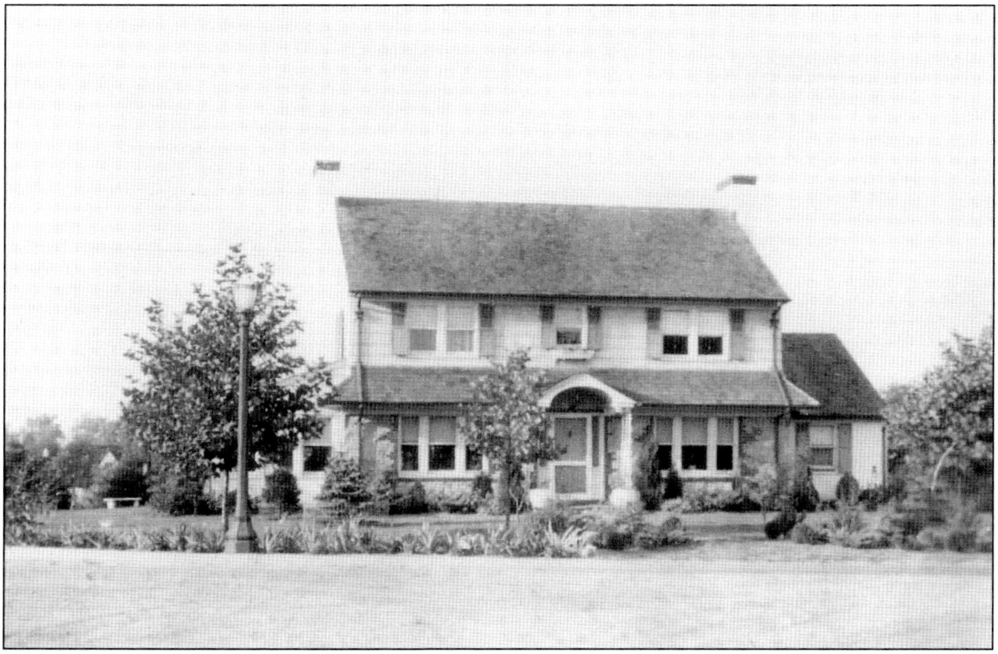

Frank Quackenbush designed a Georgian Revival center hall plan for Archibald L. Miller, a former Red Bank mayor. It was built in 1929 at the southern end of the oval and is little changed today. The garage, entered through the rear at right, has been built out, the only noteworthy change.

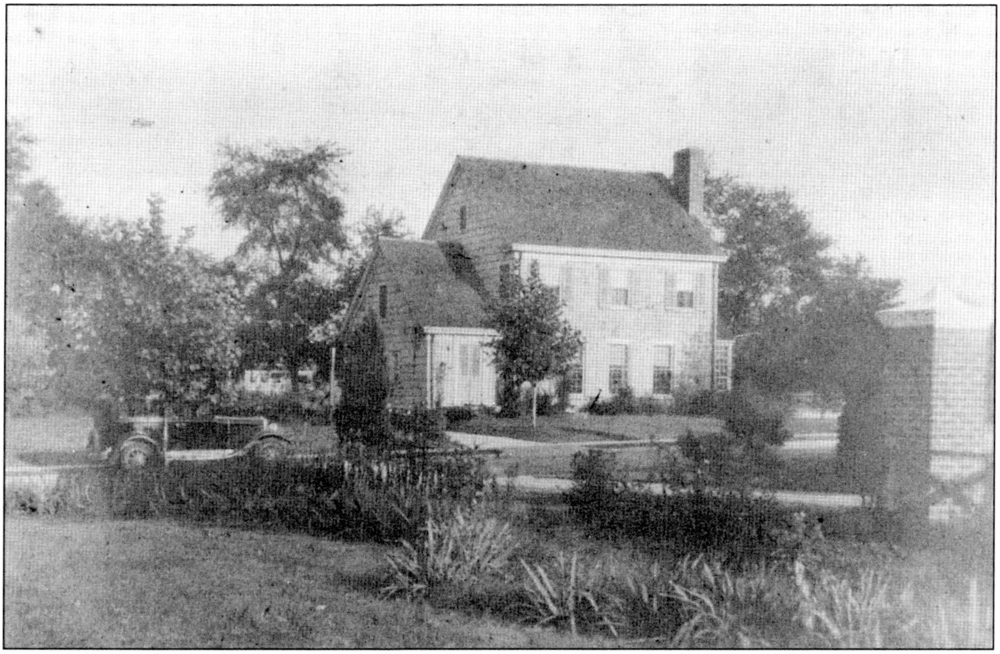

Number 34 Buttonwood on the east side of the oval was built for Thomas Wylie c. 1927 by Quackenbush & Nevius and is shown here around the time of construction. The simple, early Colonial Revival design of Frank Quackenbush has been altered by the addition of a two-car garage on the right and a hipped-roof dormer in the main block.

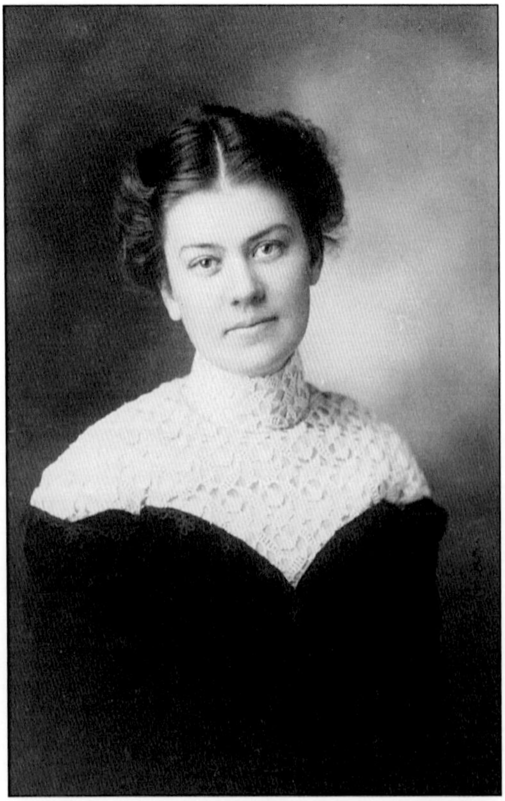

Eva Green, attractively attired in lace early in the twentieth century, was the principal of Red Bank's Shrewsbury Avenue School.

William Green's daughter Rachel is shown here leading the family's cow to a pasture at a Broad Street grove in the late 1890s. (Shrewsbury Historical Society Collection.)

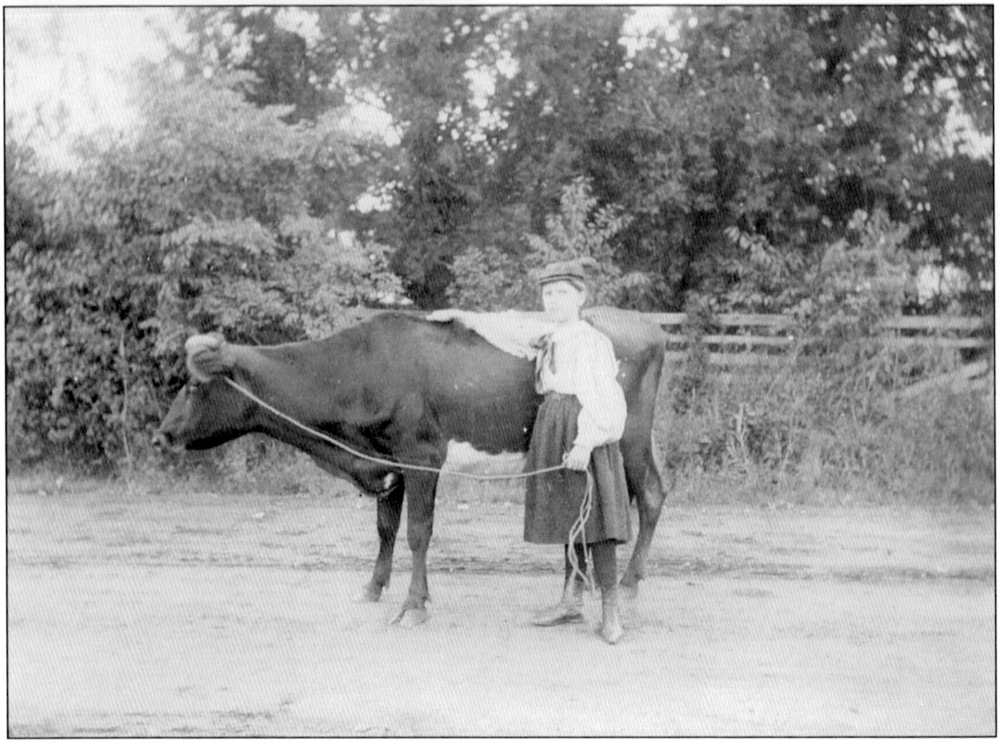

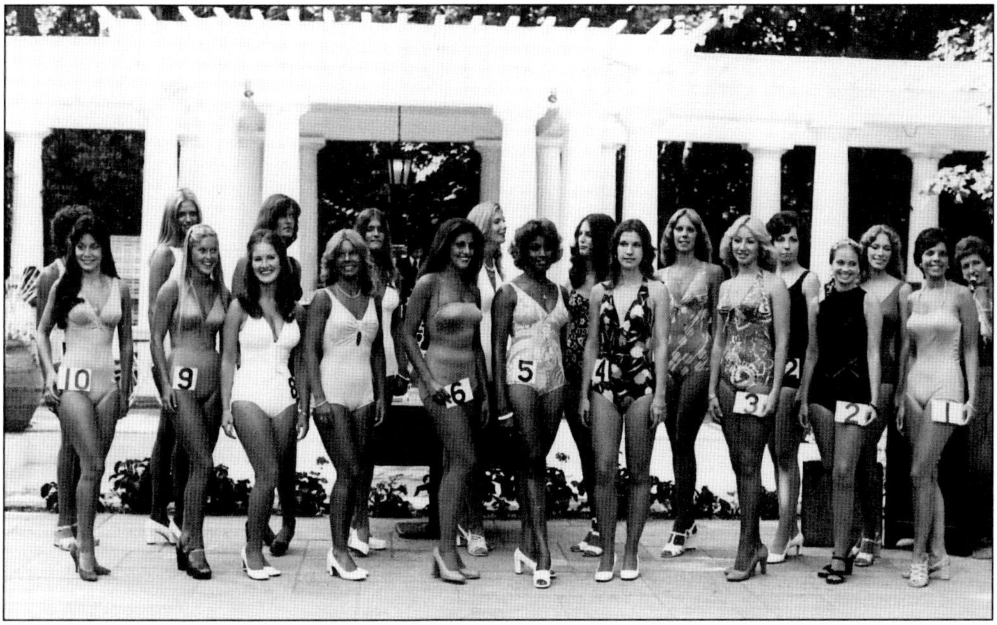

Contestants for the 1975 National Sweepstakes Regatta beauty competition are gathered at Shadowbrook's garden. Linda Sparrow of Leonardo (number 9 at left) was chosen Miss Windsor Canadian. The distiller was the major sponsor of the event that year. In the back row, above Linda's left shoulder, is Mary De Mont of Matawan, winner of the title Miss National Sweepstakes Regatta.

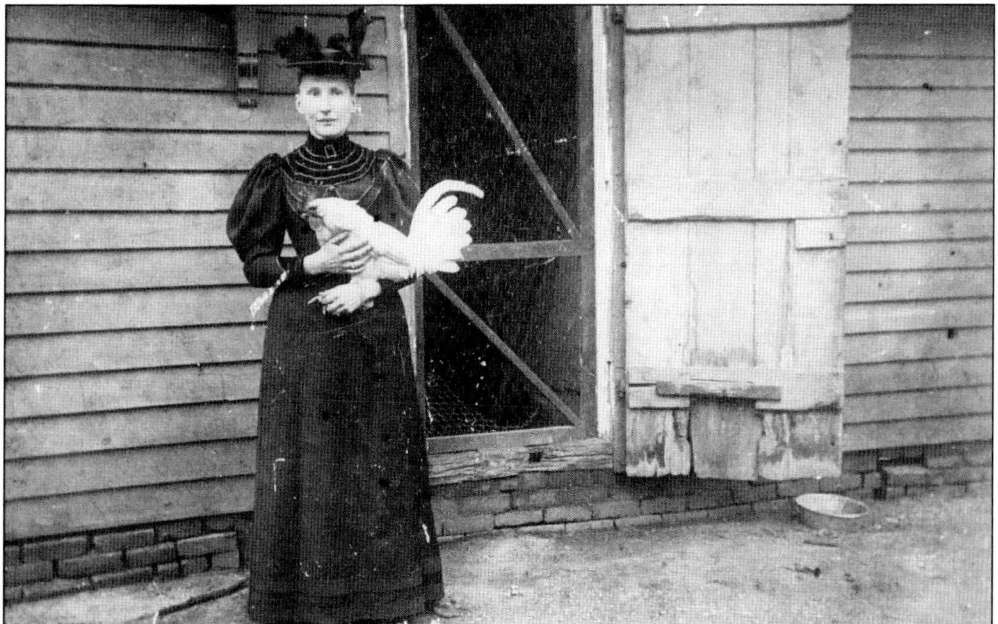

Corina Smith Baldwin (1863–1918) has a fowl to rival her hat, or is it the other way around? This daughter of E. Delafield Smith married the Reverend Albert Dorrance Baldwin, who survived her by twenty-five years. The picture, perhaps c. 1880s, is in the collection of Shrewsbury Historical Society.

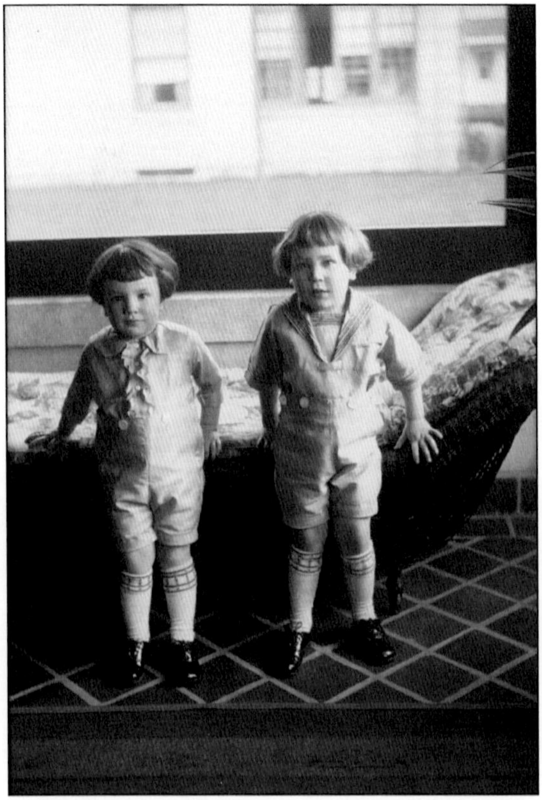

George and Monroe Marx, shown here c. 1925, were sons of Martin and Blanche Marx. They spent their careers in the family wholesale meat business. Monroe has a lengthy record of public service, notably on the Shrewsbury Board of Education. He lent the picture and will now undoubtedly hear from his many friends and associates, "Hey, I didn't know you were such a cute kid."

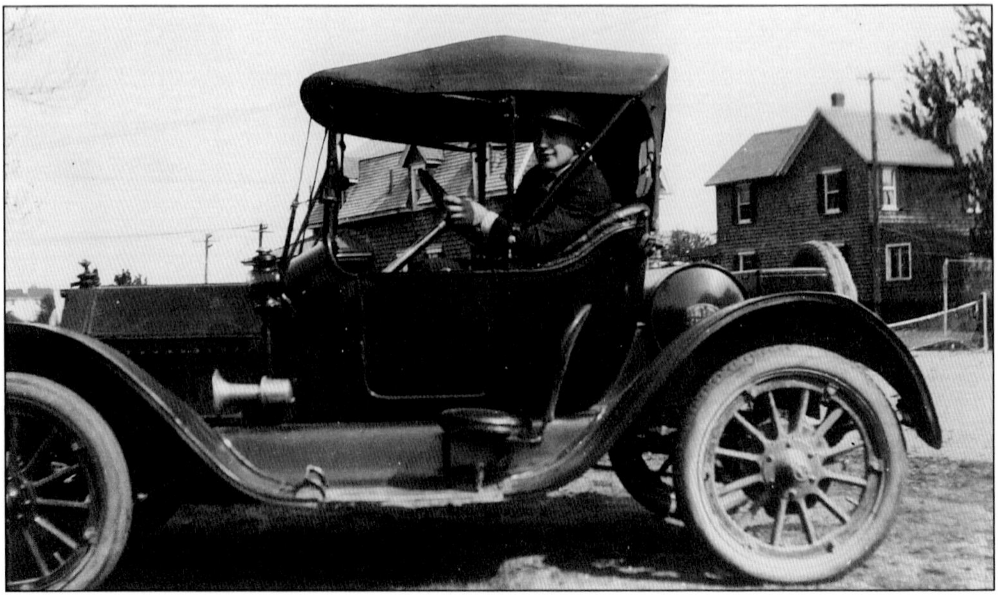

Blanche Marx proudly sits behind the wheel during the late teens.

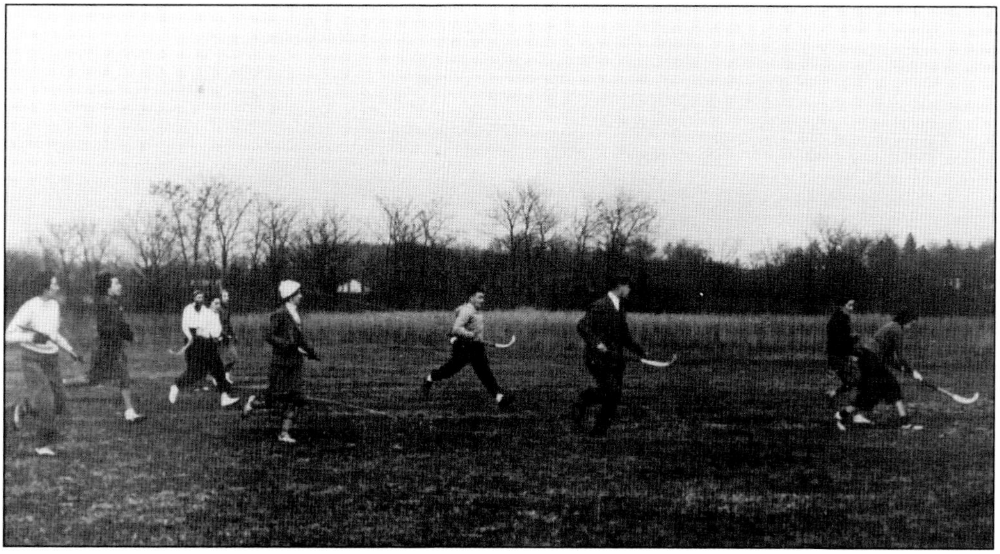

The Shrewsbury Field Hockey Association organized around October 1933, holding their first meeting on October 26 at Christ Church. Their field was on part of the Hazard property off Sycamore Avenue. Charter members were Mrs. Ira Croose, Ruth Lamarche, Mrs. Albert Willgerodt, Katherine Lamarche, Mrs. Winifred Ylvisaker, and their manager and captain, Mrs. Nye Elward. The last entry in the minute book was the final spring season meeting of June 6, 1939, making one suspect they disbanded not long afterwards. (Shrewsbury Historical Society Collection.)

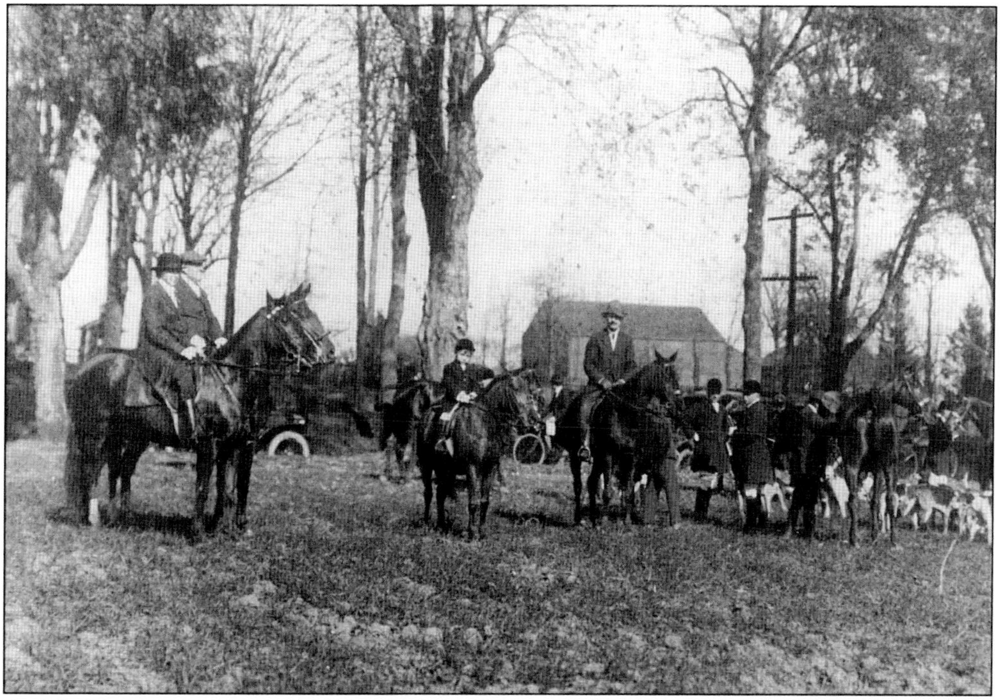

At left, Margaret Rue Campbell (p. 126) and Harry Lord Powers survey a group preparing for a fox hunt at an unidentified Shrewsbury site. Harry's son, Jessie Wood Powers, is at the center. The other figure remains unidentified.

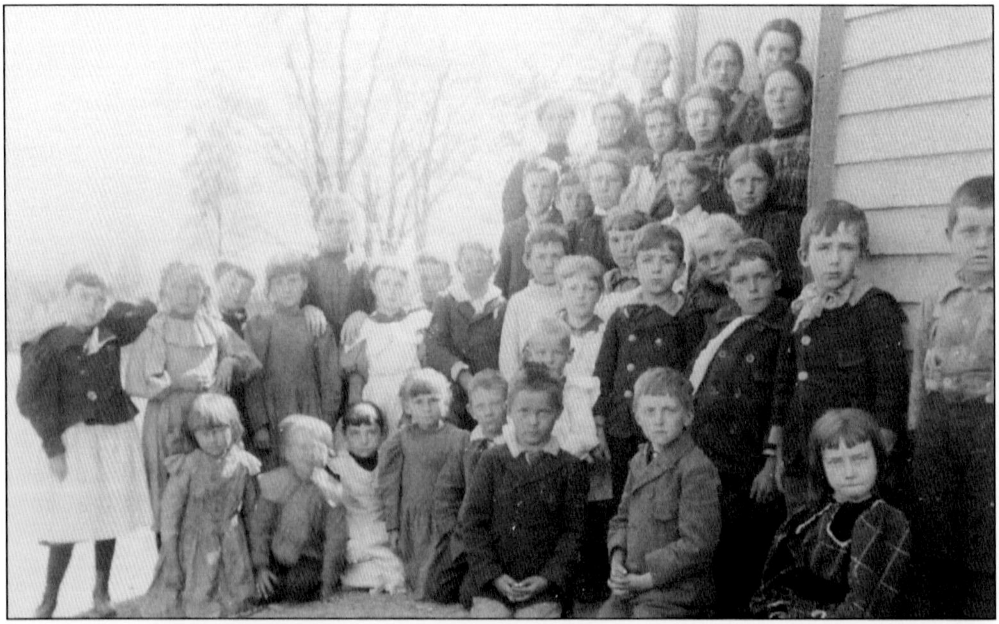

It is easy to assume Miss B. King was an unhappy, disagreeable person, based on her stern countenance; standing near the back, her expression is so severe that one wonders if it is not merely posing practice. But look at her young charges! Their expressions are little different. It is c. 1896 and Miss King probably ran a tight ship at the Sycamore Avenue grade school. The distinctiveness of their poses makes one suspect the class leaders may have been Ethel(?) Pheonic (in front with her elbow on the shoulder of May Handcock) and the tall Kattie Casey (with her hands on two fellow students). A.W. Borden was the photographer.

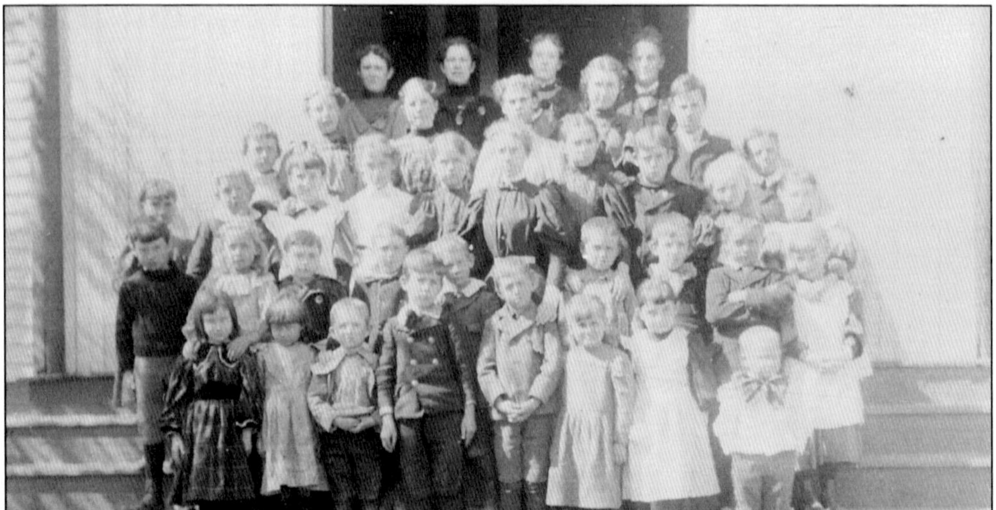

The grade school is shown here probably a year later. Charles Francis Borden (p. 81), born in 1887, recalled his classmates in 1909, forgetting a few and leaving the viewer of the original print to wonder the rows to which some belong. He recalled its location next to a barnyard was one reason for the relocation to Broad Street. He also left this sentimental inscription: "How dear to my heart are the scenes of my childhood when fond recollections present them to view: The schoolhouse, the scholars, the teacher, my friends all join in together to make up the end."

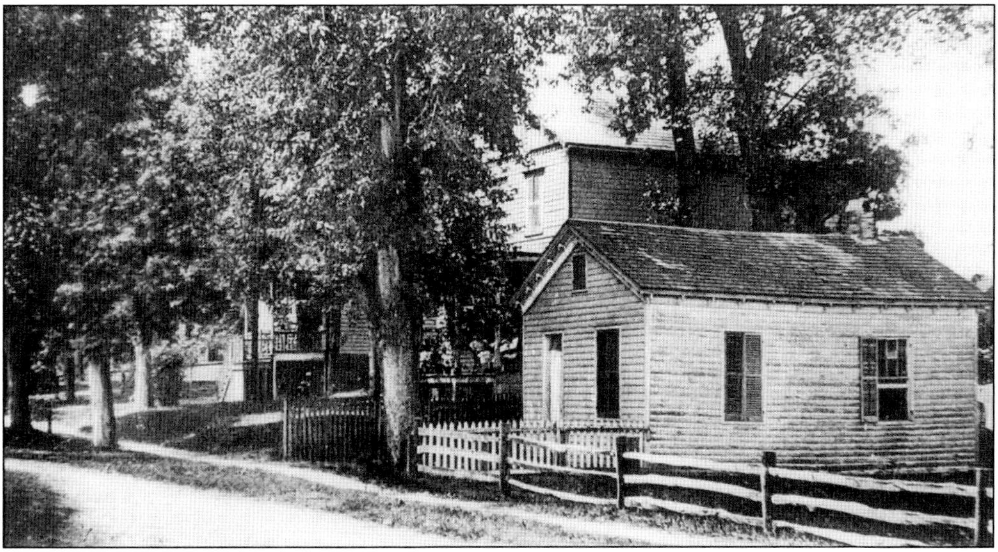

Early education in Shrewsbury was conducted by the churches. It is believed the first public school was opened *c.* 1820. This is a *c.* 1905 postcard of the fourth school, built *c.* 1860 on the north side of Sycamore Avenue adjacent to Dr. Patterson's farmhouse and opposite Peter Campbell's. Initially one room, a second was added, but the school was inadequate not long after the turn of the century. (John Rhody Collection.)

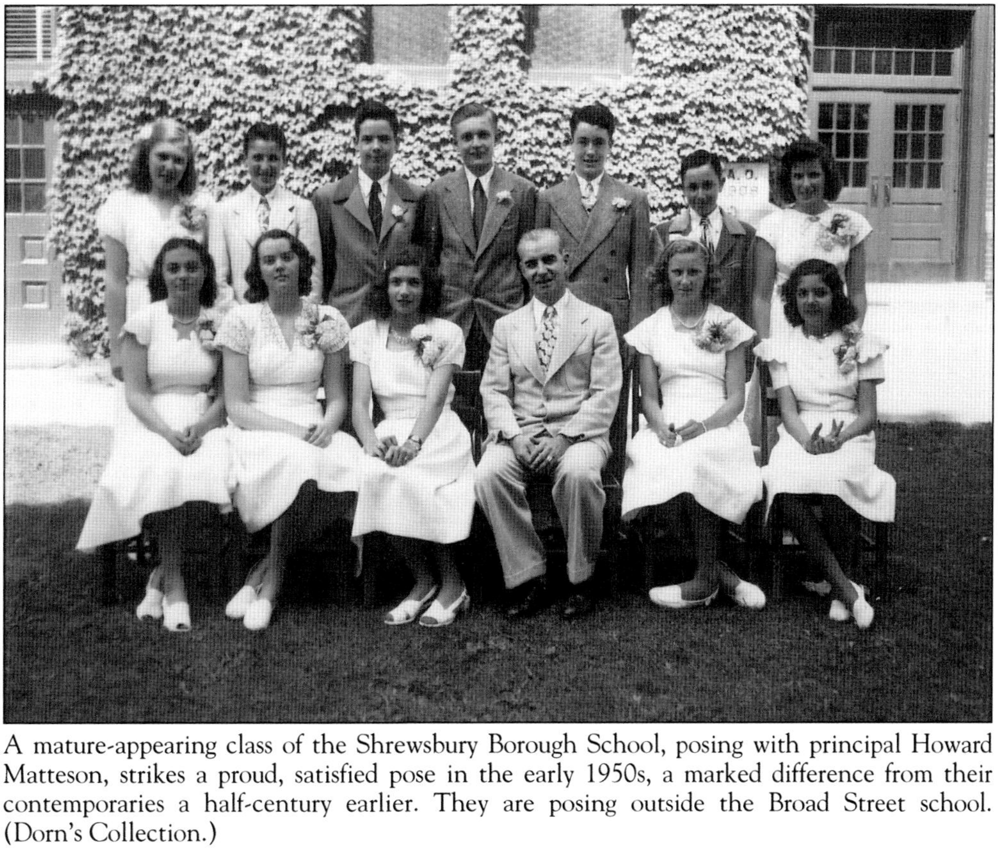

A mature-appearing class of the Shrewsbury Borough School, posing with principal Howard Matteson, strikes a proud, satisfied pose in the early 1950s, a marked difference from their contemporaries a half-century earlier. They are posing outside the Broad Street school. (Dorn's Collection.)

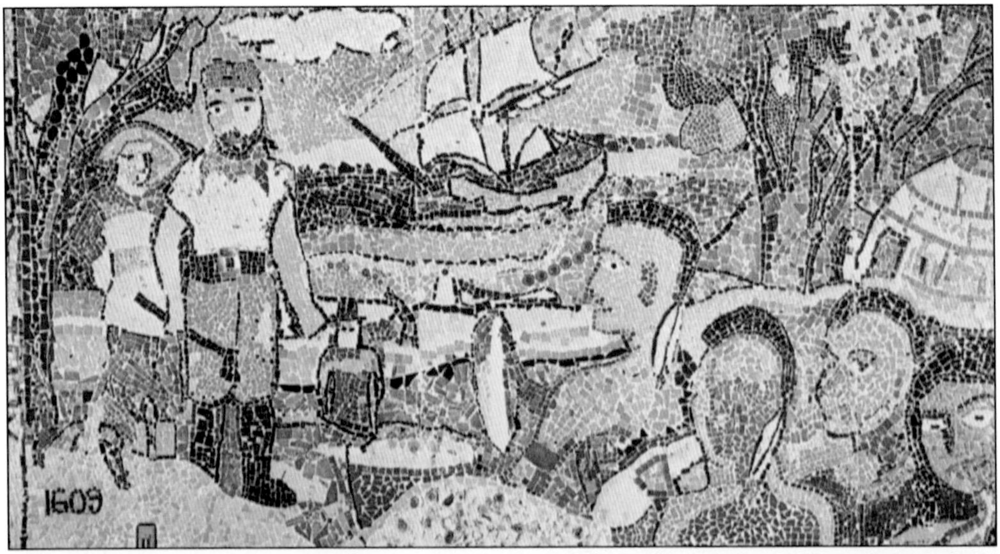

The Shrewsbury Mosaic was made by fifty-eight fourth grade pupils of Shrewsbury School during the 1961–62 school year to commemorate the 1964 New Jersey Tercentenary. They were guided by teachers J. Louise Jost and Lois Eben, chair and art director, and assisted by Adele Maclore and Margaret McNally, but the students did the work, from obtaining materials—generally objects and manufactured products found or made in New Jersey—to mounting them on plywood boards. The children studied New Jersey history in class and learned about Henry Hudson's 1609 voyage and the interactions European settlers had with Native Americans, the subjects of the first panel.

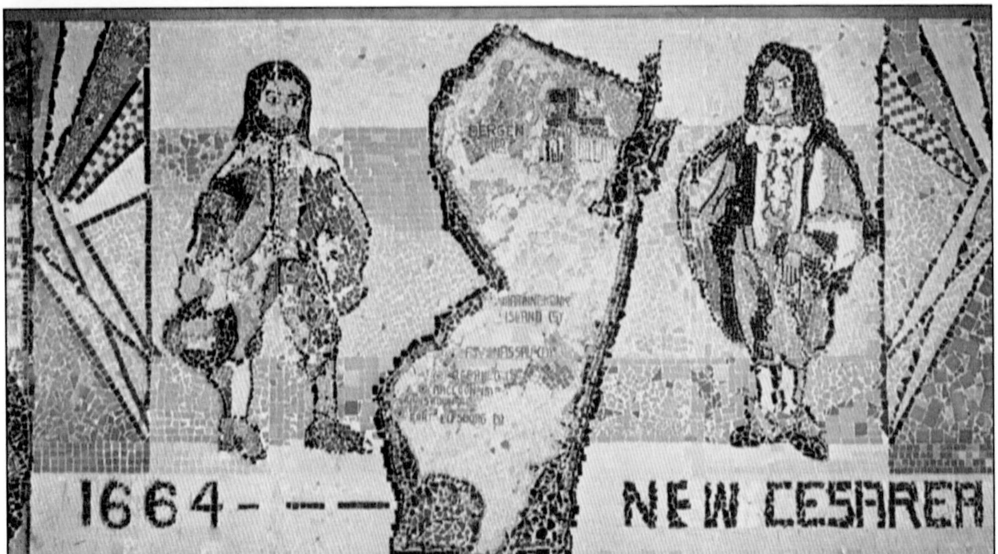

The students wrote to New Jersey businesses for donations of materials which included glass, leather, jewels, plastics, zinc, numerous varieties of tiles, and other items. Unusable materials were made part of an exhibition of New Jersey industry that June. The students corresponded with important figures in the world of New Jersey history, honing communication skills, too, in order to ascertain the aptness of their designs. The second panel has George Carteret and Lord Berkeley flanking a map of New Jersey.

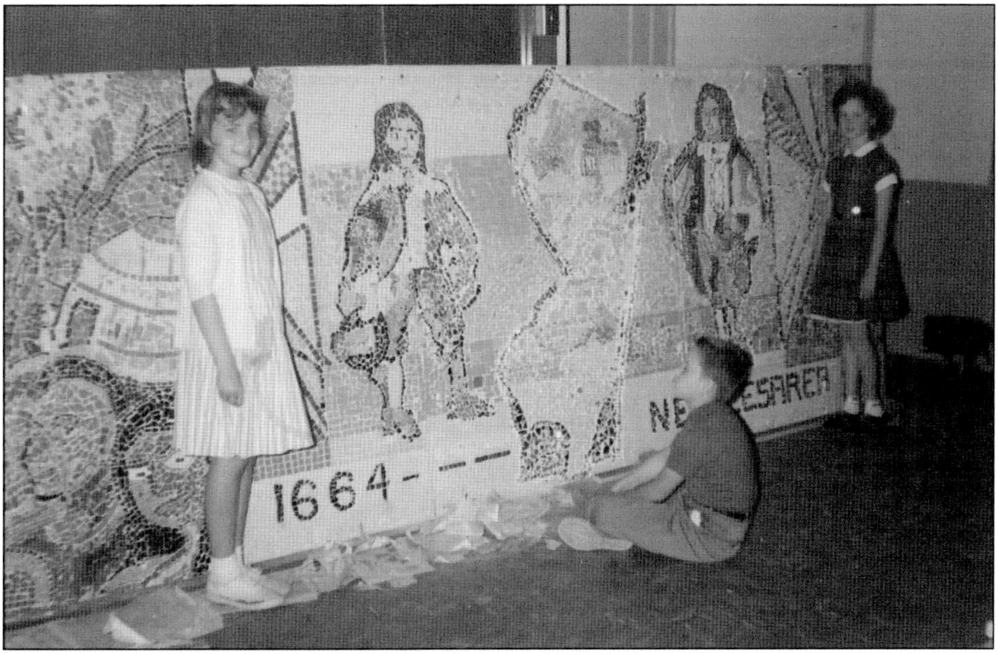

The materials had to be washed, sorted, and broken into usable pieces, requiring a large number of lunch-time and after-school hours, as well as considerable work space. This May 1962 picture shows Mrs. McNally's class working on the second panel. A large format color postcard showing the three panels is available at the Shrewsbury Historical Society.

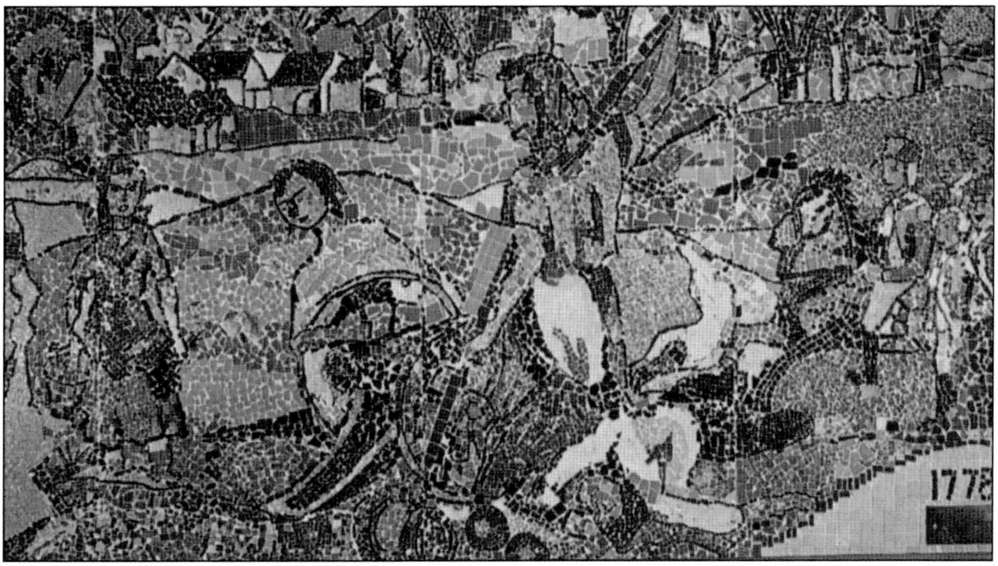

The third panel depicts the 1778 Battle of Monmouth, notably Molly Pitcher, prominent in the foreground. George Washington and his generals are pictured, along with notable buildings around the battle, drawn together with liberal use of artistic license. A June assembly program dramatized the story of The Shrewsbury Mosaic, with parents invited to see the completed work. The Mosaic was mounted on the school hall wall during the summer and formally presented to the school by its makers on Saturday, October 20, 1962. Readers are invited to visit the school and see the students' substantial work of art.

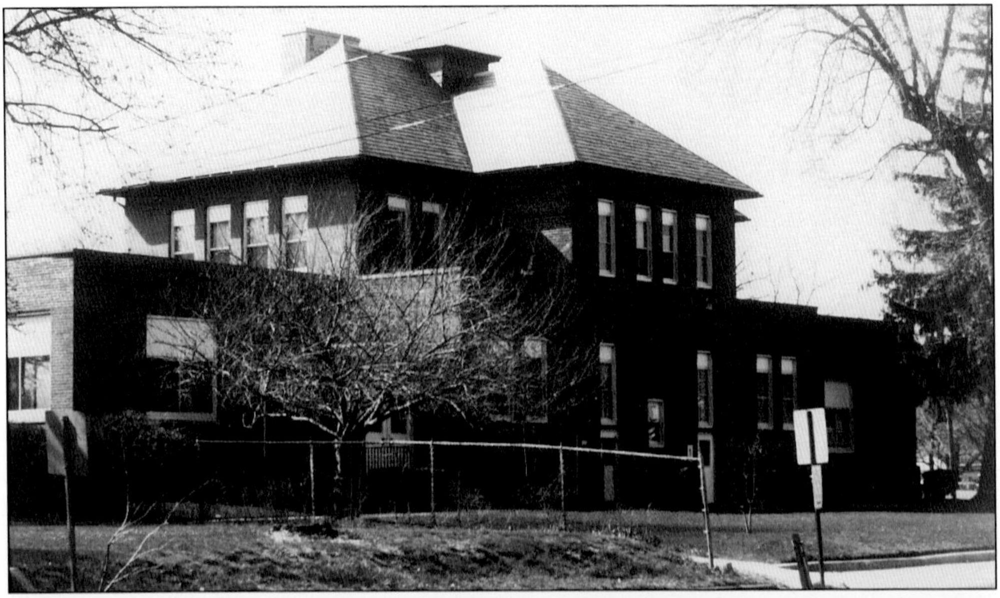

A brick, four-room school was begun in 1908 to replace the no-longer-adequate Sycamore Avenue School (p. 117). The Colonial Revival structure, designed by New York architect William T. Towner, had its cornerstone laid December 12, 1908, and was completed the next year. Several additions were made, including an auditorium in 1935 (later named for twenty-five-year school board member Monroe Marx) and classrooms in 1951, 1953, and 1958. The 1909 building was demolished for the construction of new space that opened in January 1996.

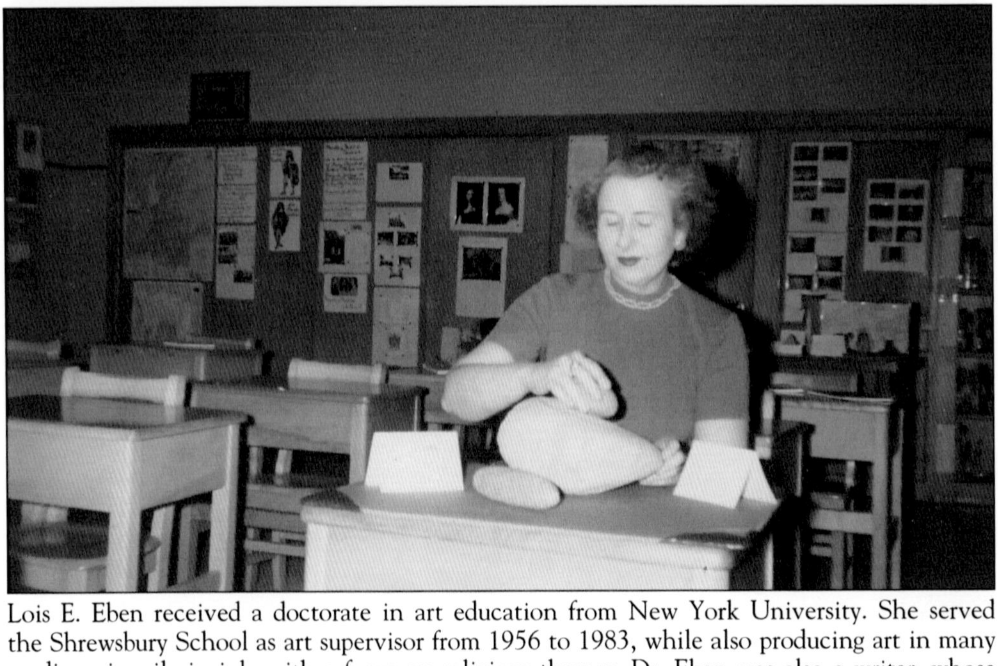

Lois E. Eben received a doctorate in art education from New York University. She served the Shrewsbury School as art supervisor from 1956 to 1983, while also producing art in many media, primarily in ink, with a focus on religious themes. Dr. Eben was also a writer, whose work included two published books and numerous articles. She is shown here working on a 1962 school project. Dr. Eben died in 1992, at age seventy. (Shrewsbury Historical Society Collection.)

Susanna Throckmorton (1814–1874) was born in Philadelphia and raised near Shrewsbury. Her father, Samuel Reading Throckmorton, who was born near Freehold, retired from a Philadelphia mercantile business in 1820 and began farming c. 1833. She is the great-great-aunt of Anna Louise Campbell Rudner (p. 99). The 28-by-36-inch oil-on-canvas portrait is attributed to Waldo & Jewett. Their names are stenciled on the back, although the portrait is unsigned. The head and shoulders were painted from life in the artist's studio, with the dress added later. Susanna married her second cousin, Samuel Reading Throckmorton, in 1833. They moved to San Francisco, where she founded an orphanage.

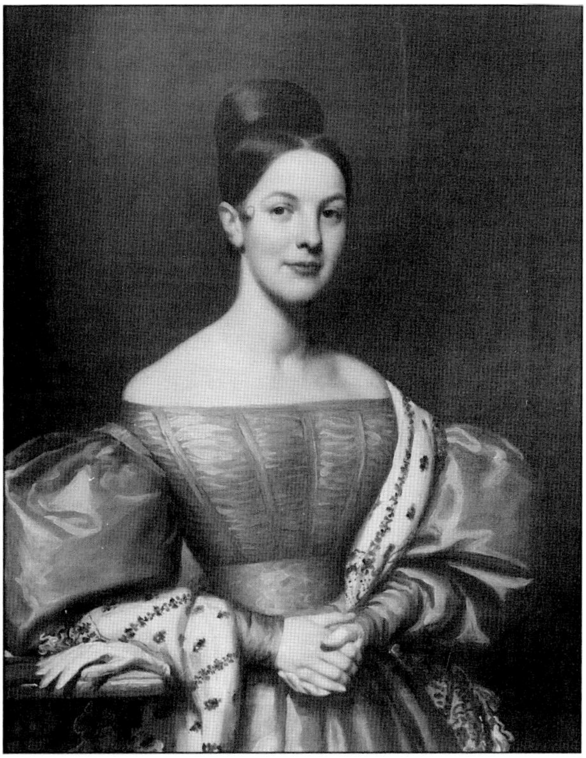

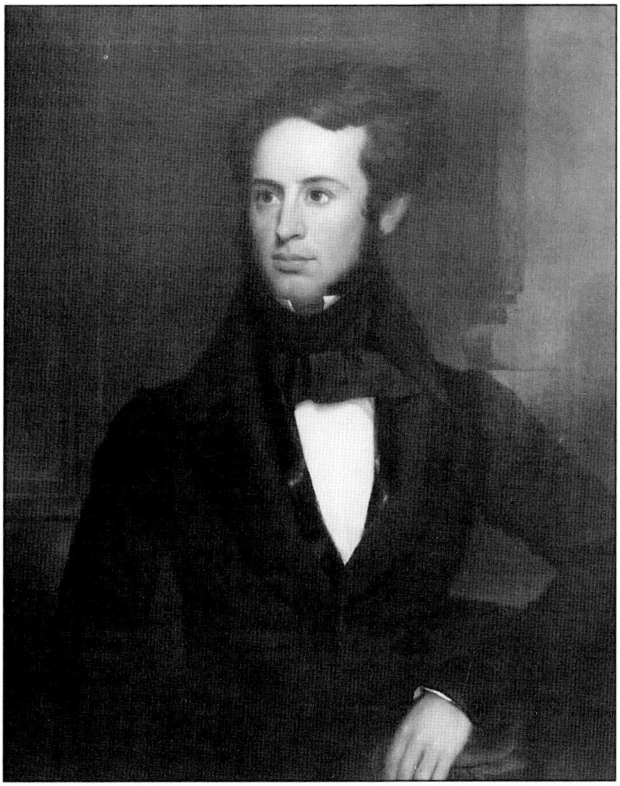

Samuel Reading Throckmorton (1808–1883) was born in Spotswood, New Jersey. He owned the Sausolito Ranch in California and was active as a fish commissioner for the state. Samuel L. Waldo (1783–1861) began his career as a sign painter, but early became one of the finest portrait artists of his day. He studied for a while with Benjamin West in London c. 1806, returning to the U.S. to open a studio in New York. William Jewett (1795–1874) joined him as a partner in 1816. Most of their portraits are signed "Waldo & Jewett" and it is difficult to distinguish between their work. Waldo continued to paint portraits by himself, which he signed. Jewett is not known to have painted portraits after Waldo's death.

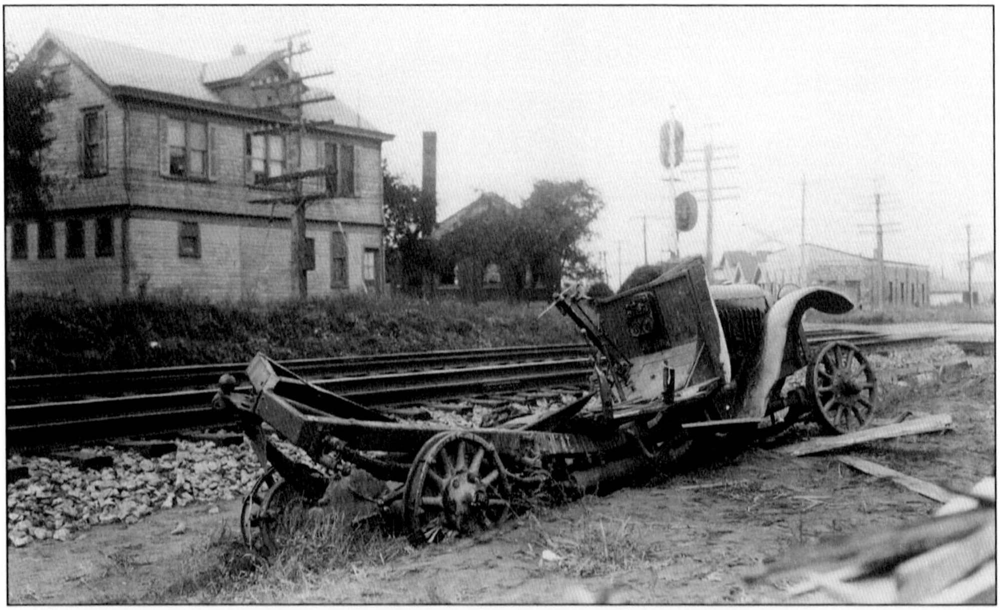

Jersey Central Power & Light Company Car no. 13, driven by Robert Swank, was heading toward Little Silver on White Road shortly after 5 pm on September 20, 1928, when it collided with a Pennsylvania Railroad train at the crossing. The crew had been working at the Smoke Shop Tavern on Broad Street. Swank and a co-worker James Peters were killed, while a third, George S. Duncan, escaped with minor injuries. This view is from the east side of the tracks, with a then-gas company facility on the left. A still-standing business building is on the right.

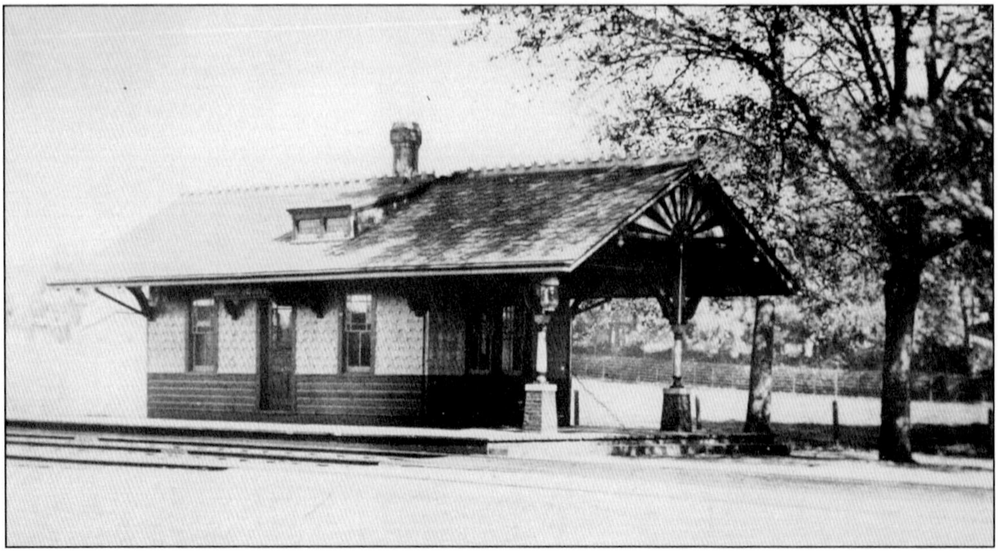

The Shrewsbury station was established on the Raritan & Delaware Bay Railroad in 1860. The line was later the New Jersey Southern Railroad, and after a second reorganization it was absorbed into the Central Railroad of New Jersey. This is a late-nineteenth-century view of the second station, built in 1876, when the earlier passenger station was turned into a freight station. The older station disappeared at an unspecified time, while this one burned in the early 1950s. It was located east of the tracks, not too far north of Sycamore Avenue. (Shrewsbury Historical Society Collection.)

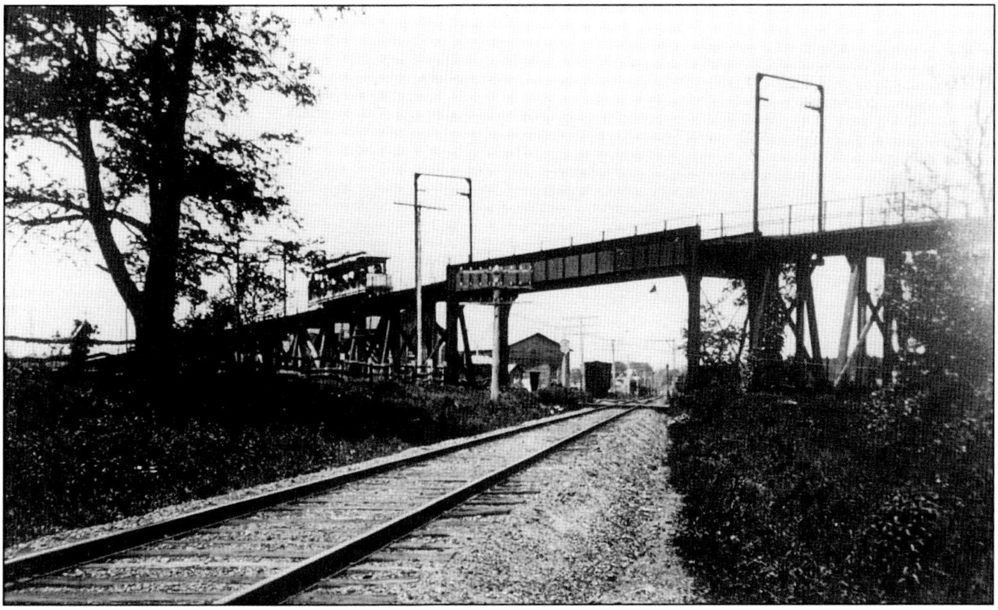

The Atlantic Highlands, Red Bank and Long Branch Electric Railway Company's efforts to run a trolley through Shrewsbury were delayed by right-of-way problems and rivalry with another line. The company altered its intended route down Broad Street to run on Shrewsbury Avenue instead, and began operations in 1896. This bridge crossed the New Jersey Southern's tracks, which still exist, just south of the Barker Avenue entrance to the present Shrewsbury Township. The 1906 picture by George Booth, lent by Joseph Eid, was published in his *Trolleys To The Fountain*, a history of the line. The bridge was demolished in 1992, after many years of service as a vehicular roadway.

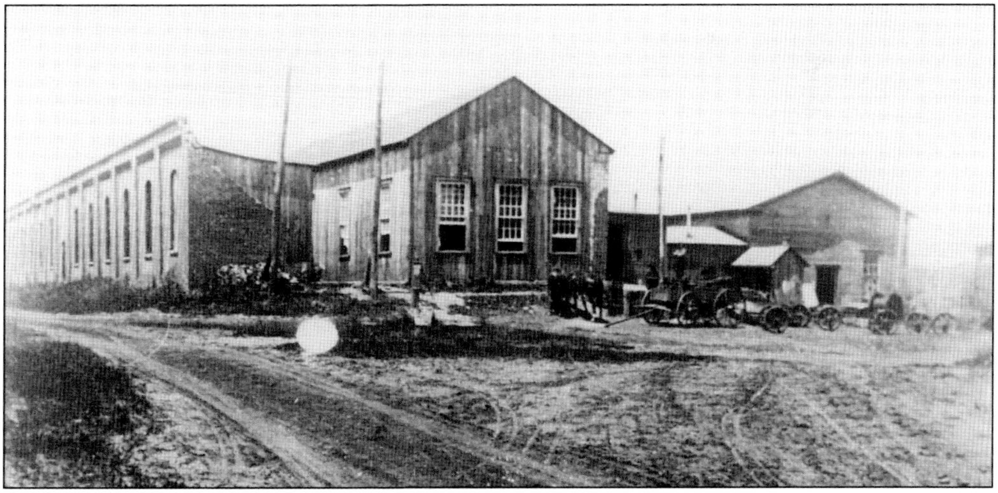

Car barns to house twenty trolleys were built in 1896 on a plot east of Shrewsbury Avenue and west of the New Jersey Southern tracks, just north of their juncture. The place and sixteen cars were substantially destroyed by an apparent incendiary fire in the early morning of May 24, 1899. Frame reconstruction can be seen adjoining the original brick walls, with a New Jersey Southern boxcar at right in this early 1900s image. The structure has long disappeared, but its footings may be found in an overgrown lot on the east side of Shrewsbury Avenue. (Joseph Eid Collection.)

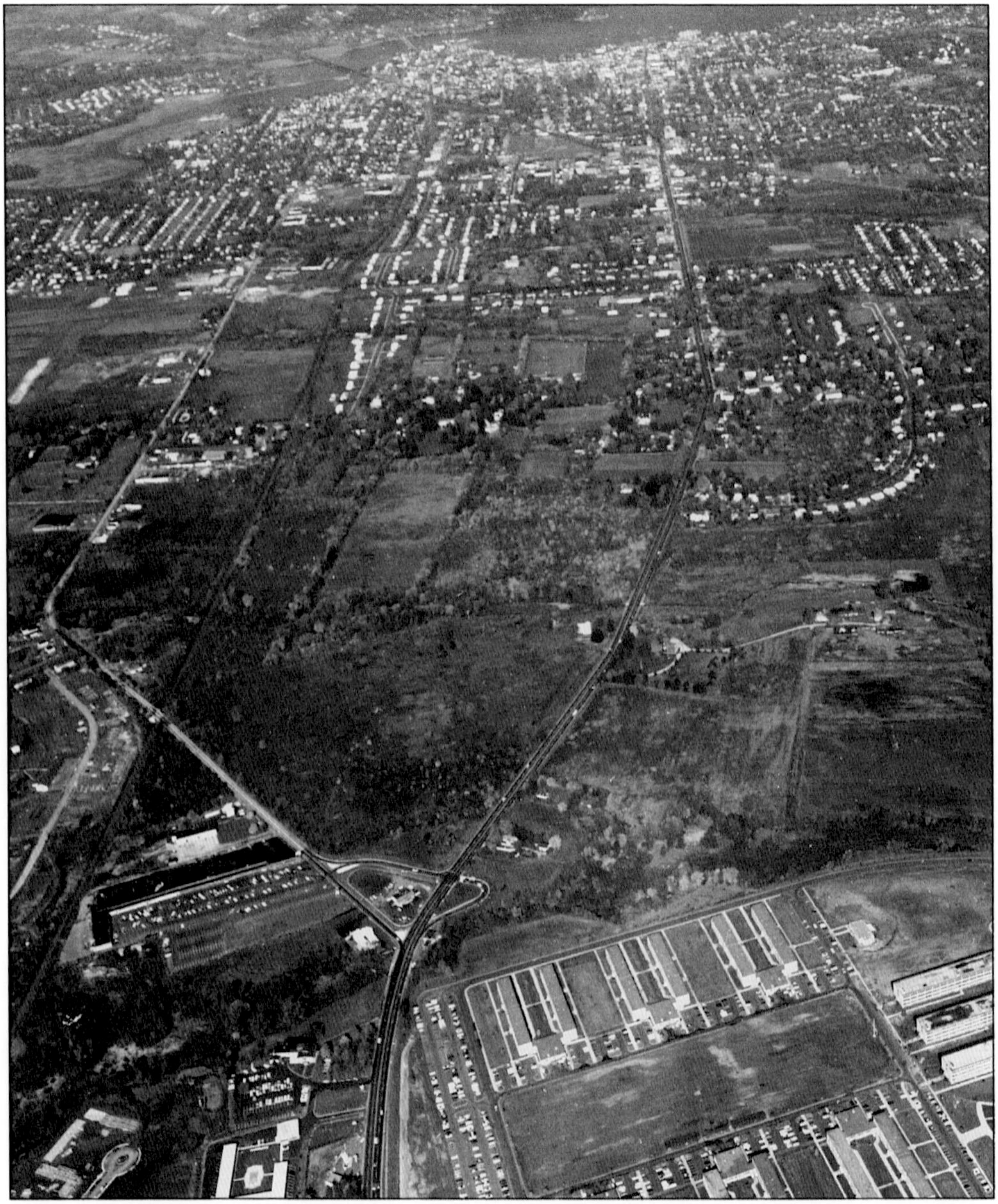

This view embraces nearly the entire borough. Shrewsbury Avenue, its western border, is the wide road at left, with the entrance to Shrewsbury Township at the bend. Parkers Creek (p. 101), with its extension Lafetras Brook, passes below the Shrewsbury Avenue-Highway 35 (Broad Street) intersection, forming the southern border. Part of the north and east border are the New York and Long Branch Railroad tracks, running on a diagonal from top to the right. Christ Church's spire, to the right and above the center, is the best visible guide to the Four Corners. Note the semi-circular driveway east of Highway 35 near the bottom, the Wallbridge estate (pp. 60–61). The J-shaped road northeast of it is Silver Brook Avenue, built through Appleby's farm (pp. 94–95).

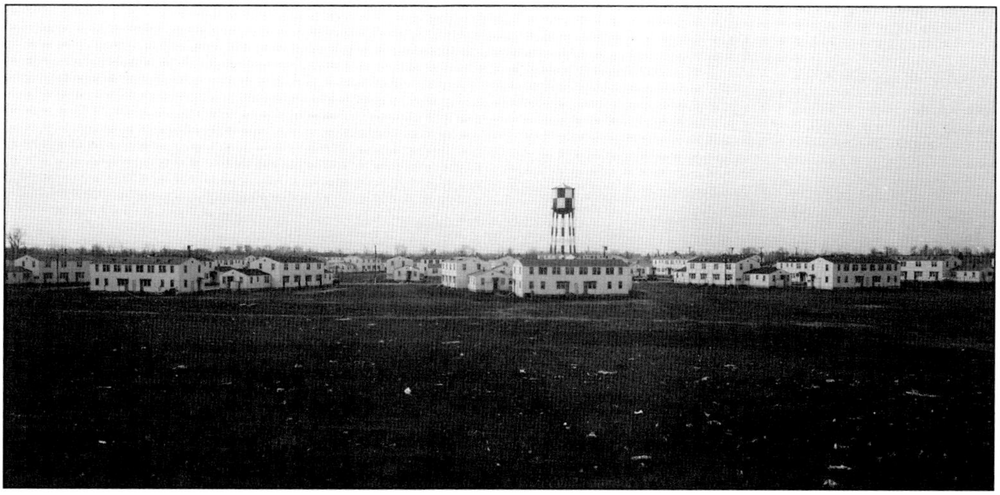

The pre-World War II expansion of the Army Signal Corp facility at nearby Fort Monmouth required housing for the growing number of personnel. The first of the Vail houses were completed in 1941 for occupancy by soldiers and families, on the borough's border with a then still-large and rural Shrewsbury Township. The enclave expanded in the early war years, built around three streets. The federal government divested the houses in the mid-1950s. This is a 1940s view from the Dorn's collection.

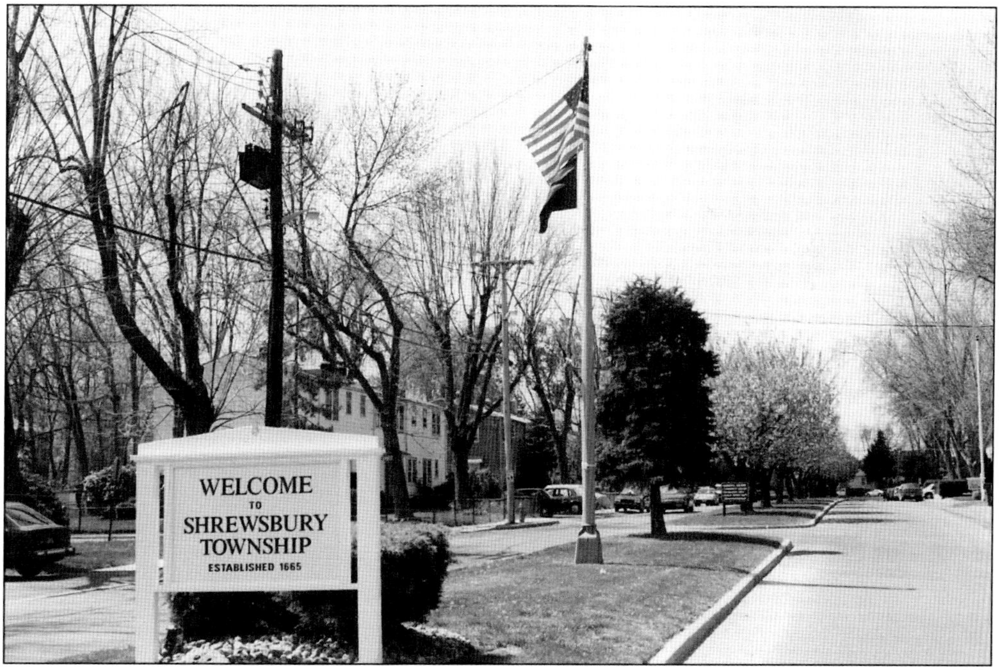

A 15-square-mile part of sparsely settled Shrewsbury Township, all of it except the tiny but densely populated Vail Homes development, seceded from the township in 1950, forming the Borough of New Shrewsbury. The borough changed its name to Tinton Falls, its oldest settlement, in 1975 in order to avoid confusion with the two other similarly named municipalities. Thus, this .09-square-mile 1940s creation has the unusual condition of having "inherited" a three-century-old municipal creation. This is the Shrewsbury Avenue entrance to Barker Avenue.

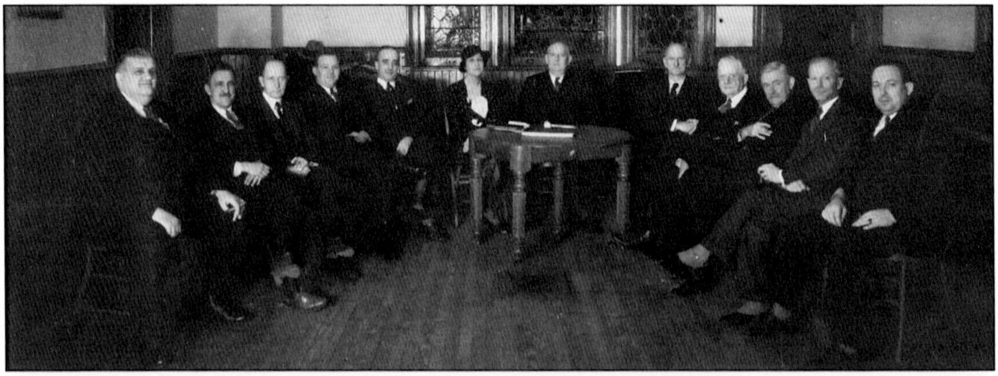

Had Shrewsbury's first borough council realized the historic significance of its meeting, perhaps they would have made sure their names were recorded with this 1926 photograph. A few are recognizable. First Mayor Benjamin J. Parker is at the table; the distinctive features of Harry Borden mark him third from the right.

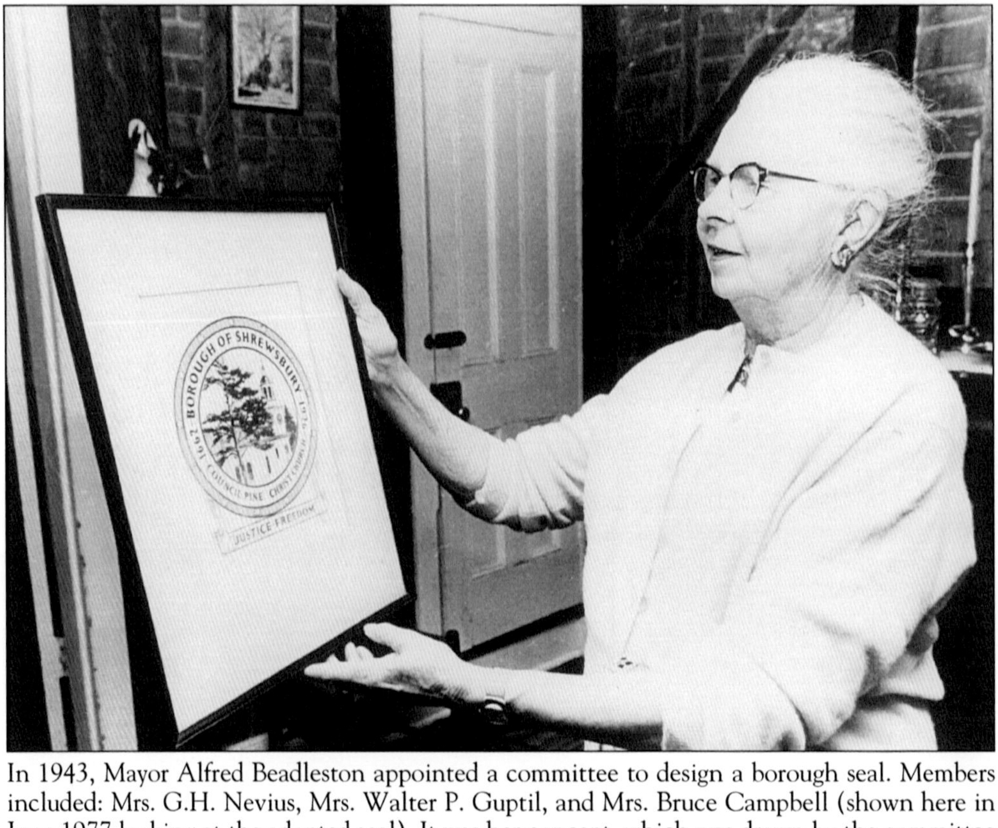

In 1943, Mayor Alfred Beadleston appointed a committee to design a borough seal. Members included: Mrs. G.H. Nevius, Mrs. Walter P. Guptil, and Mrs. Bruce Campbell (shown here in June 1977 looking at the adopted seal). It was her concept, which was drawn by the committee chairman, the noted equestrian artist George Ford Morris, that was approved and adopted on February 1, 1944. The seal pictures Christ Church and Council Pine (p. 21) and claims a settlement date of 1662, the source of current issue. The date apparently stemmed from an undated essay of Lucy Swift (1860–1936), a charter member of the Shrewsbury Reading Club, who claimed some pre-1665 Monmouth Patent settlers were a few immigrants from Connecticut who were "without religion." The date lacks substantiation. (Shrewsbury Historical Society Collection.)

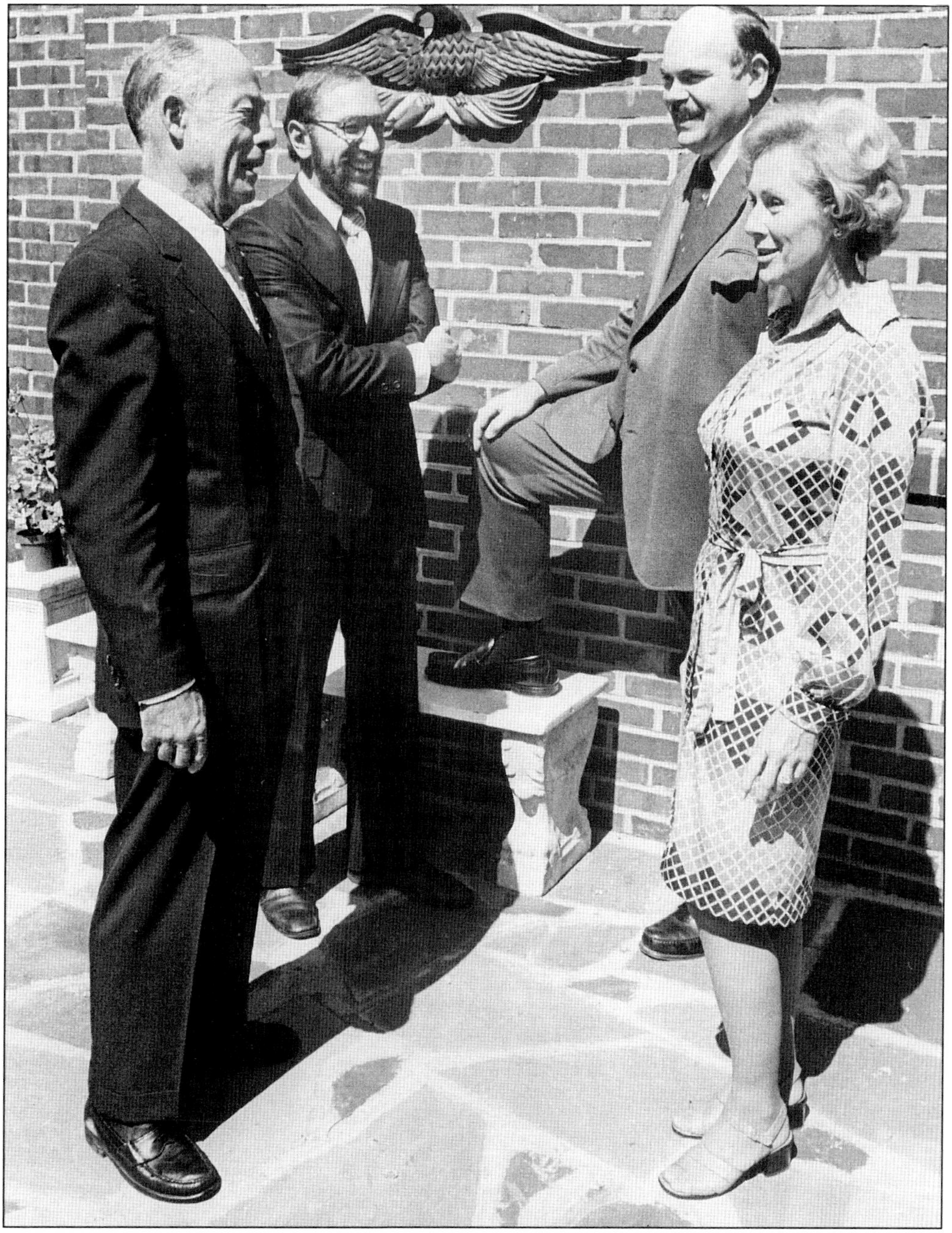

Dorothy Blair Manson, elected mayor in 1974, exchanges post-election remarks with other officeholders. She assumed the mayoralty with a goal to match the twelve years served by former mayor, Alfred N. Beadleston (at left), who was then president of the New Jersey Senate and one of the state's most respected public officials. She succeeded. Between the two are councilman Gershon Poling and then-mayor Joseph Dennis.

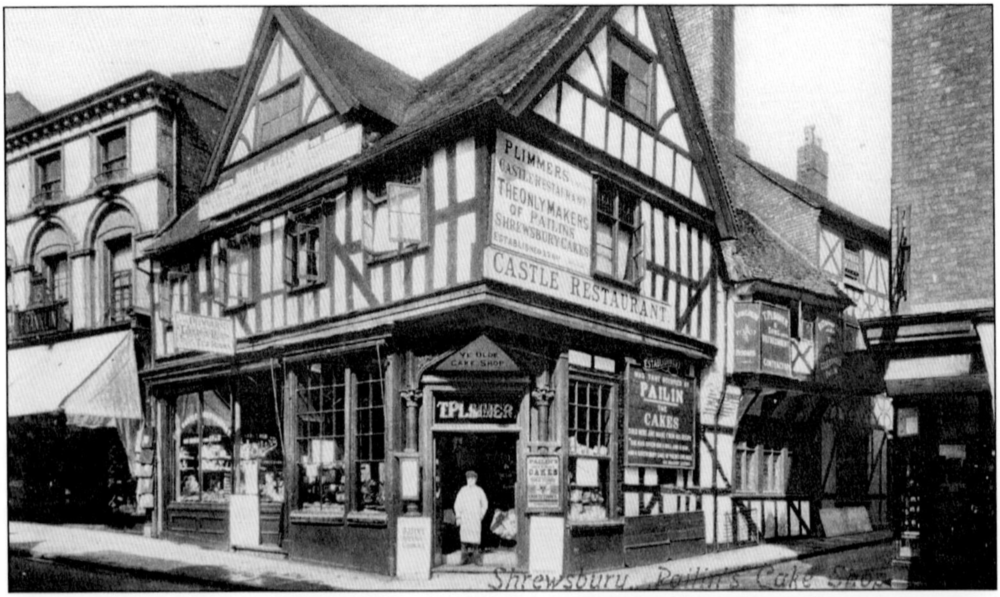

Shrewsbury, New Jersey, is believed to have been named for Shrewsbury, the county seat of Shropshire County, England. Shrewsbury, England, was long known for its small biscuits. Those produced by a nineteenth-century baker, Palin, were stamped "Palin's Original Shrewsbury Cakes." The confection is a raised biscuit flavored with caraway seeds or currents, and lemon, rather than the thin cookie now known in Monmouth County as Shrewsbury wafers. For an authentic recipe, see Theodora Fitzgibbon's *A Taste of England In Food and Pictures* (London: Pan Books, 1986), available in the U.S.

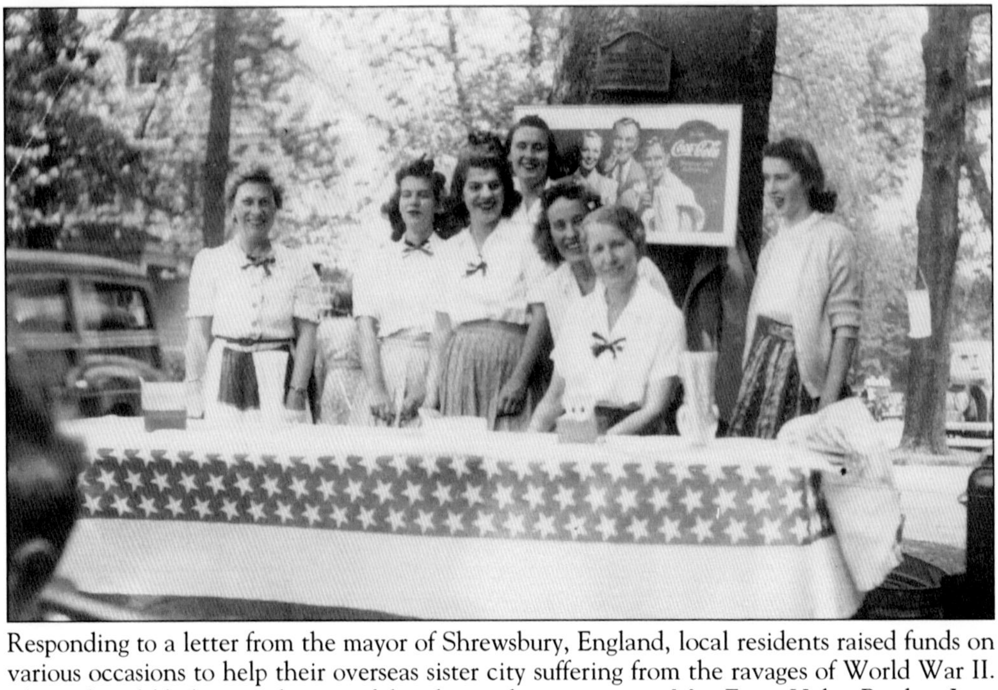

Responding to a letter from the mayor of Shrewsbury, England, local residents raised funds on various occasions to help their overseas sister city suffering from the ravages of World War II. These cheerful helpers under one of the placqued sycamores are Mrs. Frost, Helen Borden, Jane Mason, Lois Silver, Margaret Frost, Esther Hymer, and Rebecca Sieber.